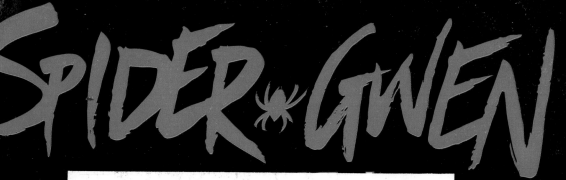

# SPIDER-GWEN

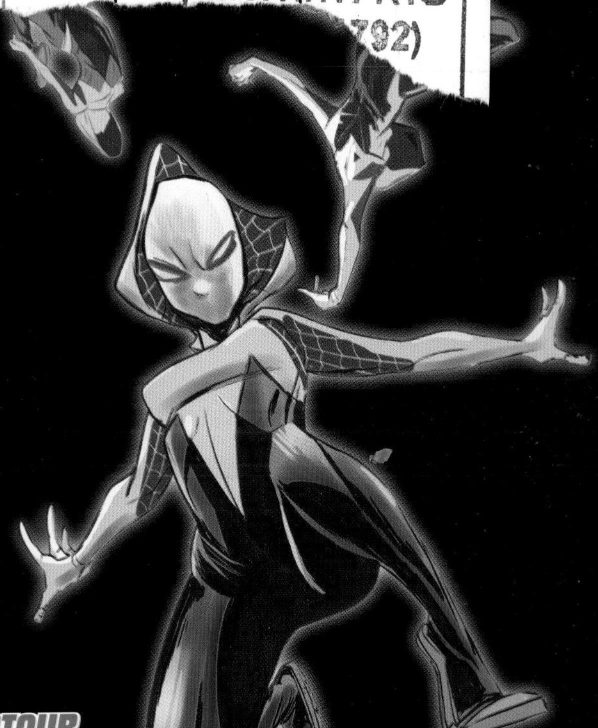

**WRITER:** JASON LATOUR
**ARTIST:** ROBBI RODRIGUEZ
**COLOURIST:** RICO RENZI
**LETTERERS:** VC's CLAYTON COWLES & TRAVIS LANHAM

**ASSOCIATE EDITOR:** DEVIN LEWIS
**EDITOR:** NICK LOWE **EDITOR-IN-CHIEF:** AXEL ALONSO
**CHIEF CREATIVE OFFICER:** JOE QUESADA **HANDBOOK ENTRY DESIGN:** JOE FRONTIRRE
**EXECUTIVE PRODUCER:** ALAN FINE **PUBLISHER:** DAN BUCKLEY
**COVER ART:** ROBBI RODRIGUEZ

Do you have any comments or queries about Spider-Gwen Vol. 2: Weapon of Cl... at graphicnovels@panini.co.uk
Join us on



TM & © 2016 Marvel & Subs. L... ...ved. First impression 2016. Published by ... ...tor. Alan O'Keefe, Managing Editor. Ma... ...y Webb, Reprint Editor. Charlotte Harve... ...ge Wells, Kent TN4 8BS. This publication ... ...n that it shall not be sold or distribute... ...rinted in Italy by Lito Terrazzi. ISBN: 978...

MARVEL
arvel.com


MIX
Paper from responsible sources
FSC
www.fsc.org
FSC® C016466

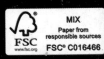

MARVEL GRAPHIC NOVEL

SPIDER-GWEN VOL. 2 #9

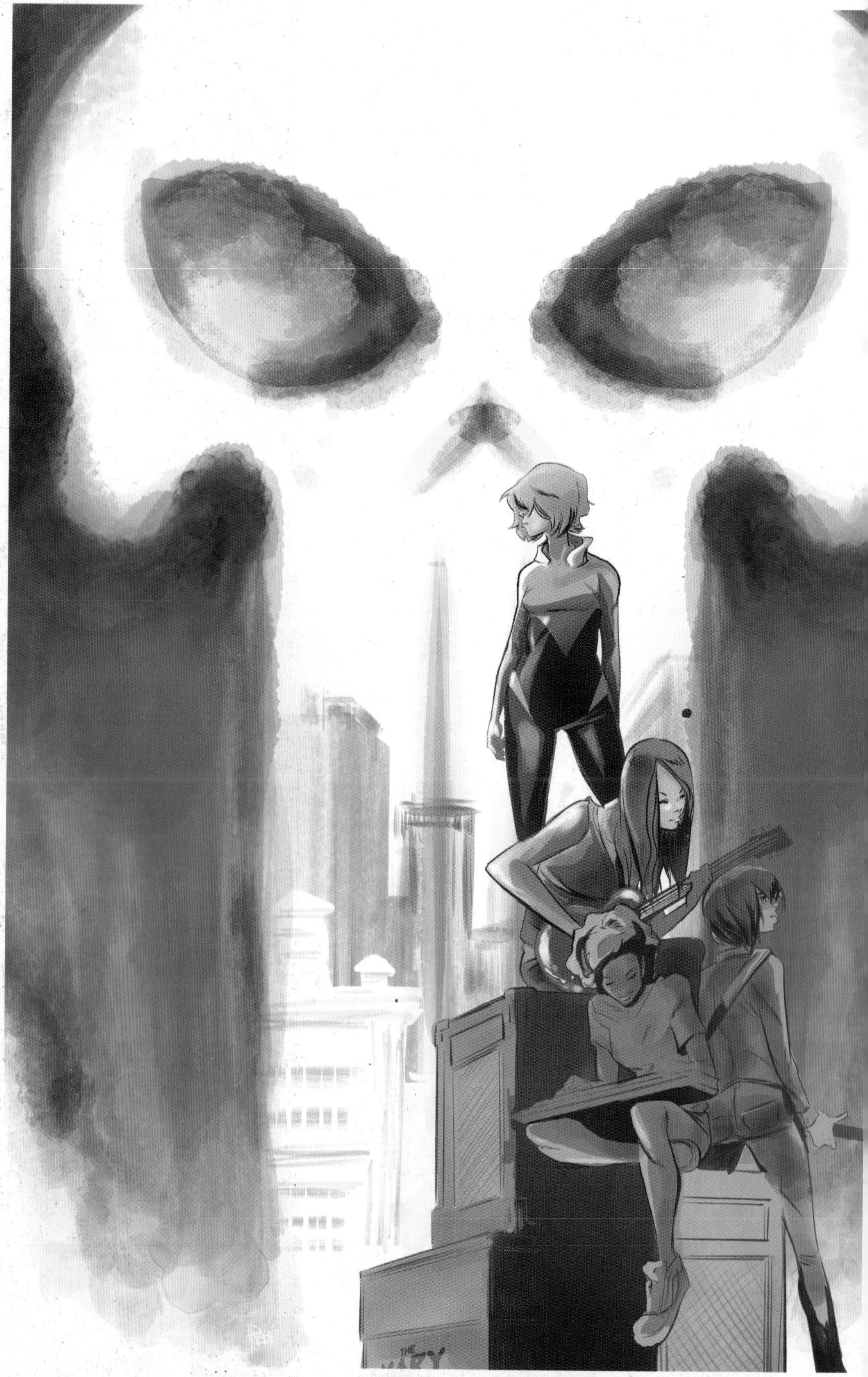

# ND JUSTICE FOR ALL?

*After years running, Spidey walks tall.*

Urich.

a few weeks since Captain America
mysterious Spider-Woman were seen
nds after a battle that swept through
blocks as well as the subway.

do
us
tum
tibu
tus
ele
e p
g a
ort
pur
cid

YOU REALLY MIGHT HAVE THE WORST TIMING ON EARTH.

THIS STUPID PHOTO OF SPIDER-WOMAN AND CAP HAS TRENDED FOR A WEEK.

EVEN J. JONAH JAMESON IS SCARED TO SAY A BAD WORD ABOUT IT.

BUT THAT'S JUST THE ICING...

I MEAN, YOU'VE *SEEN* THE *YOUWEB VIDEOS*, RIGHT?

OF GEORGE STACY, WHISTLE-BLOWING LIKE IT'S WATERGATE?

LOOK, I'M THE DISTRICT ATTORNEY, AN ELECTED OFFICIAL.

SO PUT YOURSELF IN *MY* SHOES. WHAT WOULD YOU DO...

...MY GREAT SIN. THE DEPARTMENT'S GREAT LIE...

...IS THAT SPIDER-WOMAN WAS TREATED AS GUILTY UNTIL PROVEN INNOCENT.

...WITH WHATEVER THE HELL *THIS* IS YOU JUST HANDED ME?

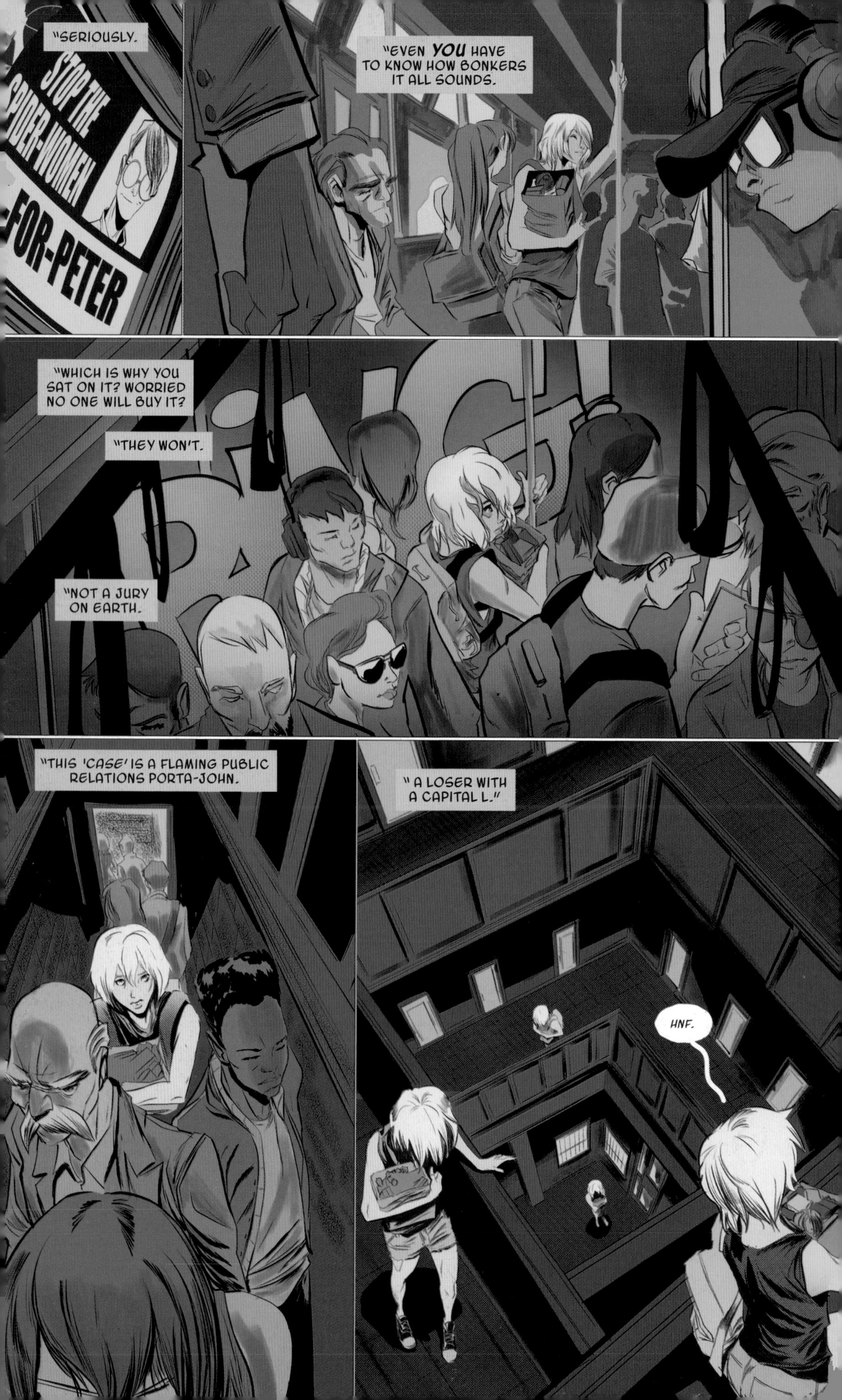
STOP THE SPIDER-WOMEN FOR-PETER
"SERIOUSLY.
"EVEN YOU HAVE TO KNOW HOW BONKERS IT ALL SOUNDS.
"WHICH IS WHY YOU SAT ON IT? WORRIED NO ONE WILL BUY IT?
"THEY WON'T.
"NOT A JURY ON EARTH.
"THIS 'CASE' IS A FLAMING PUBLIC RELATIONS PORTA-JOHN.
" A LOSER WITH A CAPITAL L."
HNF.

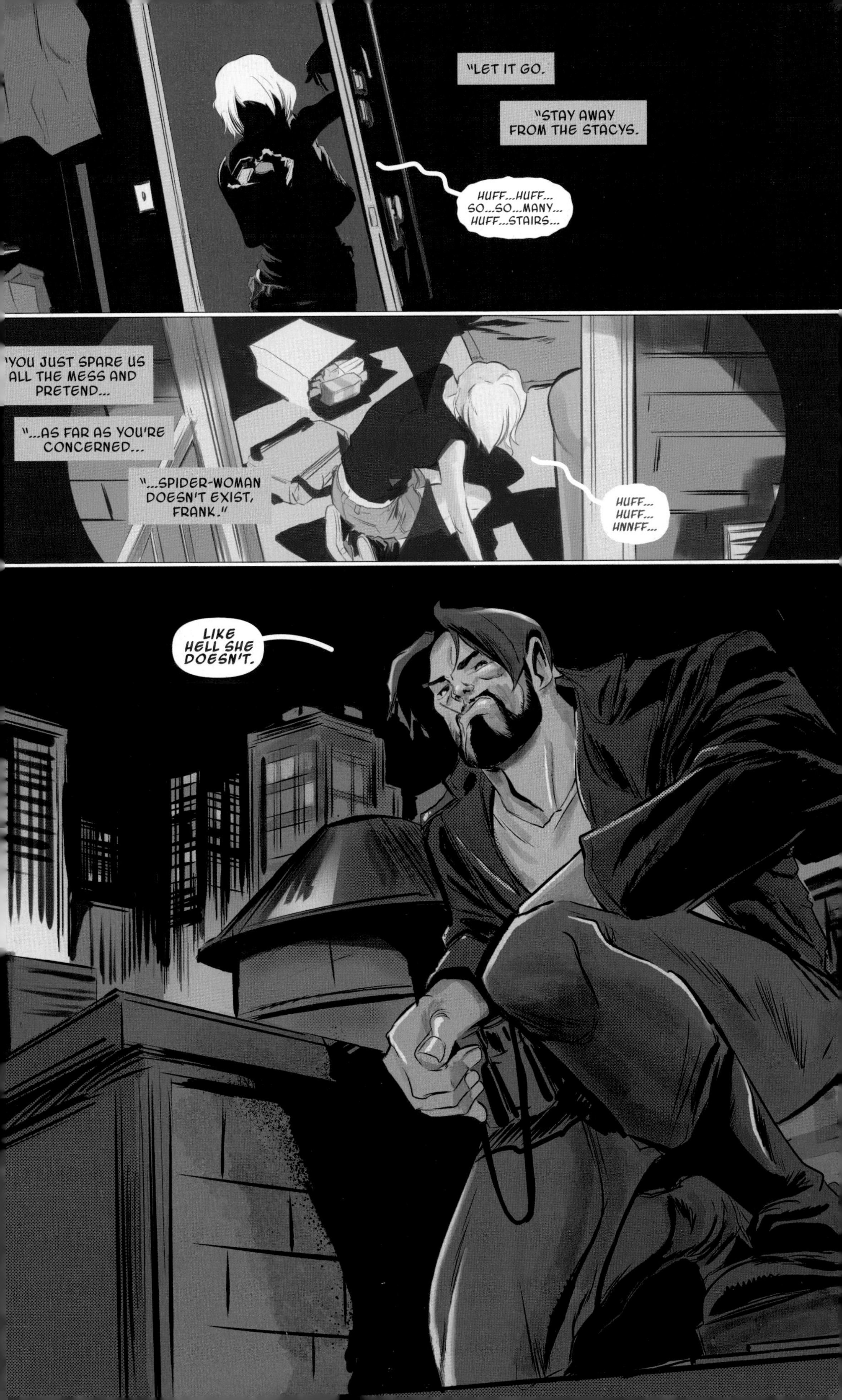
"LET IT GO.
"STAY AWAY FROM THE STACYS.
HUFF...HUFF... SO...SO...MANY... HUFF...STAIRS...
"YOU JUST SPARE US ALL THE MESS AND PRETEND...
"...AS FAR AS YOU'RE CONCERNED...
"...SPIDER-WOMAN DOESN'T EXIST, FRANK."
HUFF... HUFF... HNNFF...
LIKE HELL SHE DOESN'T.

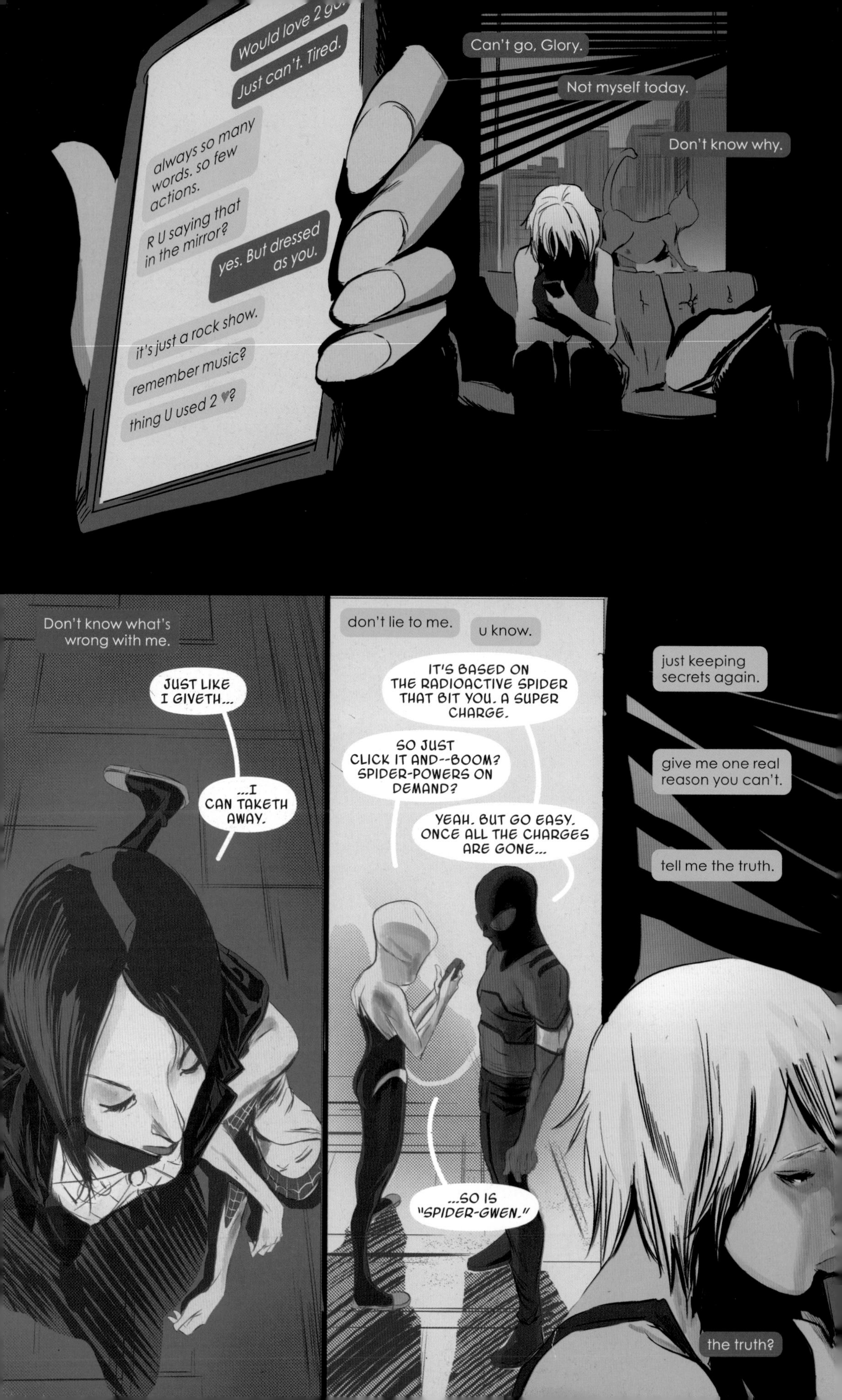

Would love 2 go.
Just can't. Tired.
always so many words. so few actions.
R U saying that in the mirror?
yes. But dressed as you.
it's just a rock show.
remember music?
thing U used 2 ♥?
Can't go, Glory.
Not myself today.
Don't know why.
Don't know what's wrong with me.
JUST LIKE I GIVETH...
...I CAN TAKETH AWAY.
don't lie to me.
u know.
IT'S BASED ON THE RADIOACTIVE SPIDER THAT BIT YOU. A SUPER CHARGE.
SO JUST CLICK IT AND--BOOM? SPIDER-POWERS ON DEMAND?
YEAH. BUT GO EASY. ONCE ALL THE CHARGES ARE GONE...
...SO IS "SPIDER-GWEN."
just keeping secrets again.
give me one real reason you can't.
tell me the truth.
the truth?

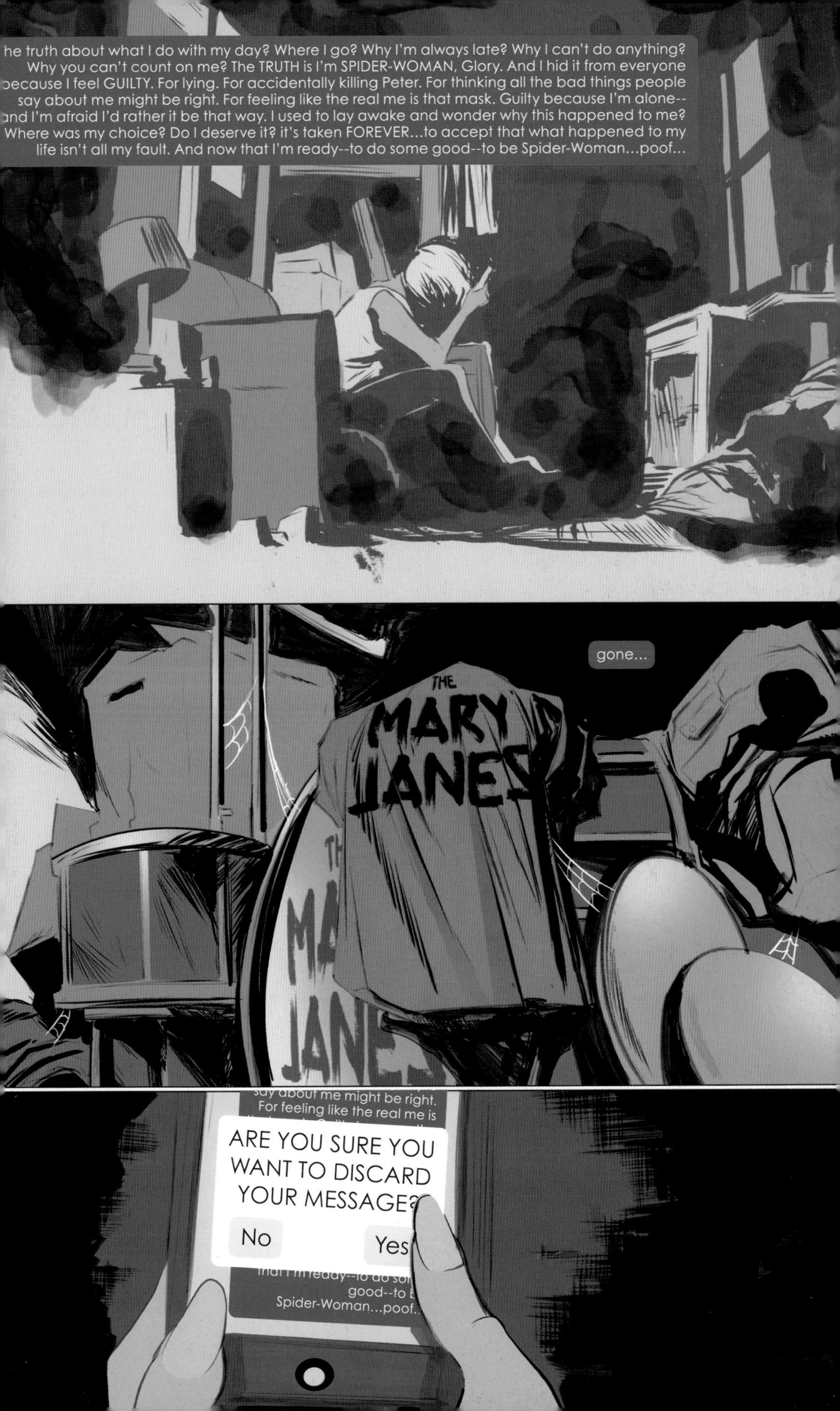
he truth about what I do with my day? Where I go? Why I'm always late? Why I can't do anything? Why you can't count on me? The TRUTH is I'm SPIDER-WOMAN, Glory. And I hid it from everyone because I feel GUILTY. For lying. For accidentally killing Peter. For thinking all the bad things people say about me might be right. For feeling like the real me is that mask. Guilty because I'm alone--and I'm afraid I'd rather it be that way. I used to lay awake and wonder why this happened to me? Where was my choice? Do I deserve it? it's taken FOREVER...to accept that what happened to my life isn't all my fault. And now that I'm ready--to do some good--to be Spider-Woman...poof...
gone...
THE MARY JANES
THE MA JANES
say about me might be right.
For feeling like the real me is
ARE YOU SURE YOU WANT TO DISCARD YOUR MESSAGE?
No
Yes
Spider-Woman...poof...

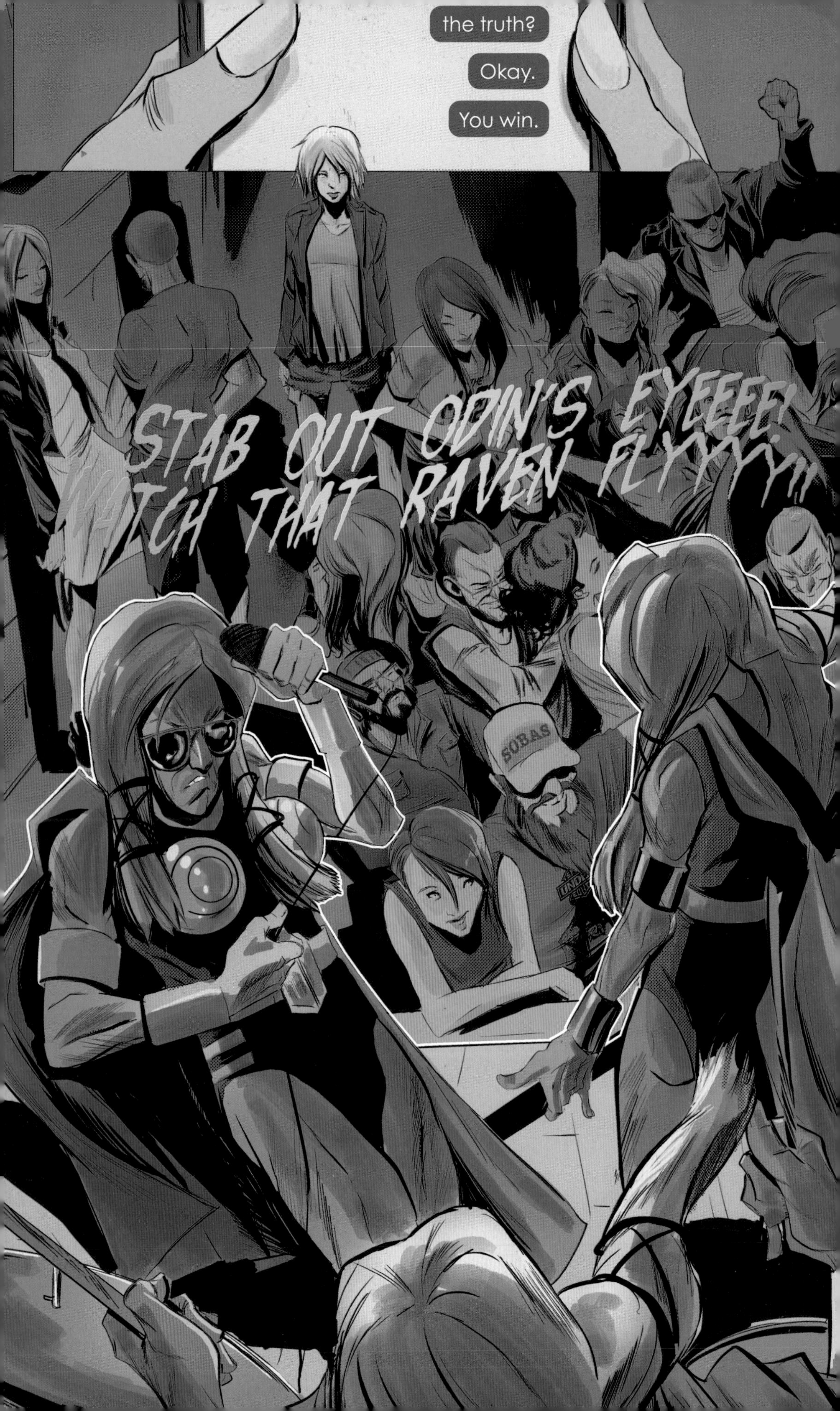
the truth?
Okay.
You win.
STAB OUT ODIN'S EYEEEE!
WATCH THAT RAVEN FLYYYY!!
SOBAS

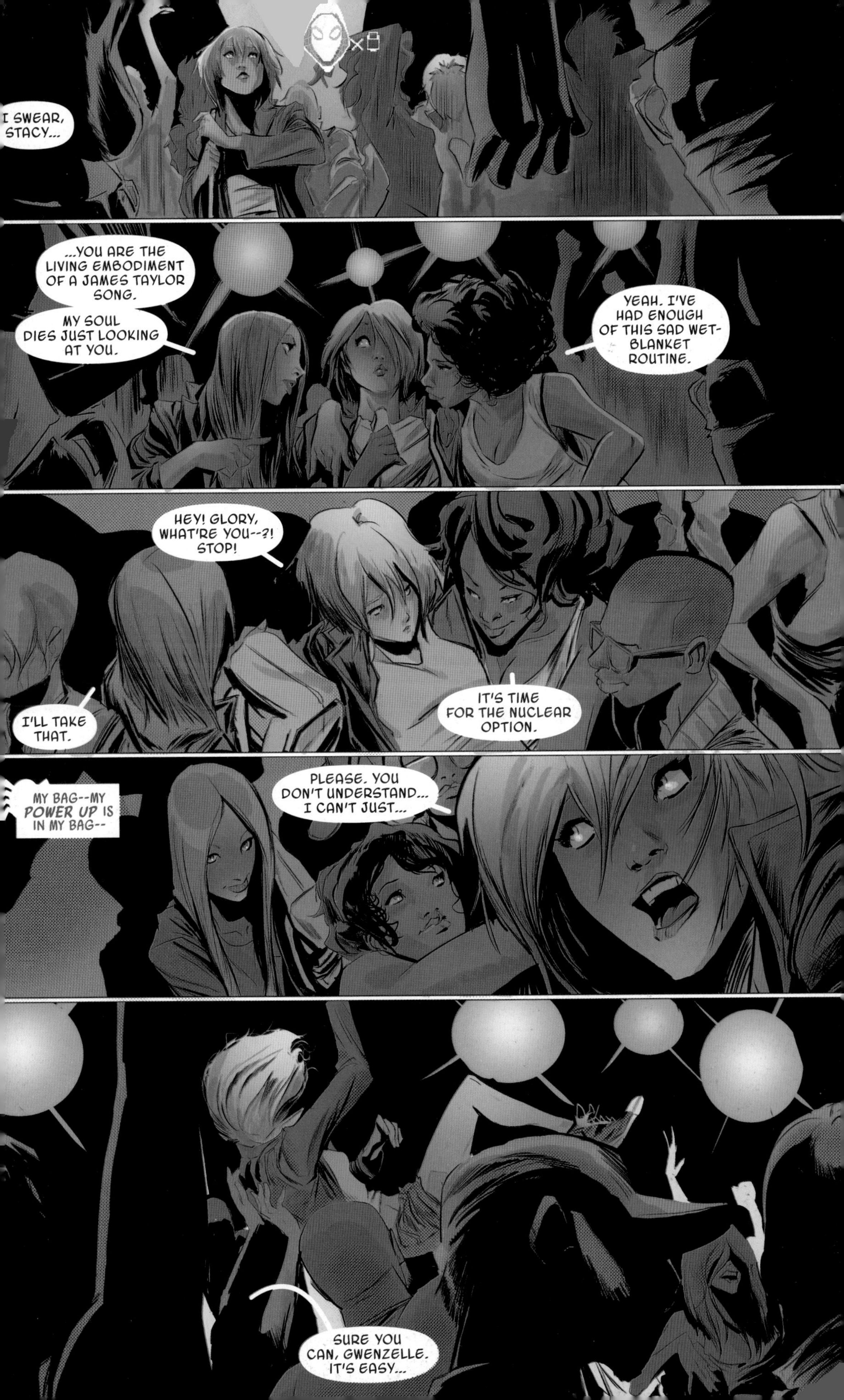
I SWEAR, STACY...
...YOU ARE THE LIVING EMBODIMENT OF A JAMES TAYLOR SONG.
MY SOUL DIES JUST LOOKING AT YOU.
YEAH. I'VE HAD ENOUGH OF THIS SAD WET-BLANKET ROUTINE.
HEY! GLORY, WHAT'RE YOU--?! STOP!
I'LL TAKE THAT.
IT'S TIME FOR THE NUCLEAR OPTION.
MY BAG--MY POWER UP IS IN MY BAG--
PLEASE. YOU DON'T UNDERSTAND... I CAN'T JUST...
SURE YOU CAN, GWENZELLE. IT'S EASY...

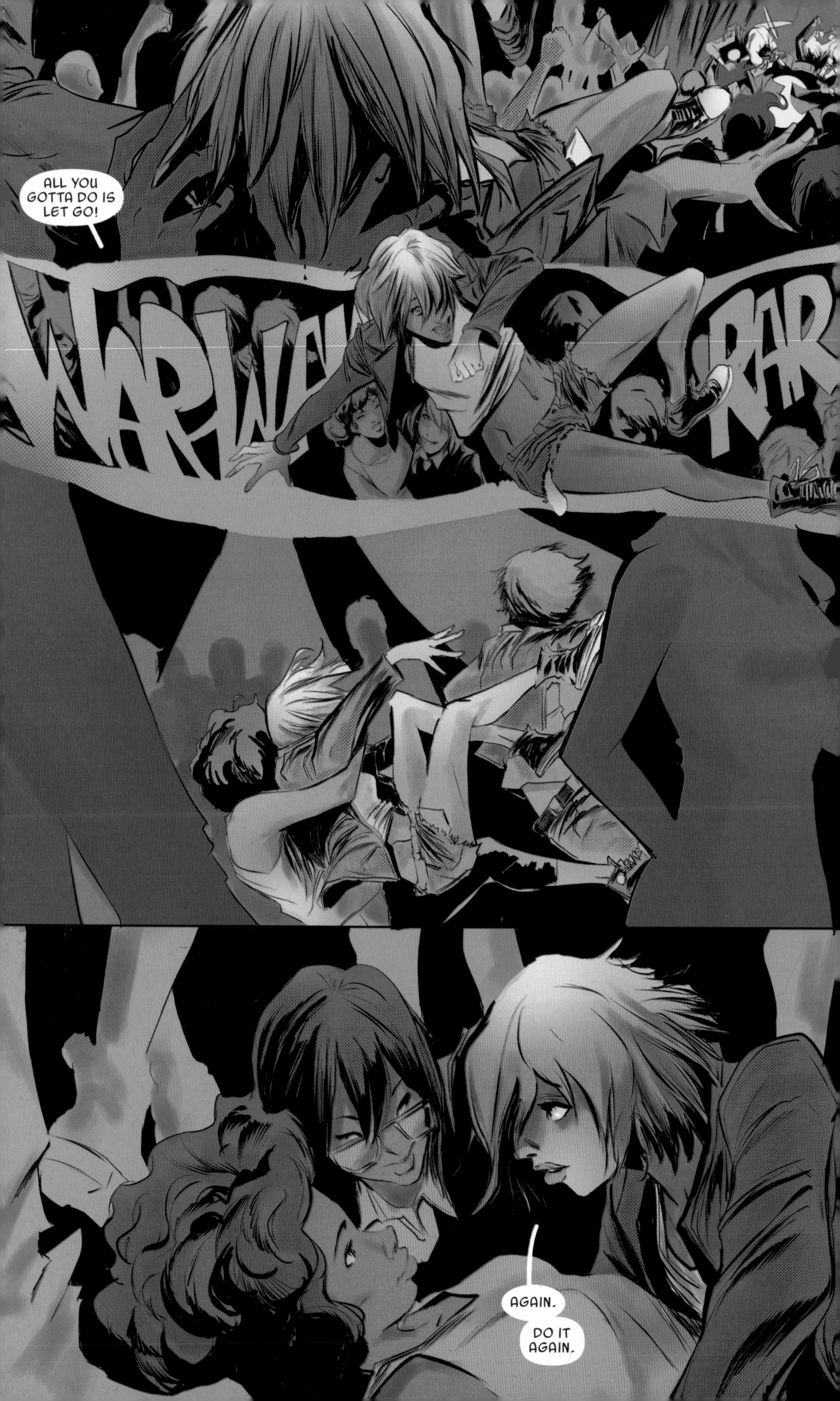
ALL YOU GOTTA DO IS LET GO!
AGAIN.
DO IT AGAIN.

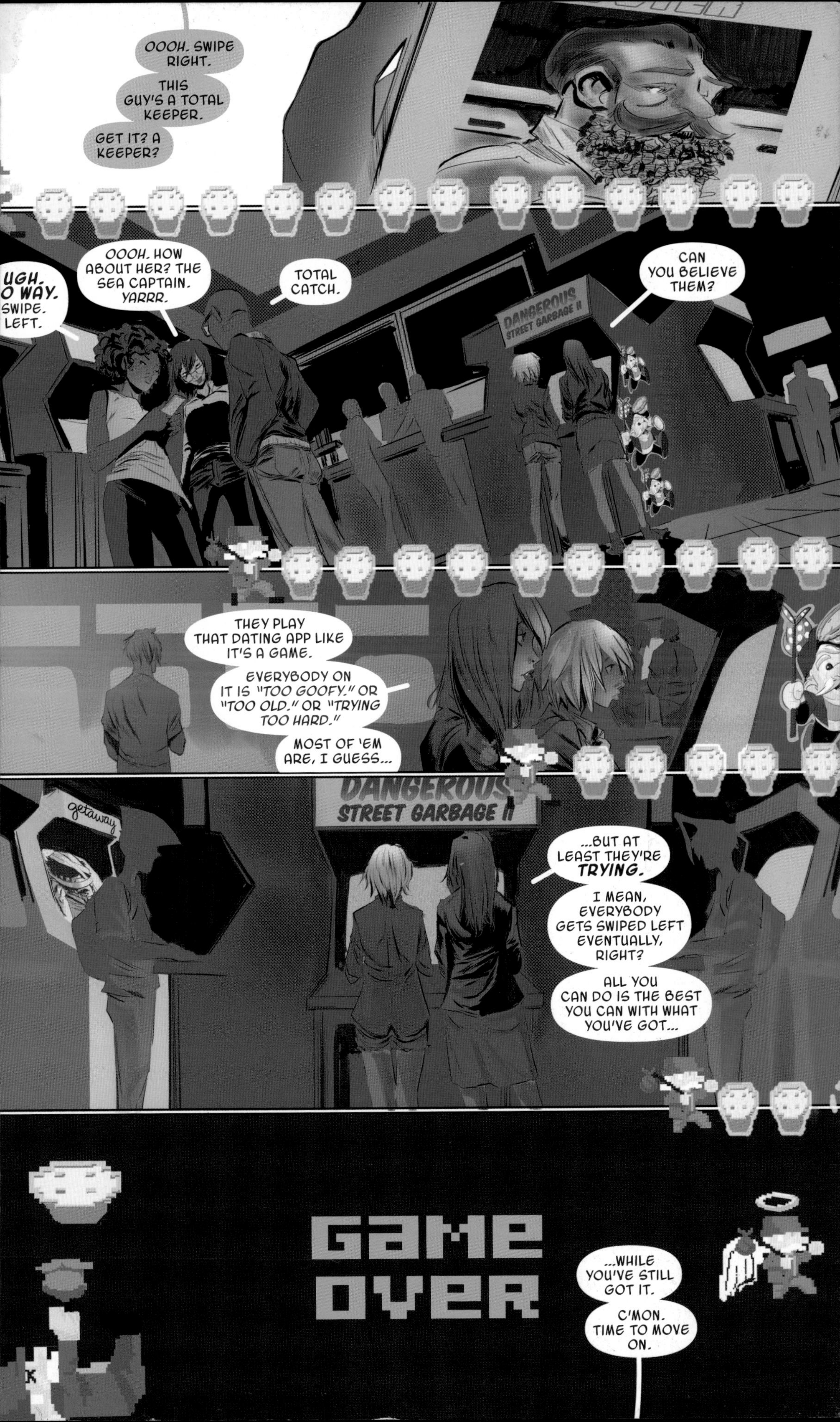
OOOH. SWIPE RIGHT.
THIS GUY'S A TOTAL KEEPER.
GET IT? A KEEPER?
UGH. O WAY. SWIPE. LEFT.
OOOH. HOW ABOUT HER? THE SEA CAPTAIN. YARRR.
TOTAL CATCH.
DANGEROUS STREET GARBAGE II
CAN YOU BELIEVE THEM?
THEY PLAY THAT DATING APP LIKE IT'S A GAME.
EVERYBODY ON IT IS "TOO GOOFY." OR "TOO OLD." OR "TRYING TOO HARD."
MOST OF 'EM ARE, I GUESS...
getaway
DANGEROUS STREET GARBAGE II
...BUT AT LEAST THEY'RE TRYING.
I MEAN, EVERYBODY GETS SWIPED LEFT EVENTUALLY, RIGHT?
ALL YOU CAN DO IS THE BEST YOU CAN WITH WHAT YOU'VE GOT...
GAME OVER
...WHILE YOU'VE STILL GOT IT.
C'MON. TIME TO MOVE ON.

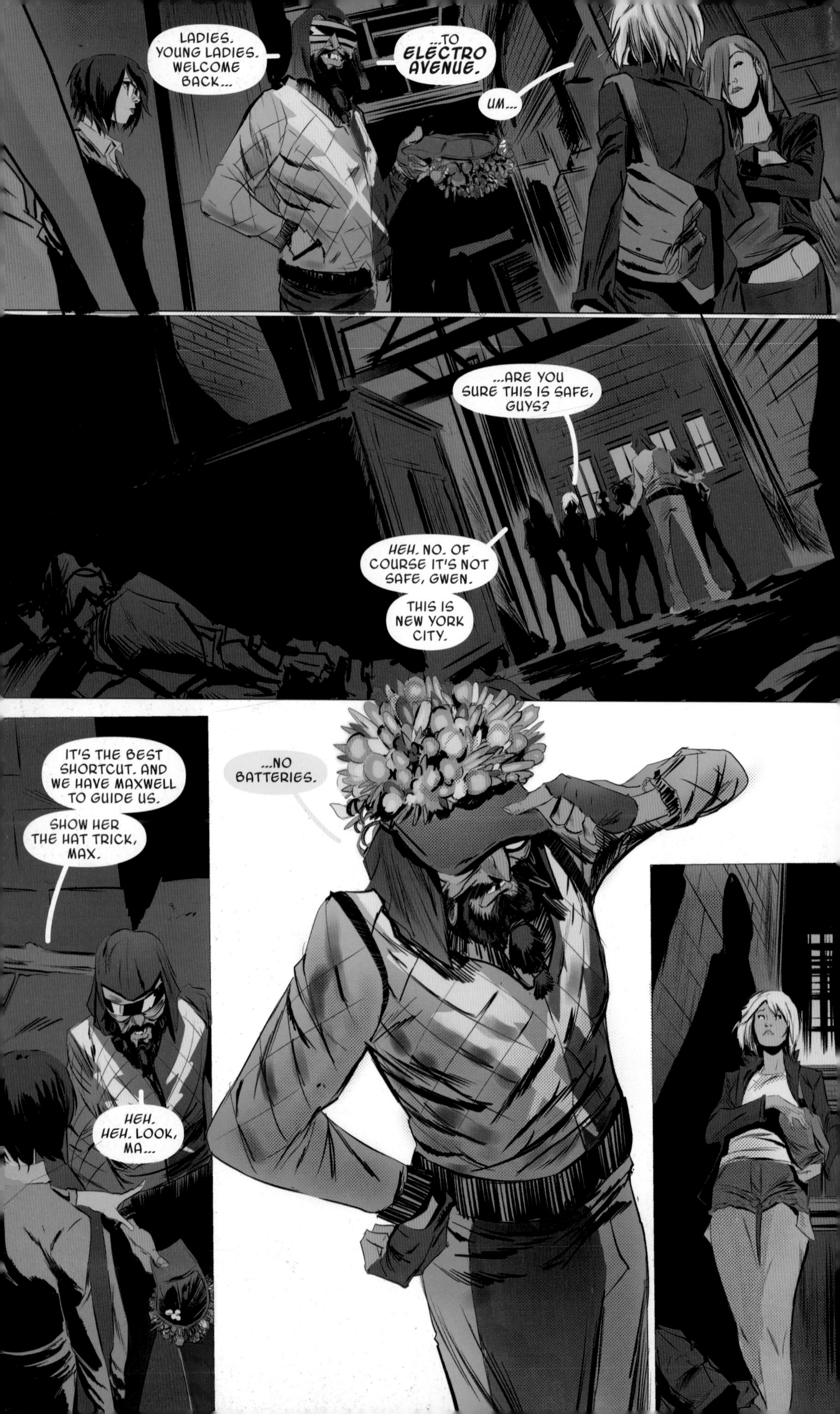
LADIES. YOUNG LADIES. WELCOME BACK...
...TO ELECTRO AVENUE.
UM...
...ARE YOU SURE THIS IS SAFE, GUYS?
HEH. NO. OF COURSE IT'S NOT SAFE, GWEN.
THIS IS NEW YORK CITY.
IT'S THE BEST SHORTCUT. AND WE HAVE MAXWELL TO GUIDE US.
SHOW HER THE HAT TRICK, MAX.
HEH. HEH. LOOK, MA...
...NO BATTERIES.

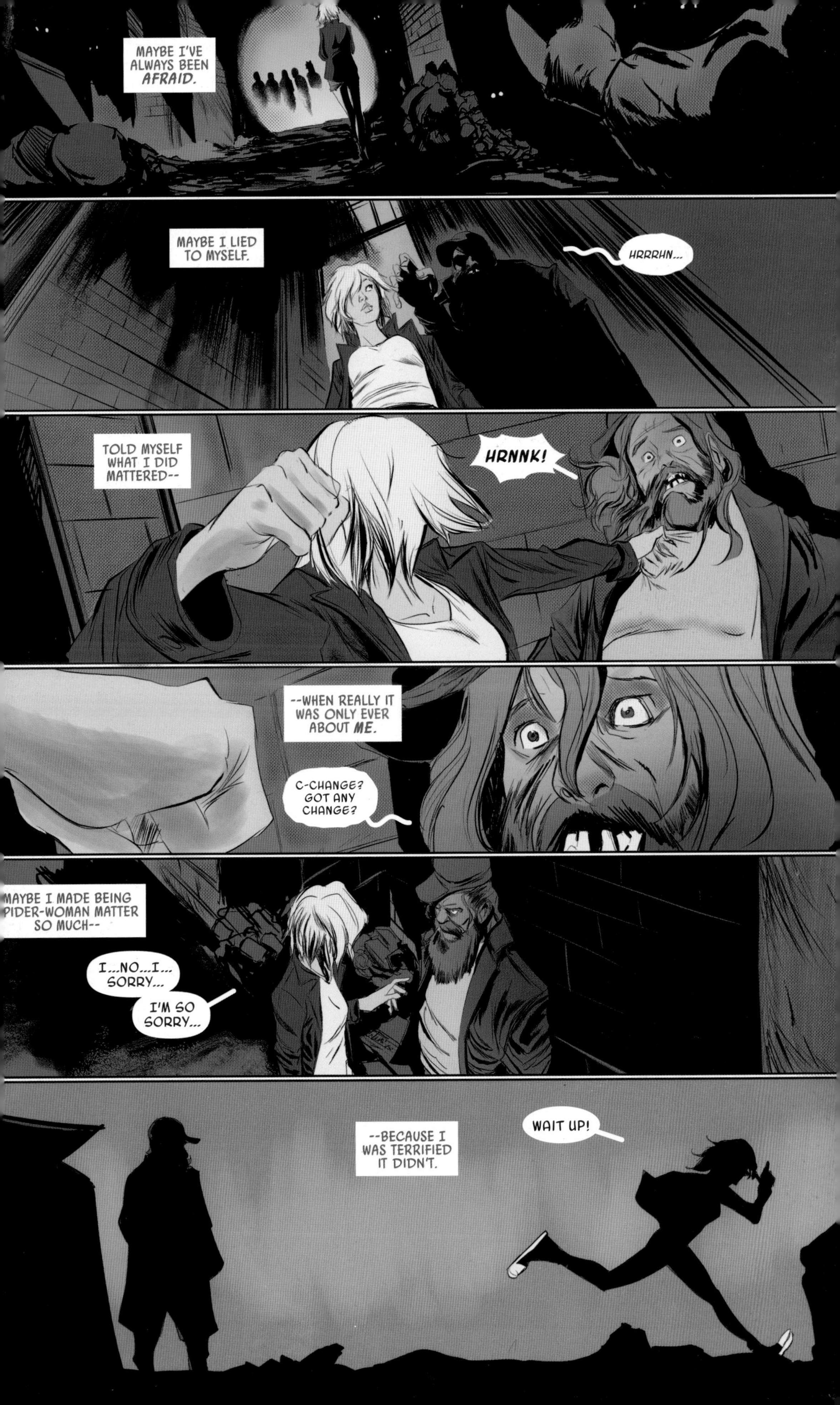
MAYBE I'VE ALWAYS BEEN AFRAID.
MAYBE I LIED TO MYSELF.
HRRRHN...
TOLD MYSELF WHAT I DID MATTERED--
HRNNK!
--WHEN REALLY IT WAS ONLY EVER ABOUT ME.
C-CHANGE? GOT ANY CHANGE?
MAYBE I MADE BEING SPIDER-WOMAN MATTER SO MUCH--
I...NO...I... SORRY...
I'M SO SORRY...
--BECAUSE I WAS TERRIFIED IT DIDN'T.
WAIT UP!

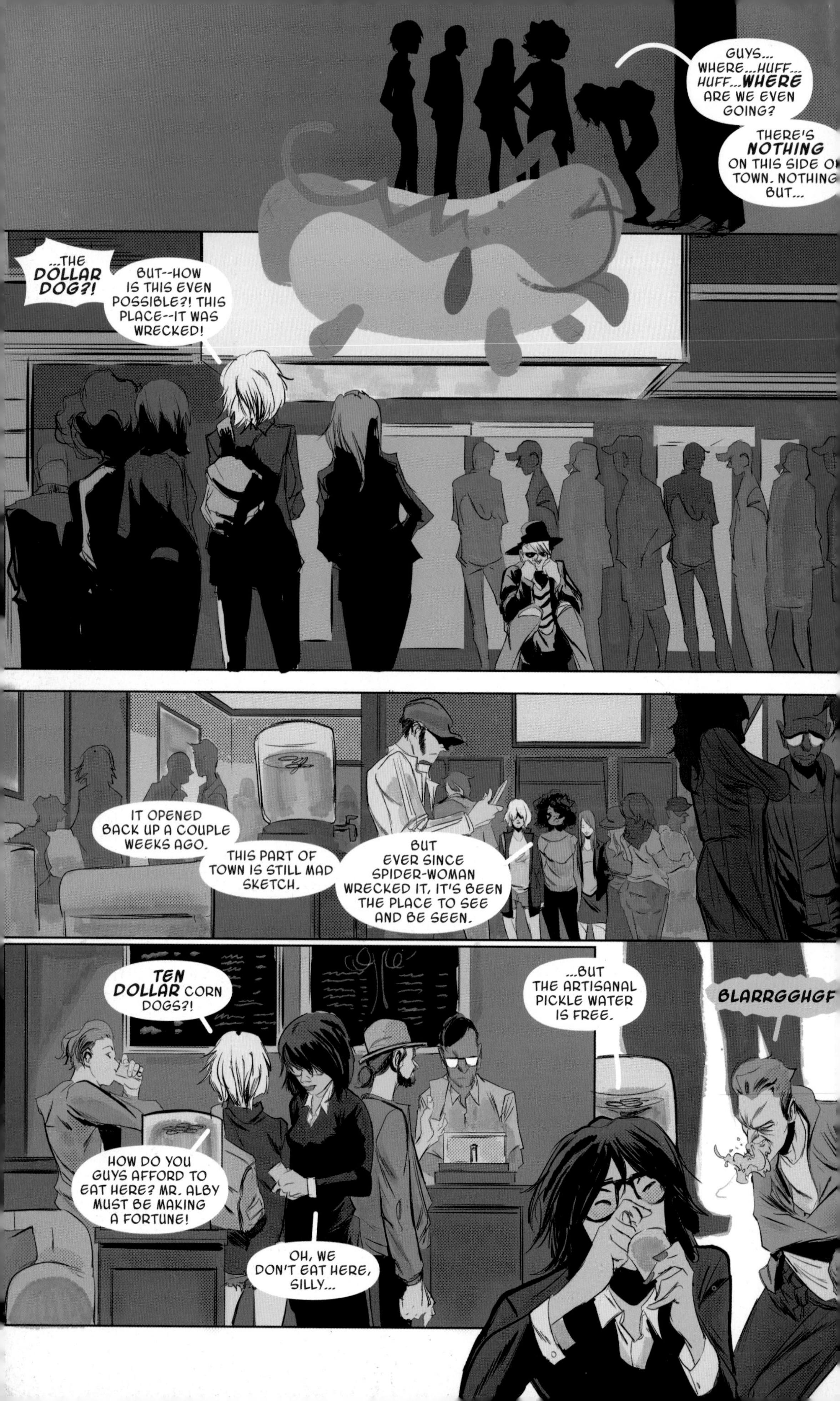

GUYS... WHERE...HUFF... HUFF...WHERE ARE WE EVEN GOING?
THERE'S NOTHING ON THIS SIDE OF TOWN. NOTHING BUT...
...THE DOLLAR DOG?!
BUT--HOW IS THIS EVEN POSSIBLE?! THIS PLACE--IT WAS WRECKED!
IT OPENED BACK UP A COUPLE WEEKS AGO.
THIS PART OF TOWN IS STILL MAD SKETCH.
BUT EVER SINCE SPIDER-WOMAN WRECKED IT, IT'S BEEN THE PLACE TO SEE AND BE SEEN.
TEN DOLLAR CORN DOGS?!
HOW DO YOU GUYS AFFORD TO EAT HERE? MR. ALBY MUST BE MAKING A FORTUNE!
OH, WE DON'T EAT HERE, SILLY...
...BUT THE ARTISANAL PICKLE WATER IS FREE.
BLARRGGHGF

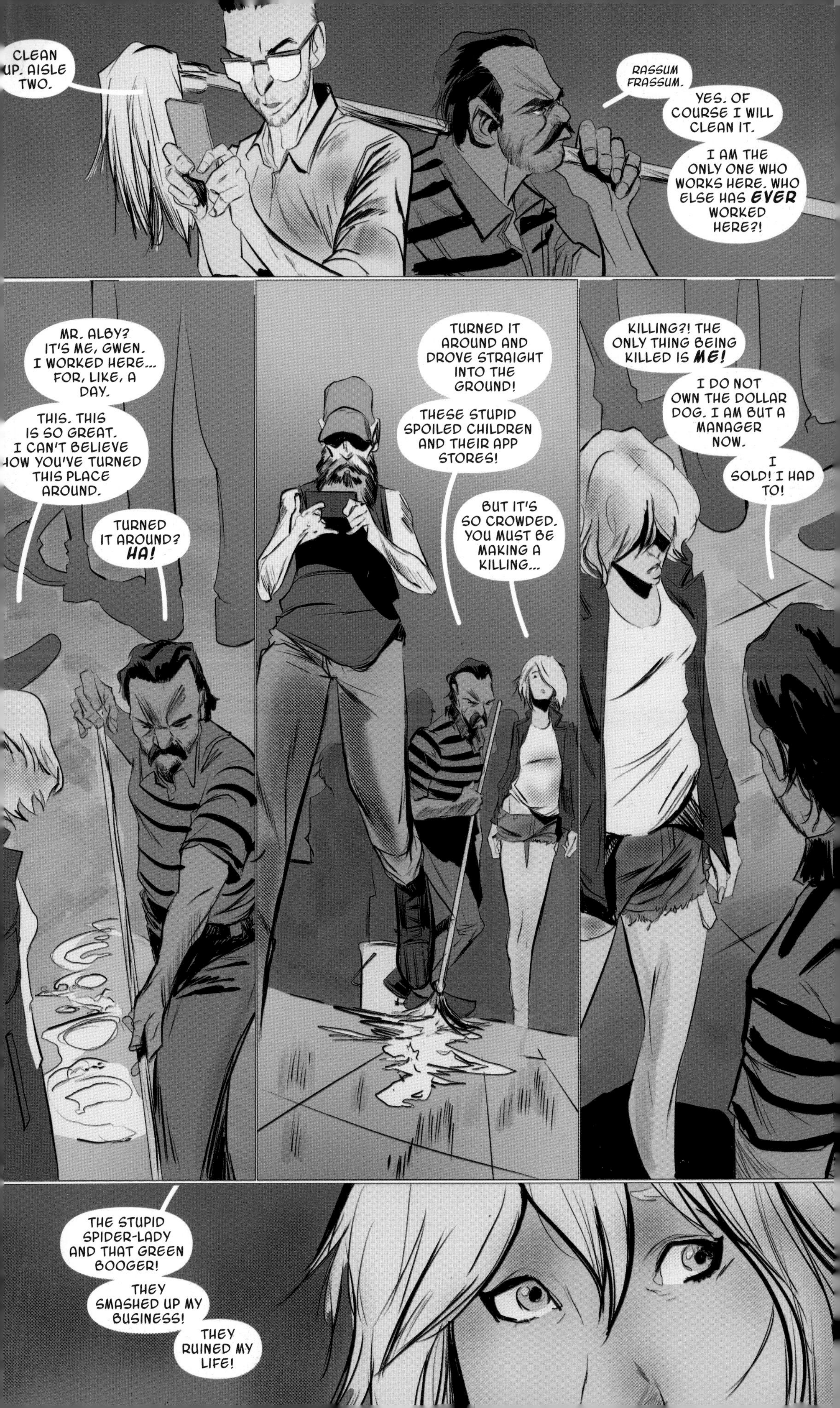
CLEAN UP. AISLE TWO.
RASSUM FRASSUM.
YES. OF COURSE I WILL CLEAN IT.
I AM THE ONLY ONE WHO WORKS HERE. WHO ELSE HAS EVER WORKED HERE?!
MR. ALBY? IT'S ME, GWEN. I WORKED HERE... FOR, LIKE, A DAY.
THIS. THIS IS SO GREAT. I CAN'T BELIEVE HOW YOU'VE TURNED THIS PLACE AROUND.
TURNED IT AROUND? HA!
TURNED IT AROUND AND DROVE STRAIGHT INTO THE GROUND!
THESE STUPID SPOILED CHILDREN AND THEIR APP STORES!
BUT IT'S SO CROWDED. YOU MUST BE MAKING A KILLING...
KILLING?! THE ONLY THING BEING KILLED IS ME!
I DO NOT OWN THE DOLLAR DOG. I AM BUT A MANAGER NOW.
I SOLD! I HAD TO!
THE STUPID SPIDER-LADY AND THAT GREEN BOOGER!
THEY SMASHED UP MY BUSINESS!
THEY RUINED MY LIFE!

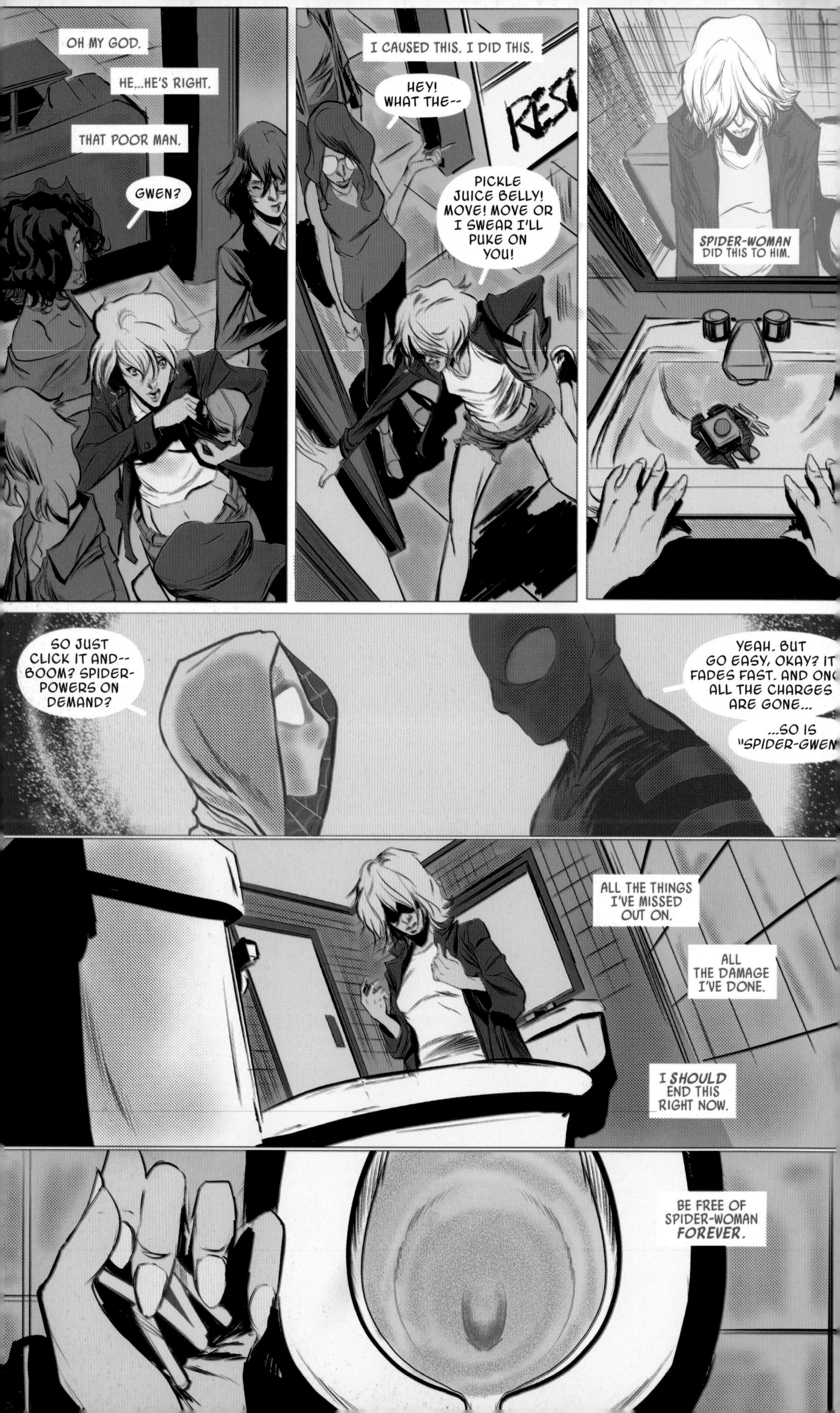
OH MY GOD.
HE...HE'S RIGHT.
THAT POOR MAN.
GWEN?
I CAUSED THIS. I DID THIS.
HEY! WHAT THE--
PICKLE JUICE BELLY! MOVE! MOVE OR I SWEAR I'LL PUKE ON YOU!
SPIDER-WOMAN DID THIS TO HIM.
SO JUST CLICK IT AND-- BOOM? SPIDER-POWERS ON DEMAND?
YEAH. BUT GO EASY, OKAY? IT FADES FAST. AND ONC ALL THE CHARGES ARE GONE...
...SO IS "SPIDER-GWEN
ALL THE THINGS I'VE MISSED OUT ON.
ALL THE DAMAGE I'VE DONE.
I SHOULD END THIS RIGHT NOW.
BE FREE OF SPIDER-WOMAN FOREVER.

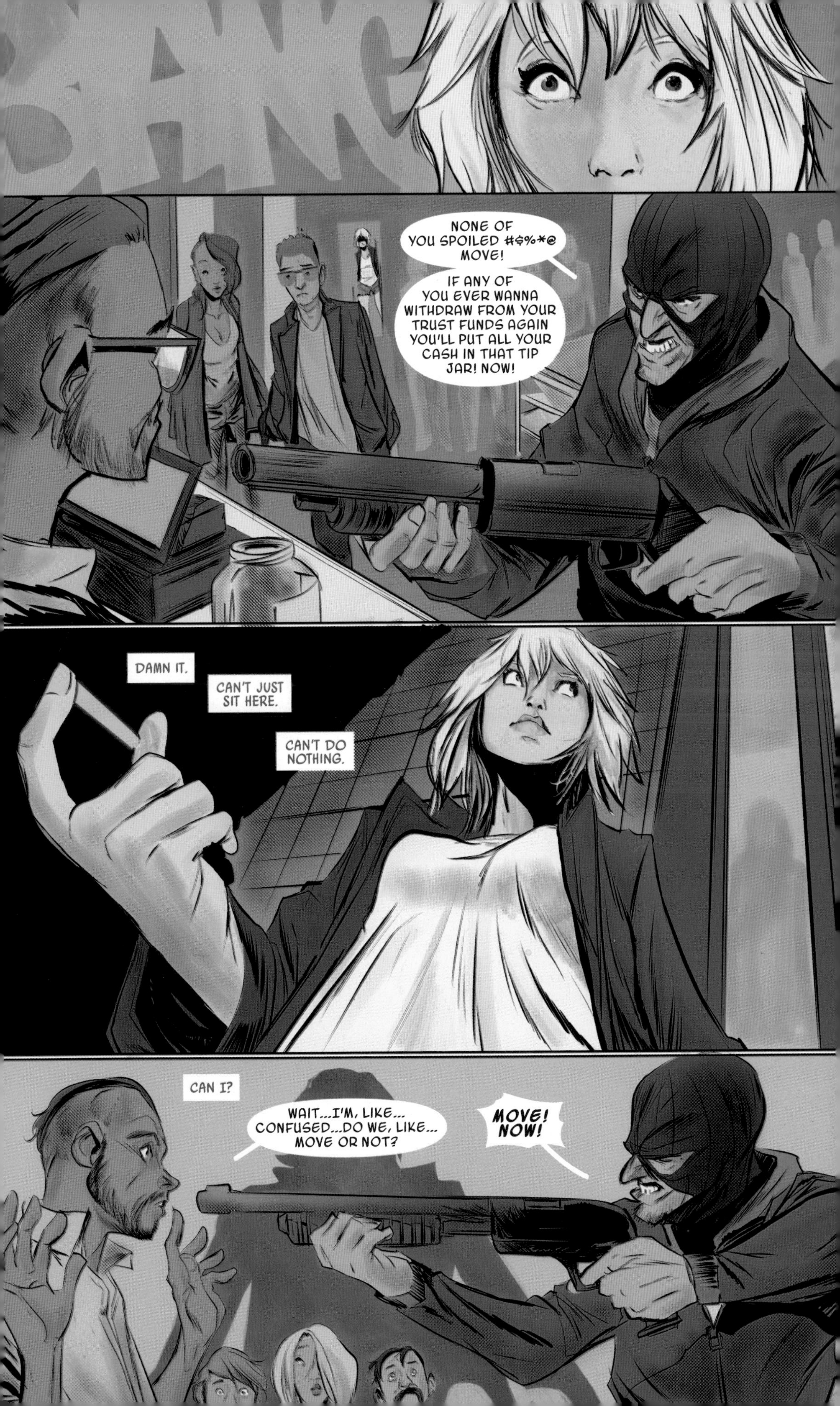
NONE OF YOU SPOILED #$%*@ MOVE!
IF ANY OF YOU EVER WANNA WITHDRAW FROM YOUR TRUST FUNDS AGAIN YOU'LL PUT ALL YOUR CASH IN THAT TIP JAR! NOW!
DAMN IT.
CAN'T JUST SIT HERE.
CAN'T DO NOTHING.
CAN I?
WAIT...I'M, LIKE... CONFUSED...DO WE, LIKE... MOVE OR NOT?
MOVE! NOW!

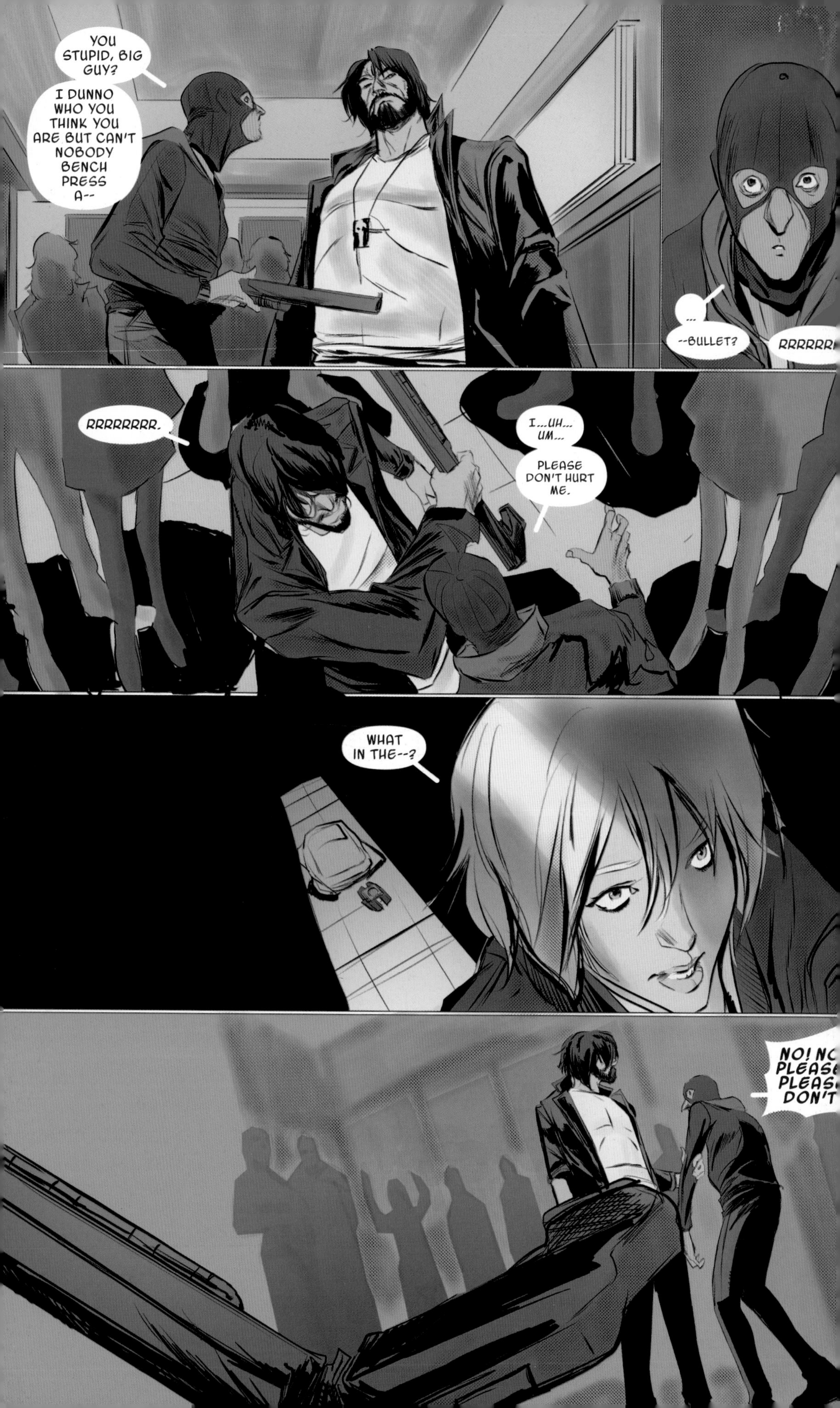
YOU STUPID, BIG GUY?
I DUNNO WHO YOU THINK YOU ARE BUT CAN'T NOBODY BENCH PRESS A--
...
--BULLET?
RRRRRR
RRRRRRRR.
I...UH... UM...
PLEASE DON'T HURT ME.
WHAT IN THE--?
NO! NO PLEASE PLEASE DON'T

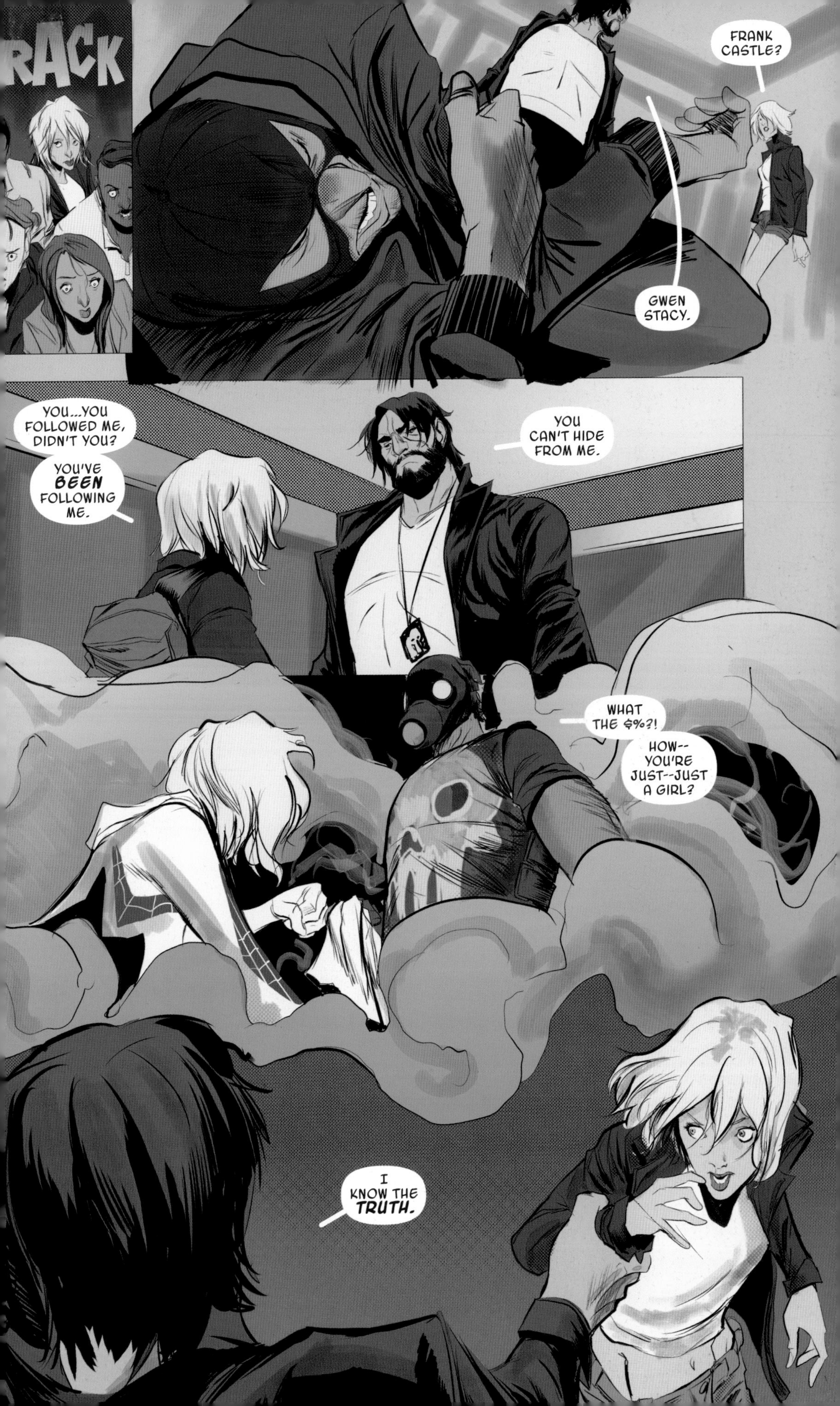
RACK
FRANK CASTLE?
GWEN STACY.
YOU...YOU FOLLOWED ME, DIDN'T YOU?
YOU'VE BEEN FOLLOWING ME.
YOU CAN'T HIDE FROM ME.
WHAT THE $%?!
HOW-- YOU'RE JUST--JUST A GIRL?
I KNOW THE TRUTH.

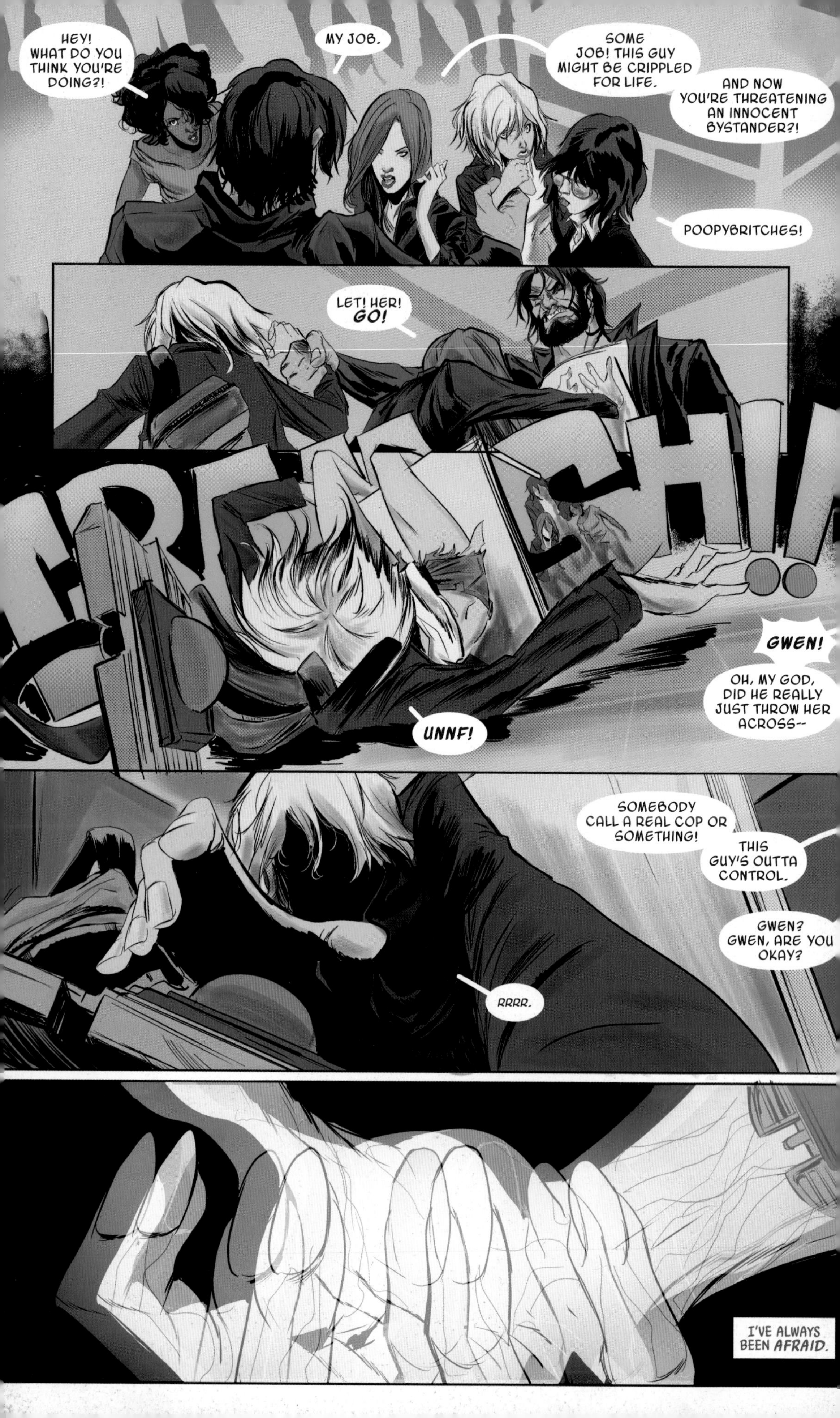
HEY! WHAT DO YOU THINK YOU'RE DOING?!
MY JOB.
SOME JOB! THIS GUY MIGHT BE CRIPPLED FOR LIFE.
AND NOW YOU'RE THREATENING AN INNOCENT BYSTANDER?!
POOPYBRITCHES!
LET! HER! GO!
UNNF!
GWEN!
OH, MY GOD, DID HE REALLY JUST THROW HER ACROSS--
SOMEBODY CALL A REAL COP OR SOMETHING!
THIS GUY'S OUTTA CONTROL.
GWEN? GWEN, ARE YOU OKAY?
RRRR.
I'VE ALWAYS BEEN AFRAID.

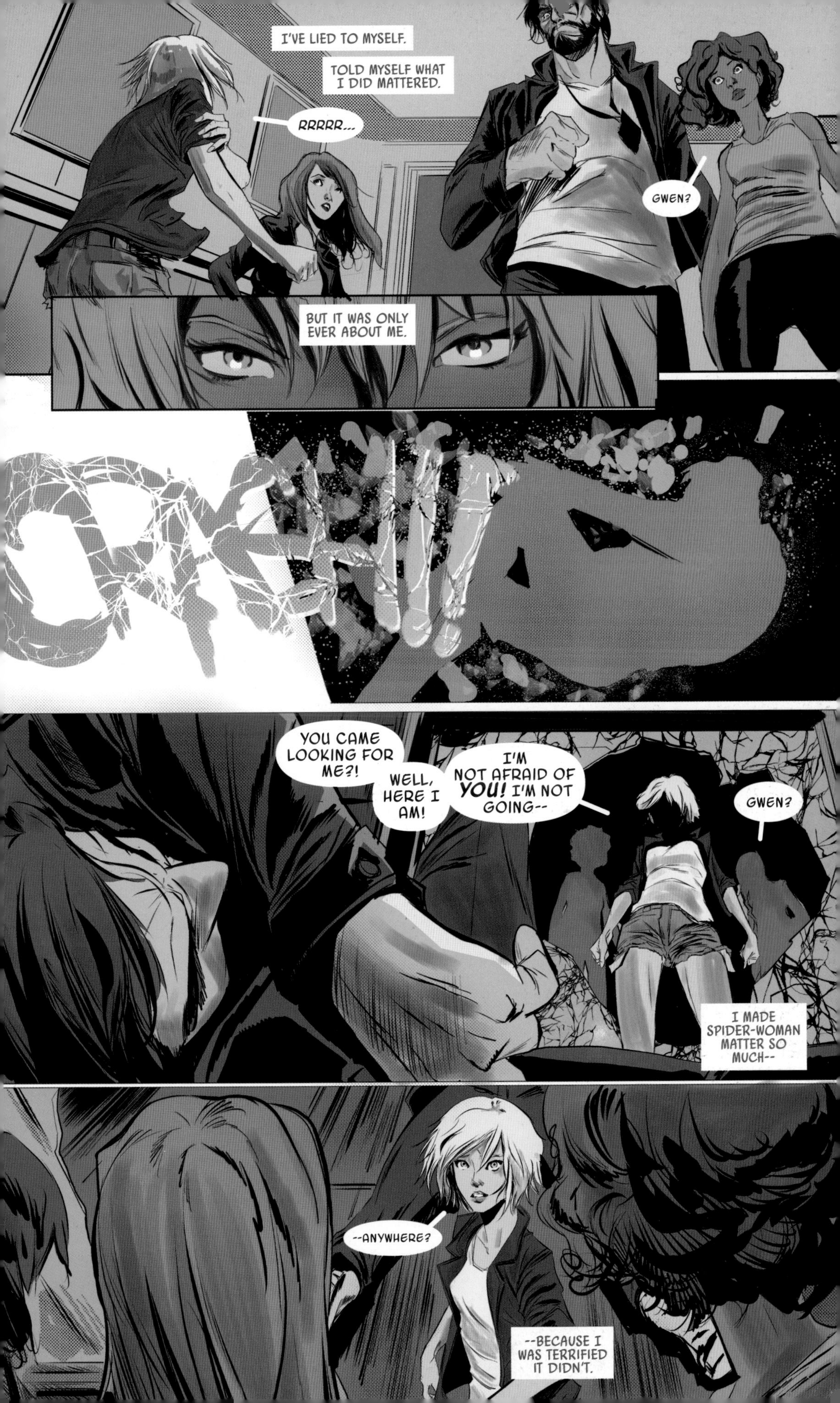
I'VE LIED TO MYSELF.
TOLD MYSELF WHAT I DID MATTERED.
RRRRR...
GWEN?
BUT IT WAS ONLY EVER ABOUT ME.
YOU CAME LOOKING FOR ME?!
WELL, HERE I AM!
I'M NOT AFRAID OF YOU! I'M NOT GOING--
GWEN?
I MADE SPIDER-WOMAN MATTER SO MUCH--
--ANYWHERE?
--BECAUSE I WAS TERRIFIED IT DIDN'T.

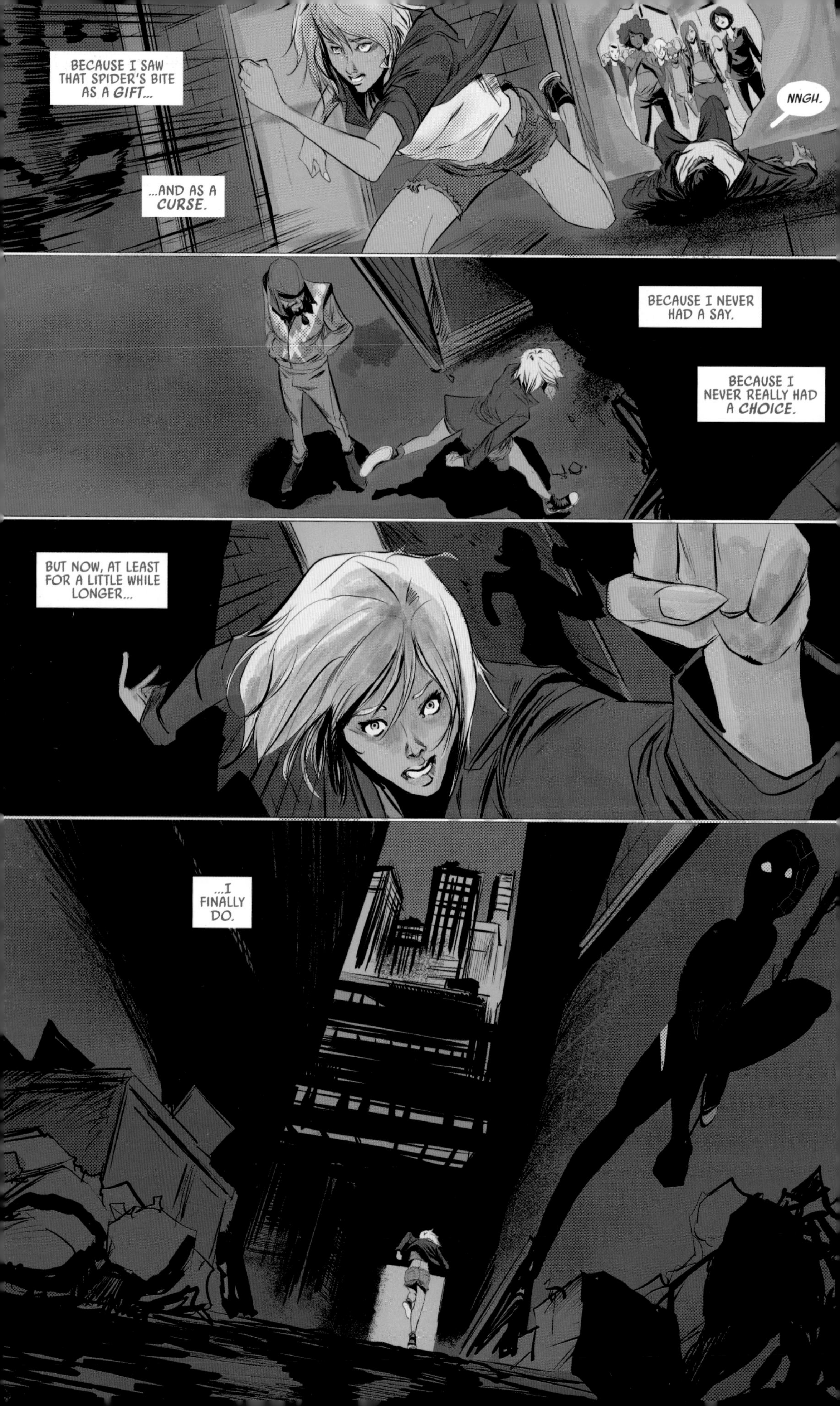

BECAUSE I SAW THAT SPIDER'S BITE AS A *GIFT*...
...AND AS A *CURSE*.
NNGH.
BECAUSE I NEVER HAD A SAY.
BECAUSE I NEVER REALLY HAD A *CHOICE*.
BUT NOW, AT LEAST FOR A LITTLE WHILE LONGER...
...I FINALLY DO.

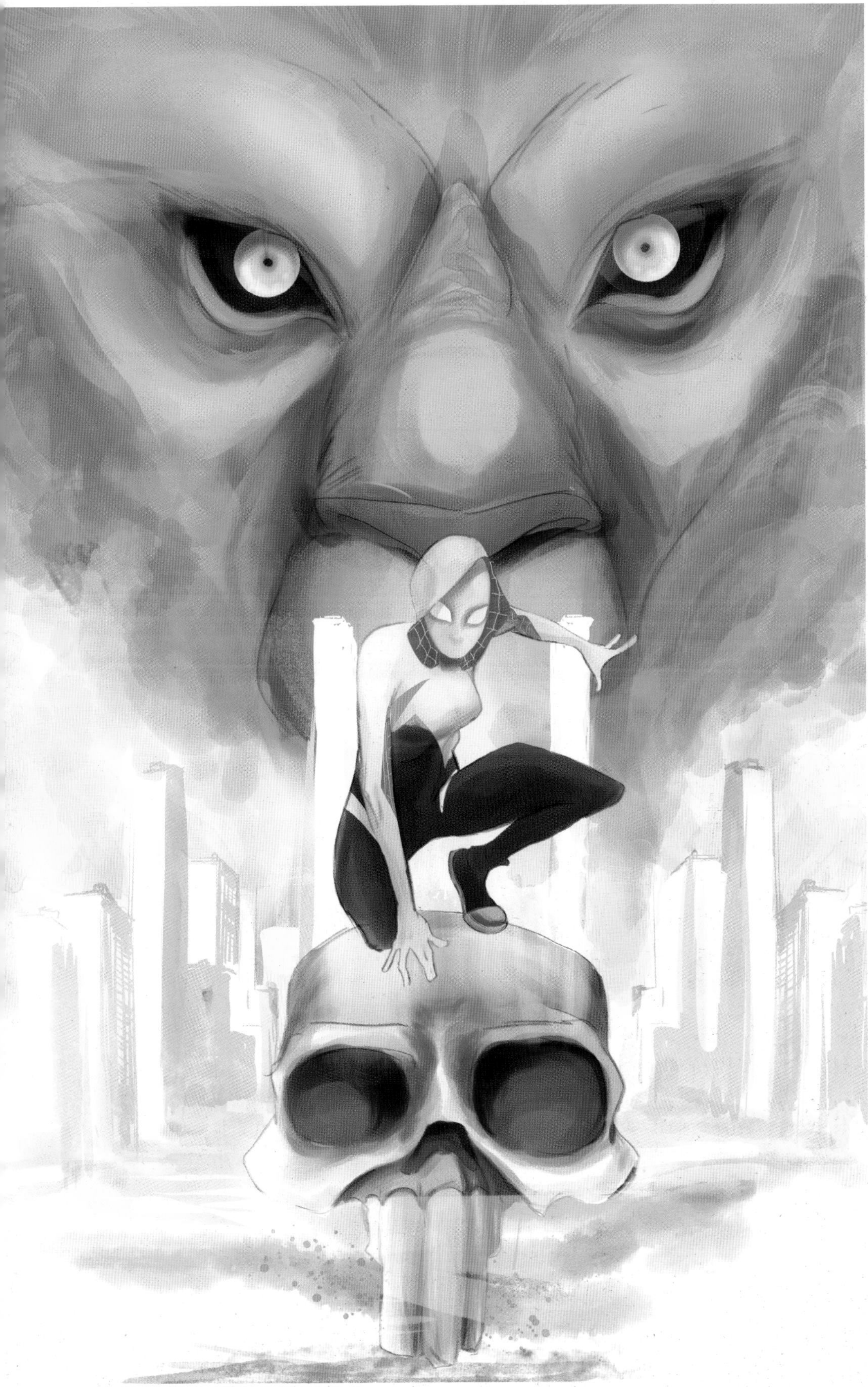

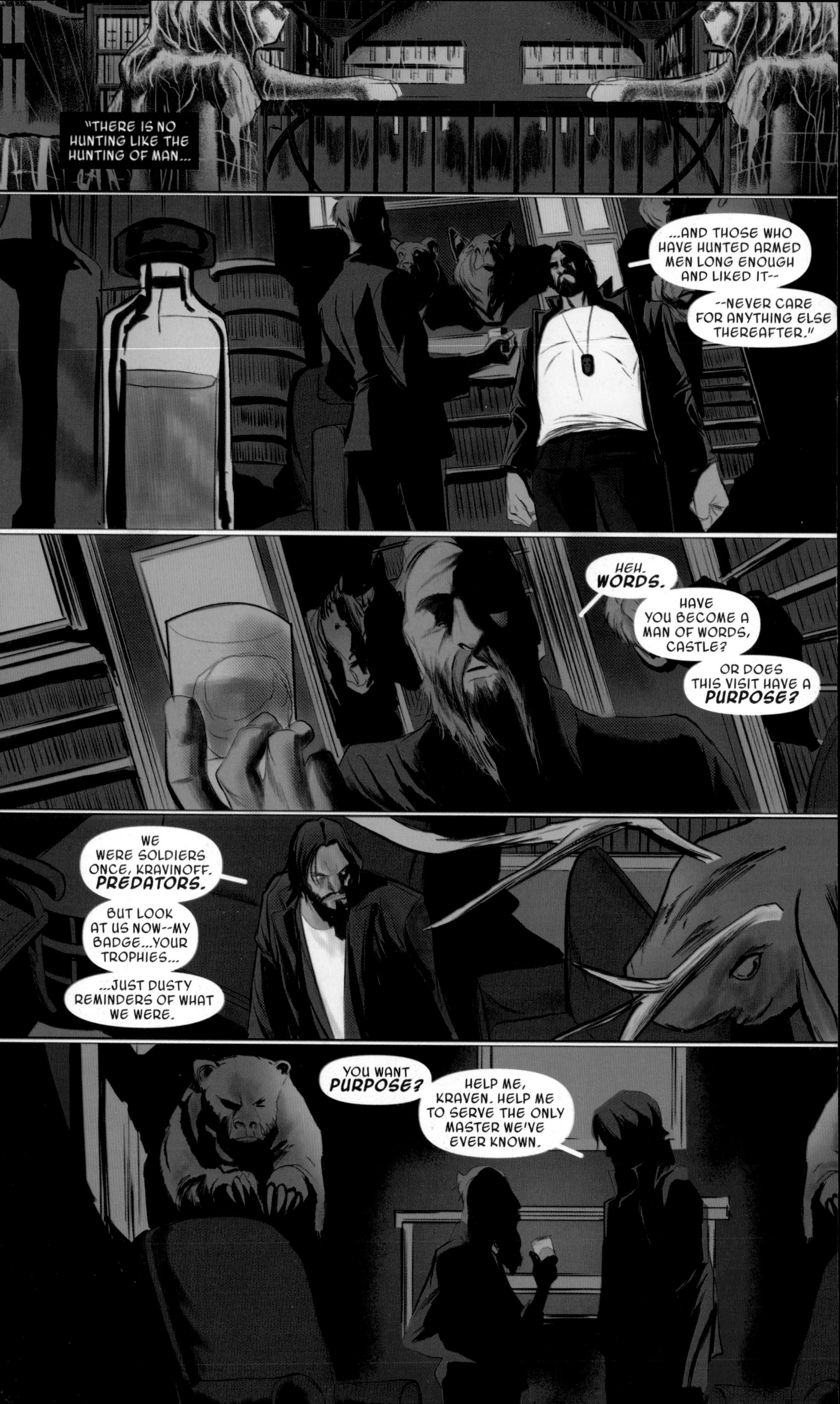
"THERE IS NO HUNTING LIKE THE HUNTING OF MAN...
...AND THOSE WHO HAVE HUNTED ARMED MEN LONG ENOUGH AND LIKED IT--
--NEVER CARE FOR ANYTHING ELSE THEREAFTER."
HEH. WORDS.
HAVE YOU BECOME A MAN OF WORDS, CASTLE?
OR DOES THIS VISIT HAVE A PURPOSE?
WE WERE SOLDIERS ONCE, KRAVINOFF. PREDATORS.
BUT LOOK AT US NOW--MY BADGE...YOUR TROPHIES...
...JUST DUSTY REMINDERS OF WHAT WE WERE.
YOU WANT PURPOSE?
HELP ME, KRAVEN. HELP ME TO SERVE THE ONLY MASTER WE'VE EVER KNOWN.

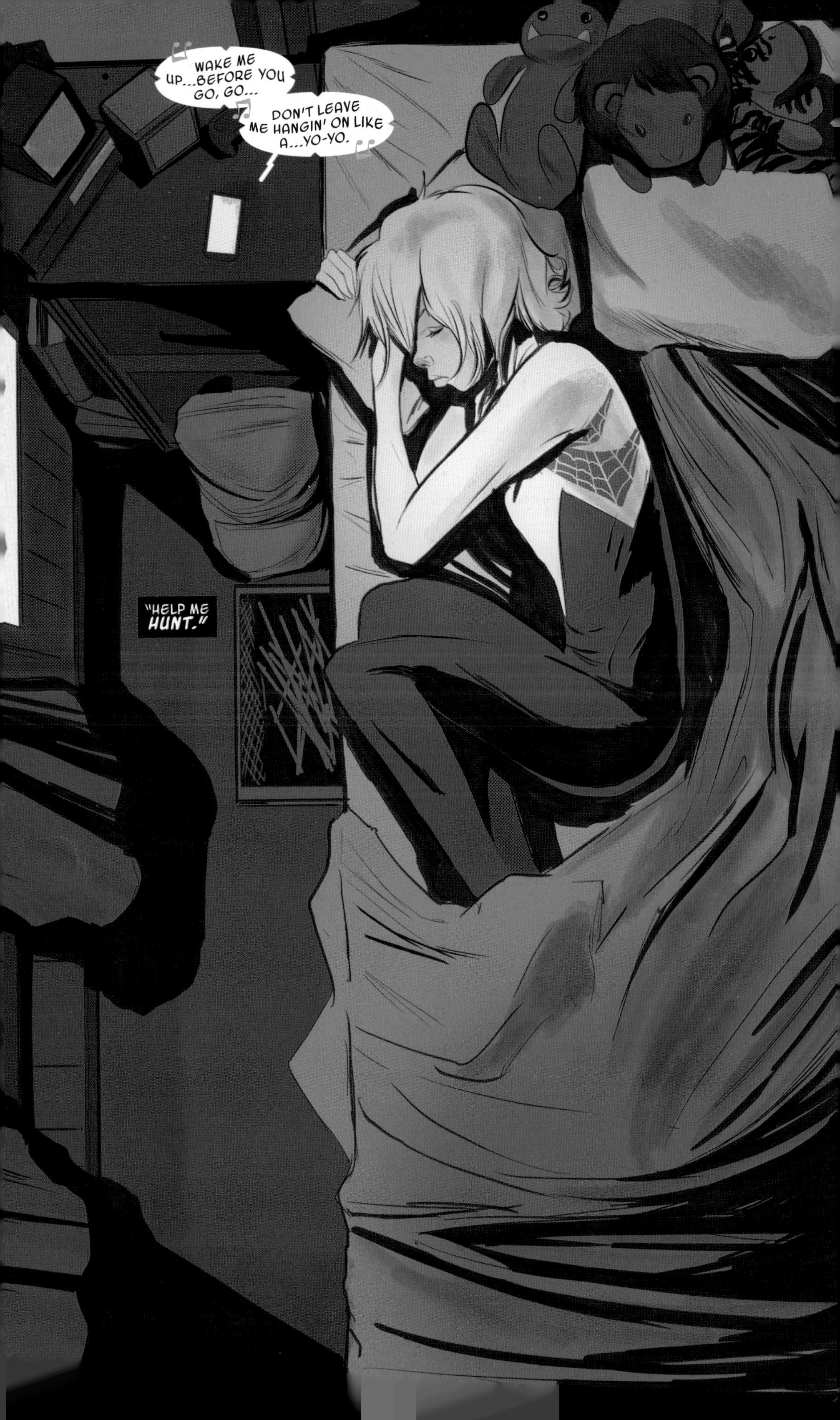
WAKE ME UP...BEFORE YOU GO, GO...
DON'T LEAVE ME HANGIN' ON LIKE A...YO-YO.
"HELP ME HUNT."

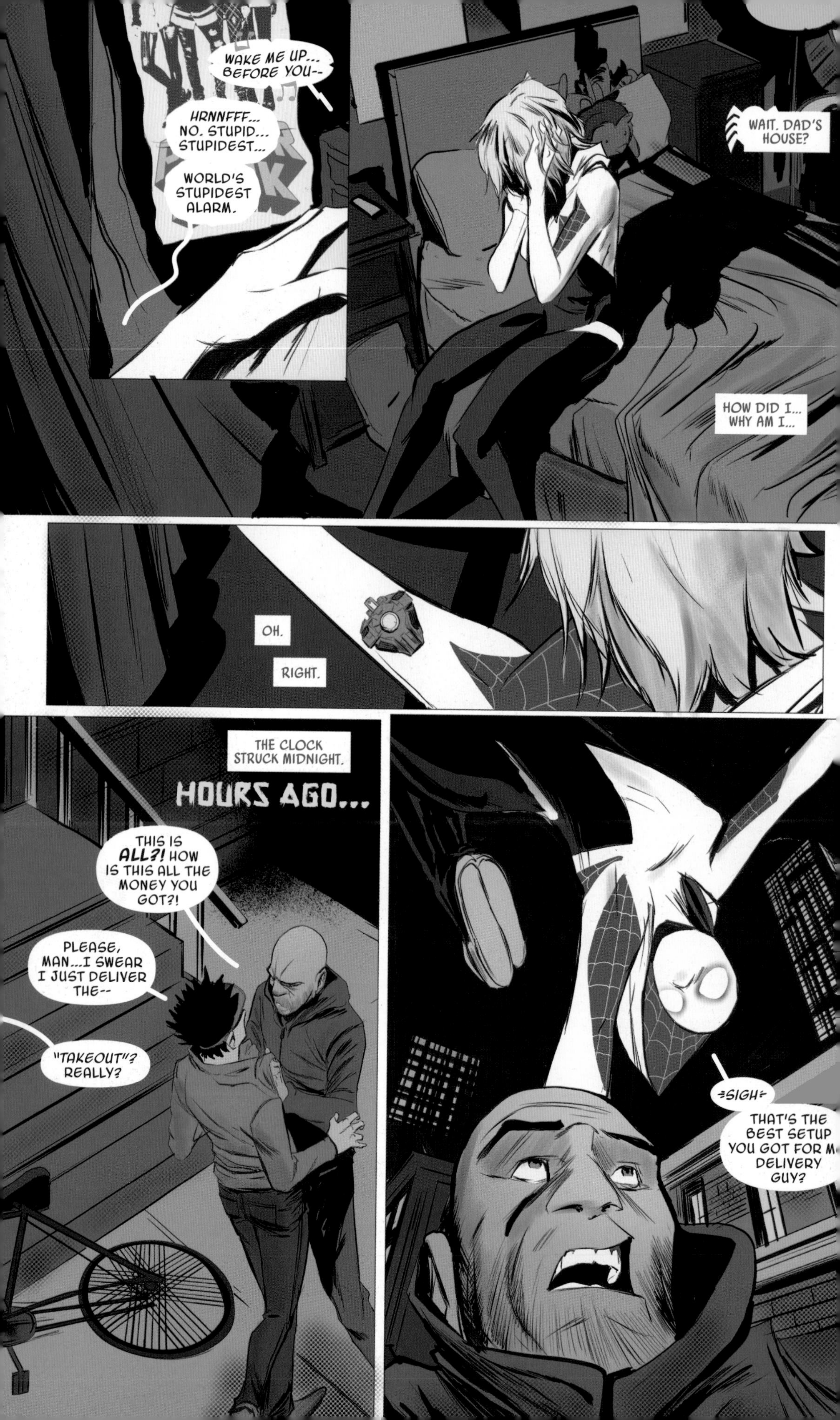

WAKE ME UP... BEFORE YOU--
HRNNFFF... NO. STUPID... STUPIDEST...
WORLD'S STUPIDEST ALARM.
WAIT. DAD'S HOUSE?
HOW DID I... WHY AM I...
OH.
RIGHT.
THE CLOCK STRUCK MIDNIGHT.
HOURS AGO...
THIS IS ALL?! HOW IS THIS ALL THE MONEY YOU GOT?!
PLEASE, MAN...I SWEAR I JUST DELIVER THE--
"TAKEOUT"? REALLY?
=SIGH=
THAT'S THE BEST SETUP YOU GOT FOR M DELIVERY GUY?

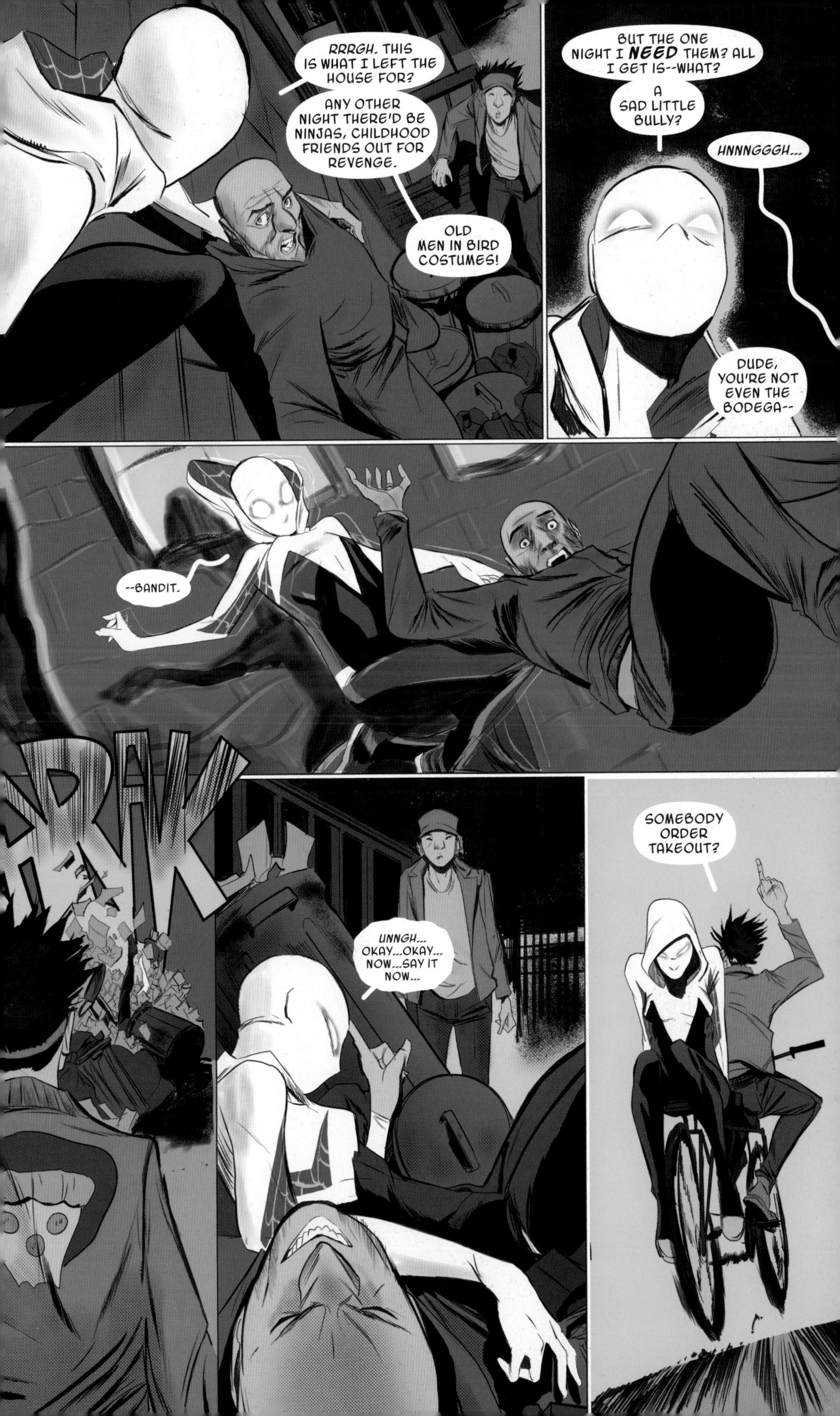
RRRGH. THIS IS WHAT I LEFT THE HOUSE FOR?
ANY OTHER NIGHT THERE'D BE NINJAS, CHILDHOOD FRIENDS OUT FOR REVENGE.
OLD MEN IN BIRD COSTUMES!
BUT THE ONE NIGHT I **NEED** THEM? ALL I GET IS--WHAT?
A SAD LITTLE BULLY?
HNNNGGGH...
DUDE, YOU'RE NOT EVEN THE BODEGA--
--BANDIT.
UNNGH... OKAY...OKAY... NOW...SAY IT NOW...
SOMEBODY ORDER TAKEOUT?

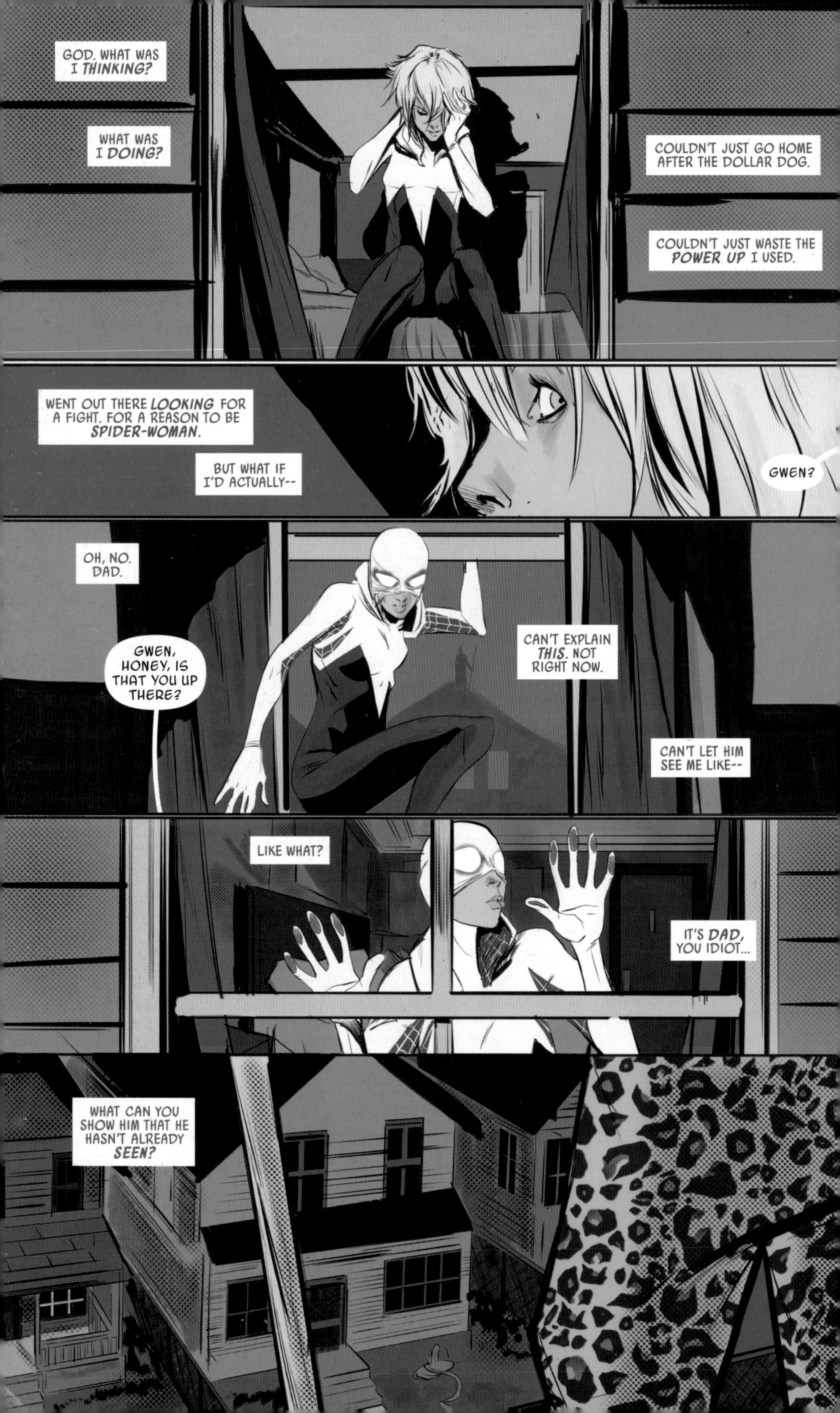
GOD. WHAT WAS I THINKING?
WHAT WAS I DOING?
COULDN'T JUST GO HOME AFTER THE DOLLAR DOG.
COULDN'T JUST WASTE THE POWER UP I USED.
WENT OUT THERE LOOKING FOR A FIGHT. FOR A REASON TO BE SPIDER-WOMAN.
BUT WHAT IF I'D ACTUALLY--
GWEN?
OH, NO. DAD.
GWEN, HONEY, IS THAT YOU UP THERE?
CAN'T EXPLAIN THIS. NOT RIGHT NOW.
CAN'T LET HIM SEE ME LIKE--
LIKE WHAT?
IT'S DAD, YOU IDIOT...
WHAT CAN YOU SHOW HIM THAT HE HASN'T ALREADY SEEN?

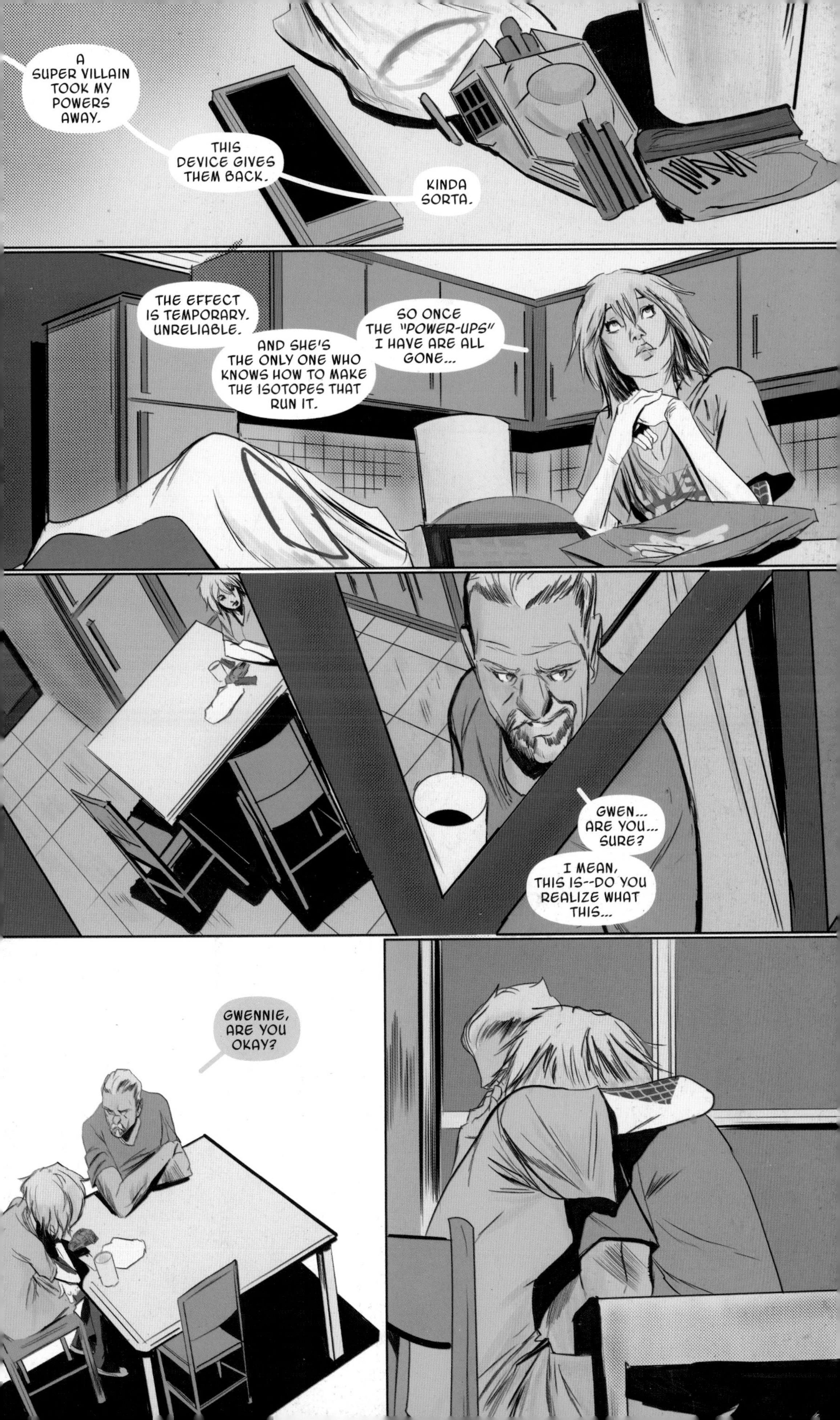
A SUPER VILLAIN TOOK MY POWERS AWAY.
THIS DEVICE GIVES THEM BACK.
KINDA SORTA.
THE EFFECT IS TEMPORARY. UNRELIABLE.
AND SHE'S THE ONLY ONE WHO KNOWS HOW TO MAKE THE ISOTOPES THAT RUN IT.
SO ONCE THE "POWER-UPS" I HAVE ARE ALL GONE...
GWEN... ARE YOU... SURE?
I MEAN, THIS IS--DO YOU REALIZE WHAT THIS...
GWENNIE, ARE YOU OKAY?

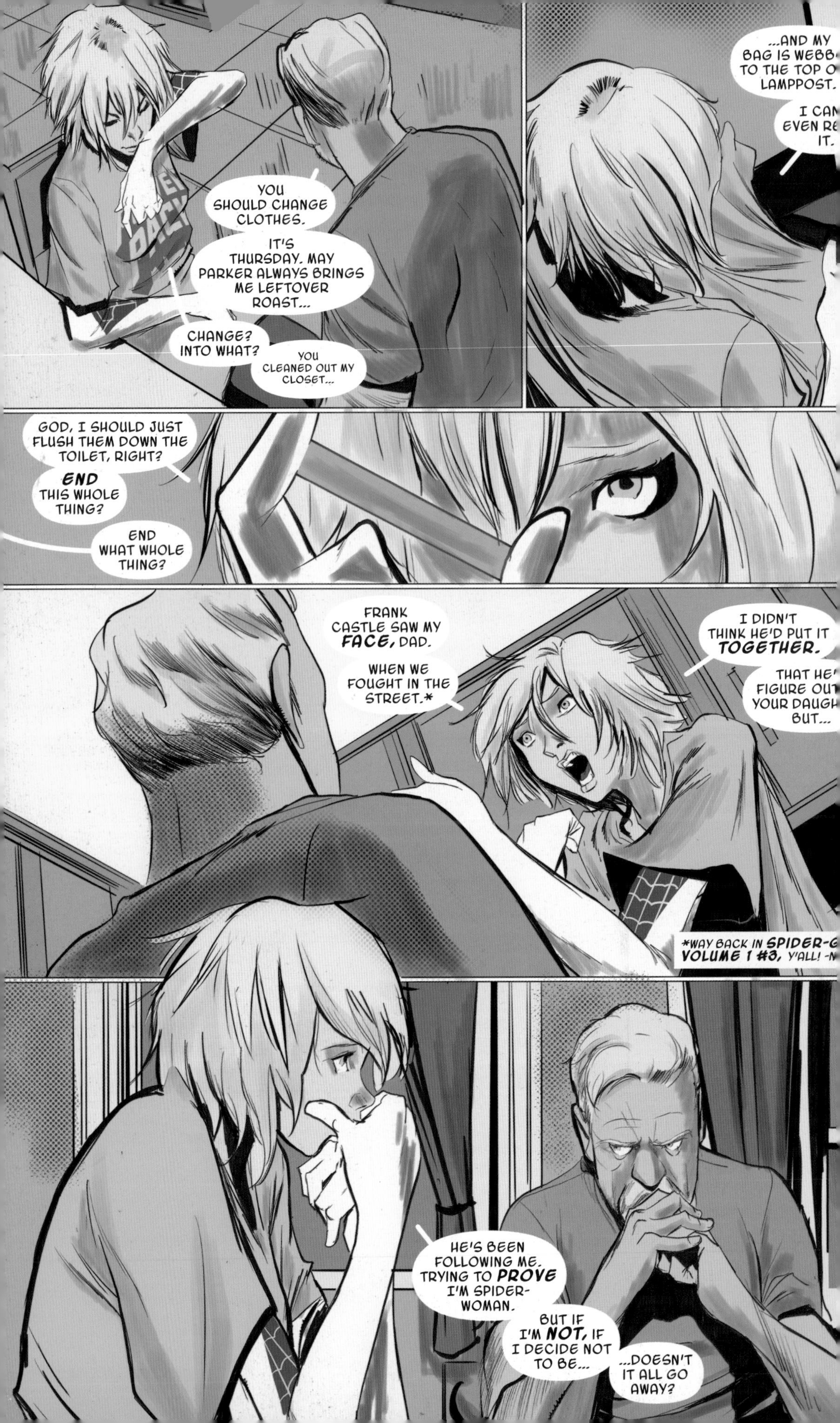
YOU SHOULD CHANGE CLOTHES.
IT'S THURSDAY. MAY PARKER ALWAYS BRINGS ME LEFTOVER ROAST...
CHANGE? INTO WHAT?
YOU CLEANED OUT MY CLOSET...
...AND MY BAG IS WEBB
TO THE TOP O
LAMPPOST.
I CAN
EVEN RE
IT.
GOD, I SHOULD JUST FLUSH THEM DOWN THE TOILET, RIGHT?
END THIS WHOLE THING?
END WHAT WHOLE THING?
FRANK CASTLE SAW MY FACE, DAD.
WHEN WE FOUGHT IN THE STREET.*
I DIDN'T THINK HE'D PUT IT TOGETHER.
THAT HE'
FIGURE OUT
YOUR DAUGH
BUT...
*WAY BACK IN SPIDER-G
VOLUME 1 #3, Y'ALL! -N
HE'S BEEN FOLLOWING ME. TRYING TO PROVE I'M SPIDER-WOMAN.
BUT IF I'M NOT, IF I DECIDE NOT TO BE...
...DOESN'T IT ALL GO AWAY?

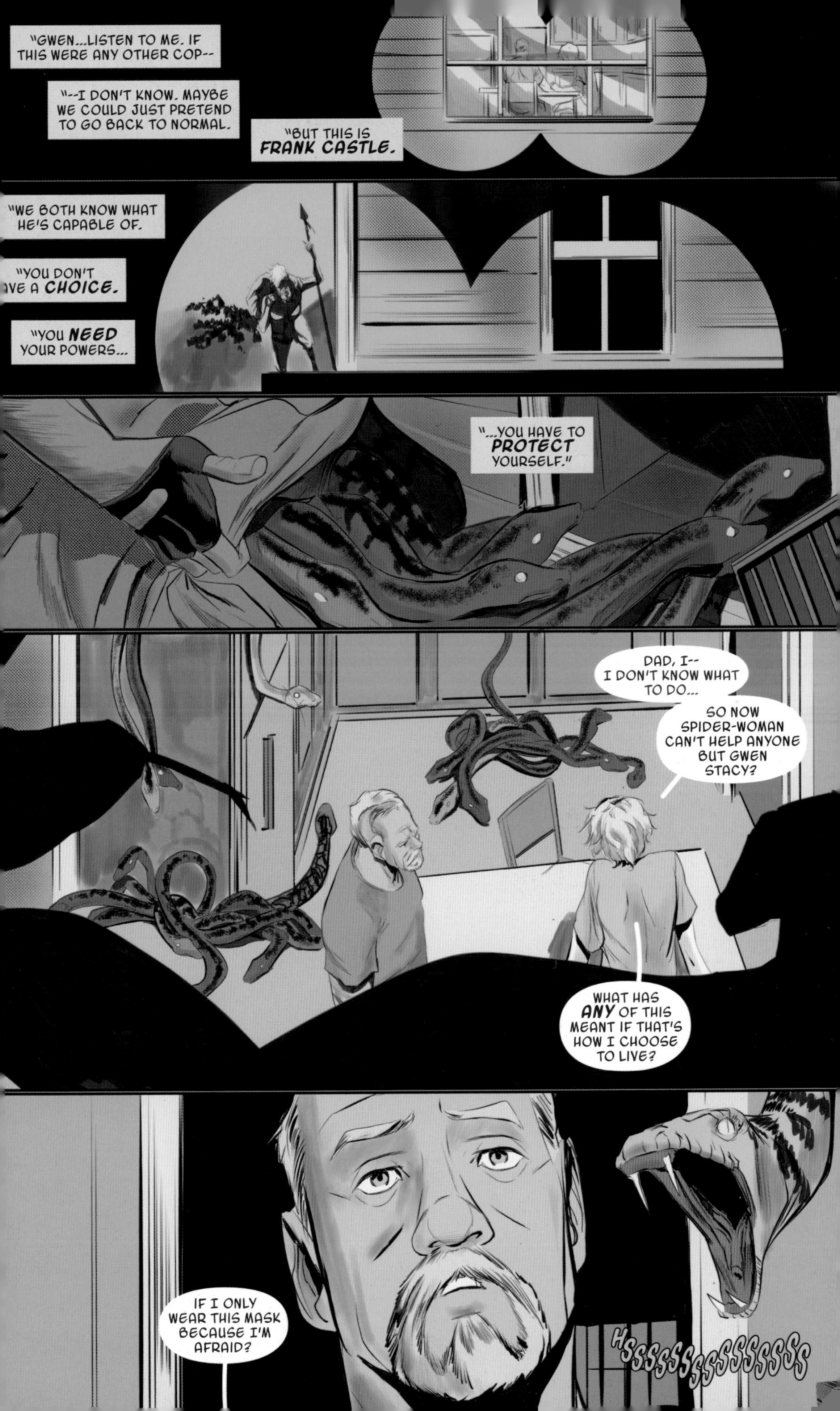
"GWEN...LISTEN TO ME. IF THIS WERE ANY OTHER COP--
"--I DON'T KNOW. MAYBE WE COULD JUST PRETEND TO GO BACK TO NORMAL.
"BUT THIS IS FRANK CASTLE.
"WE BOTH KNOW WHAT HE'S CAPABLE OF.
"YOU DON'T AVE A CHOICE.
"YOU NEED YOUR POWERS...
"...YOU HAVE TO PROTECT YOURSELF."
DAD, I-- I DON'T KNOW WHAT TO DO...
SO NOW SPIDER-WOMAN CAN'T HELP ANYONE BUT GWEN STACY?
WHAT HAS ANY OF THIS MEANT IF THAT'S HOW I CHOOSE TO LIVE?
IF I ONLY WEAR THIS MASK BECAUSE I'M AFRAID?
HSSSSSSSSSSSSSSSS

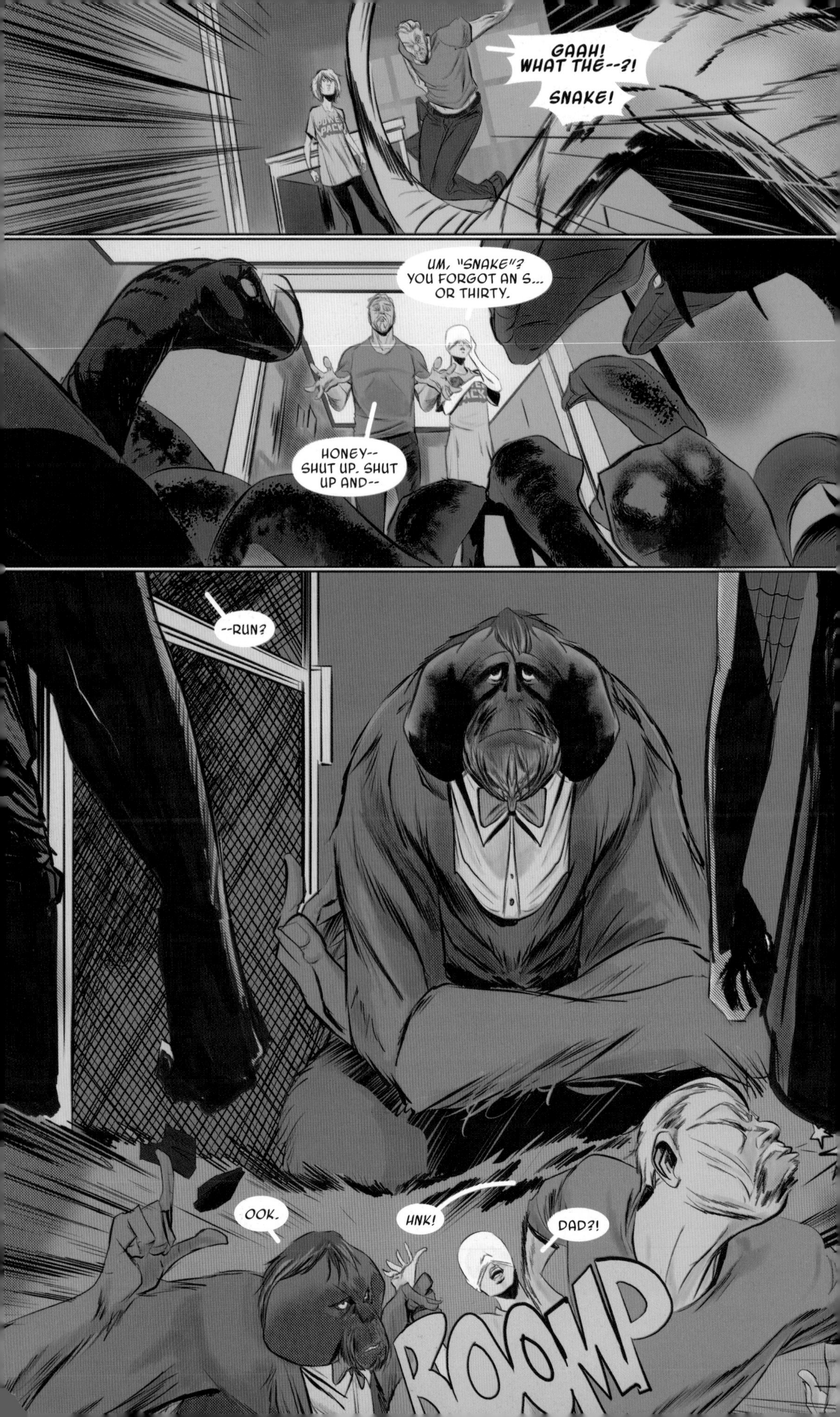
GAAH! WHAT THE--?!
SNAKE!
UM, "SNAKE"? YOU FORGOT AN S... OR THIRTY.
HONEY-- SHUT UP. SHUT UP AND--
--RUN?
OOK.
HNK!
DAD?!
BOOMP

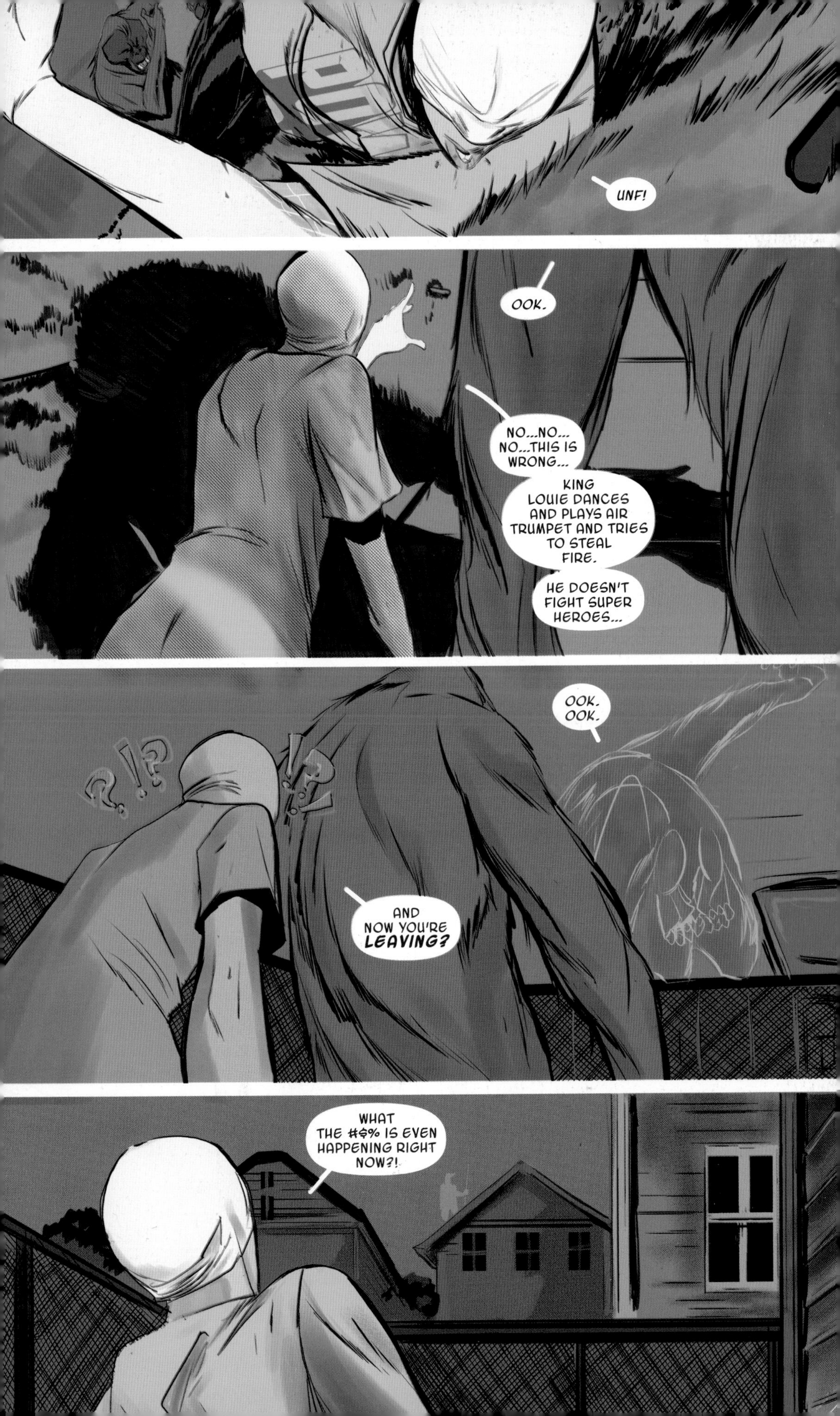
UNF!
OOK.
NO...NO... NO...THIS IS WRONG...
KING LOUIE DANCES AND PLAYS AIR TRUMPET AND TRIES TO STEAL FIRE.
HE DOESN'T FIGHT SUPER HEROES...
OOK. OOK.
?!?
!?!
AND NOW YOU'RE LEAVING?
WHAT THE #$% IS EVEN HAPPENING RIGHT NOW?!

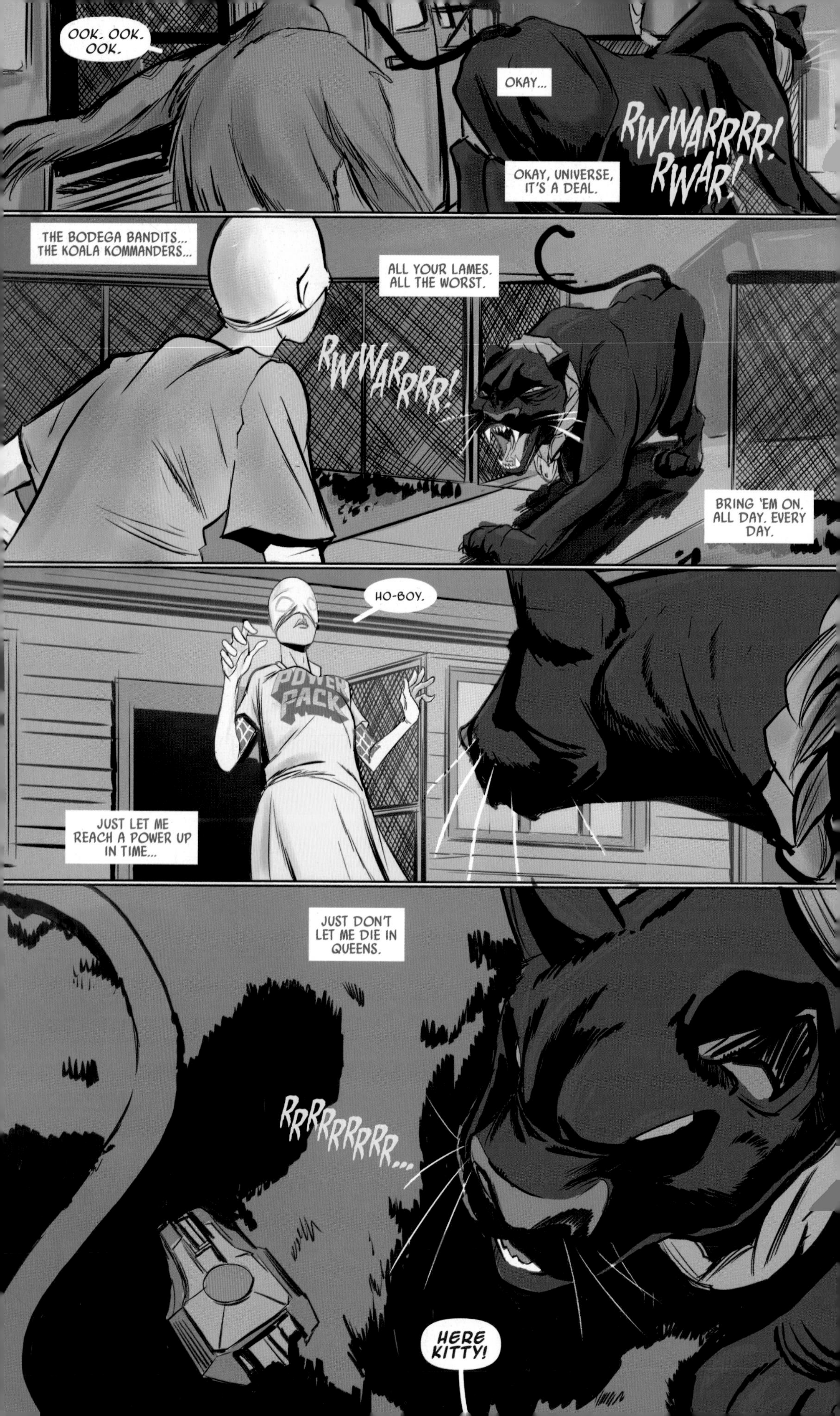
OOK. OOK. OOK.
OKAY...
RWWARRRR! RWAR!
OKAY, UNIVERSE, IT'S A DEAL.
THE BODEGA BANDITS... THE KOALA KOMMANDERS...
ALL YOUR LAMES. ALL THE WORST.
RWWARRRR!
BRING 'EM ON. ALL DAY. EVERY DAY.
HO-BOY.
POWER PACK
JUST LET ME REACH A POWER UP IN TIME...
JUST DON'T LET ME DIE IN QUEENS.
RRRRRRRRR...
HERE KITTY!

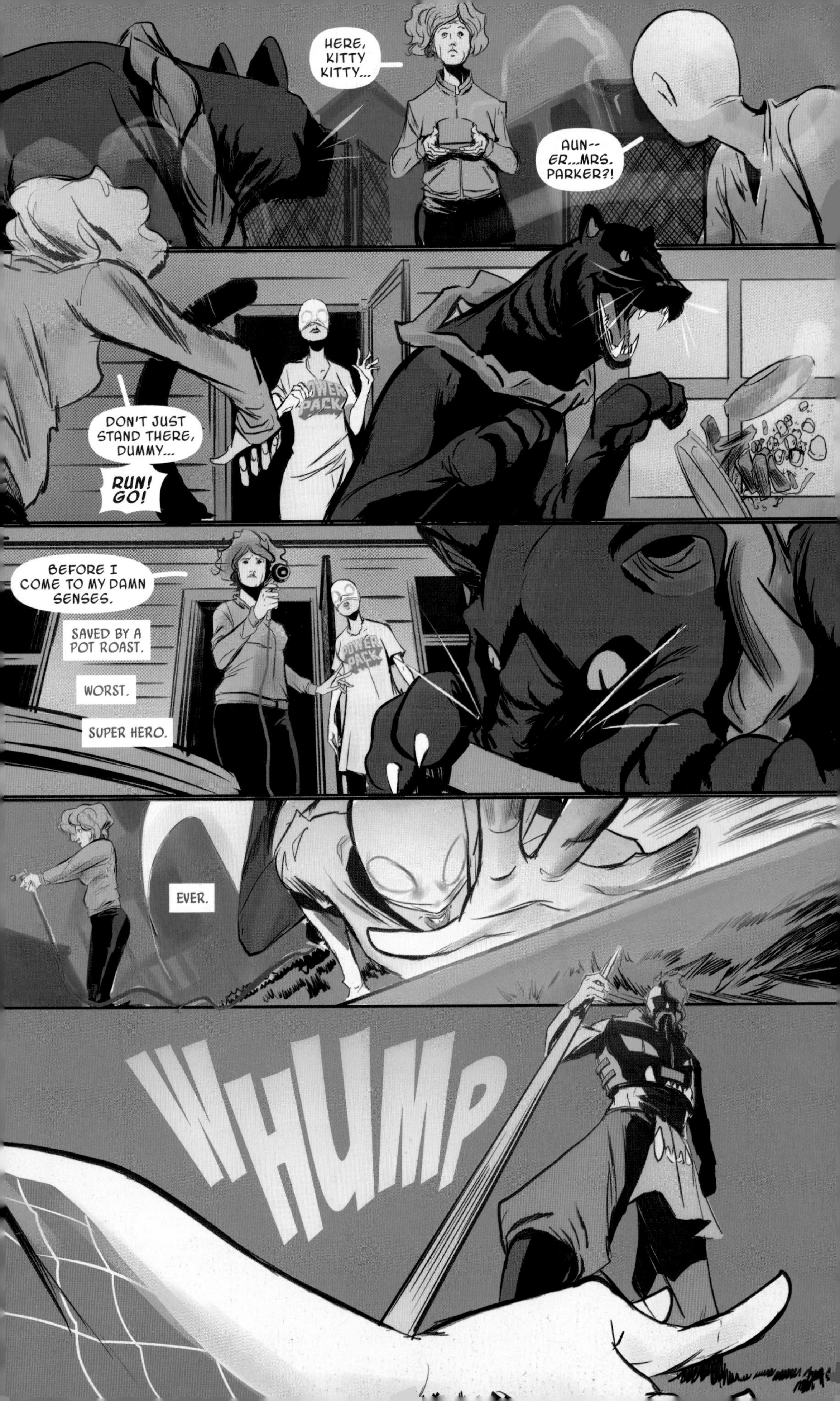

HERE, KITTY KITTY...
AUN-- ER...MRS. PARKER?!
DON'T JUST STAND THERE, DUMMY...
RUN! GO!
BEFORE I COME TO MY DAMN SENSES.
SAVED BY A POT ROAST.
WORST.
SUPER HERO.
EVER.
WHUMP

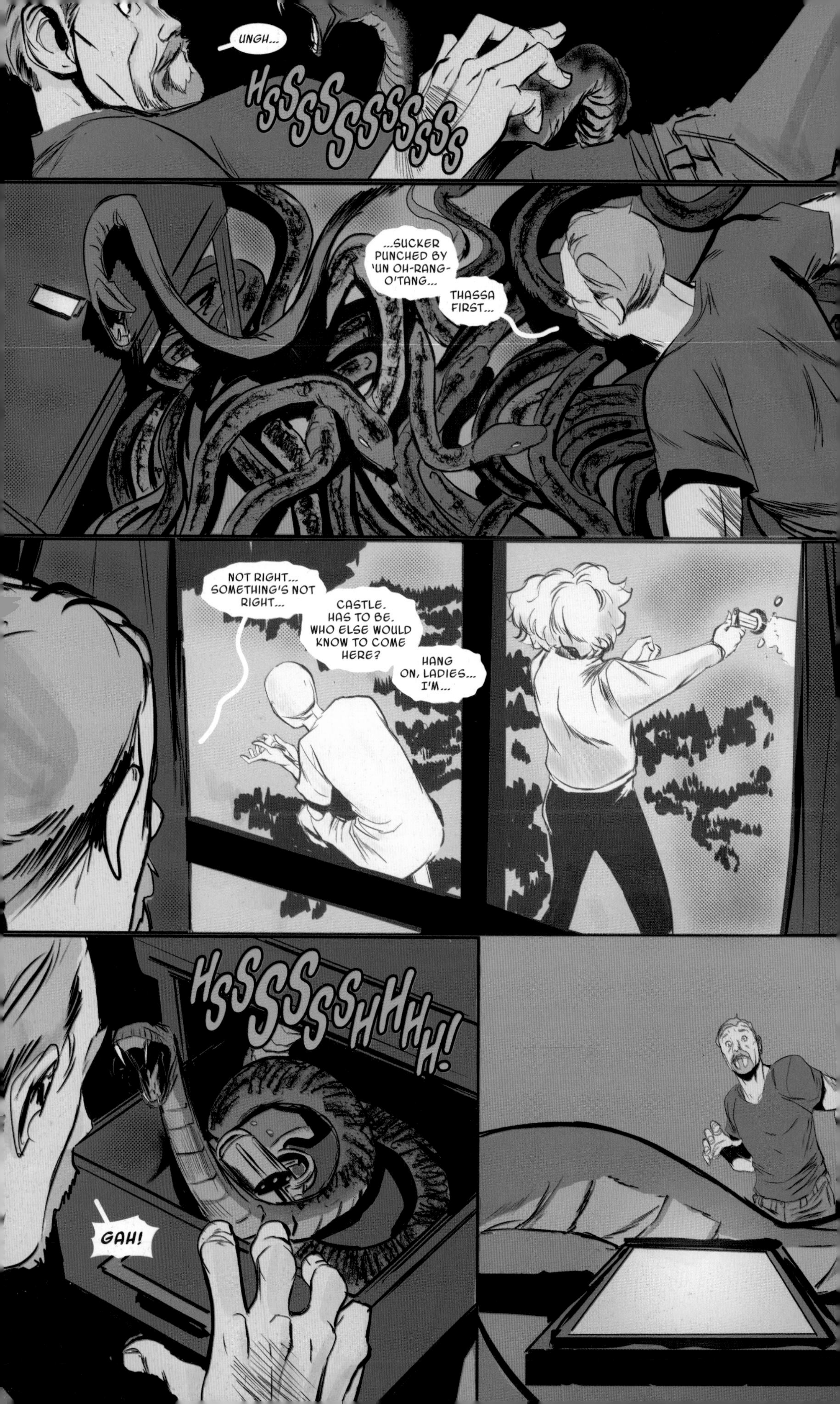
UNGH...
HSSSSSSSSSSSS
...SUCKER PUNCHED BY 'UN OH-RANG-O'TANG...
THASSA FIRST...
NOT RIGHT... SOMETHING'S NOT RIGHT...
CASTLE. HAS TO BE. WHO ELSE WOULD KNOW TO COME HERE?
HANG ON, LADIES... I'M...
HSSSSSSHHHHH!
GAH!

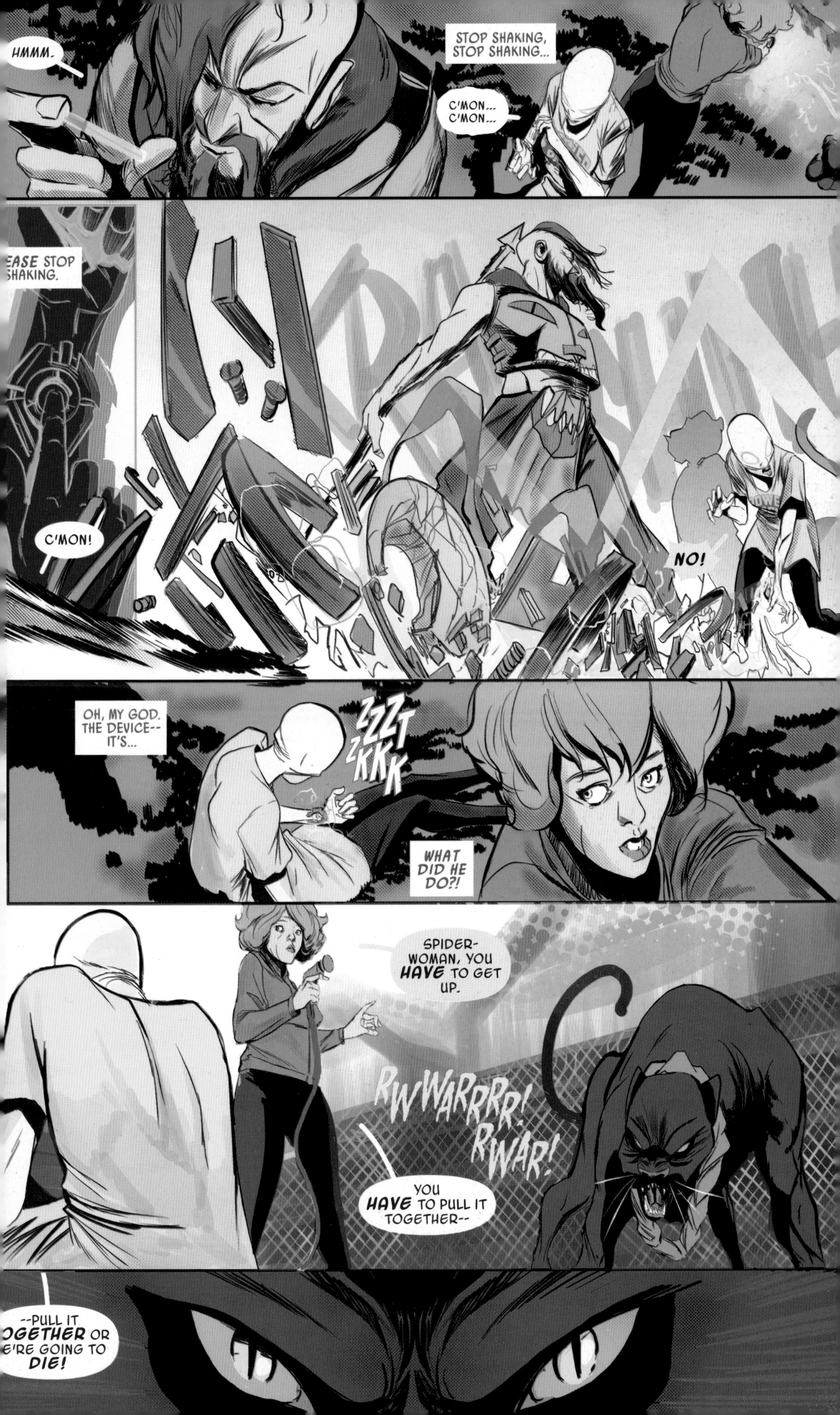

HMMM.
STOP SHAKING, STOP SHAKING...
C'MON... C'MON...
EASE STOP SHAKING.
C'MON!
NO!
OH, MY GOD. THE DEVICE-- IT'S...
ZZZT ZKKK
WHAT DID HE DO?!
SPIDER-WOMAN, YOU HAVE TO GET UP.
RWWARRRR! RWAR!
YOU HAVE TO PULL IT TOGETHER--
--PULL IT OGETHER OR E'RE GOING TO DIE!

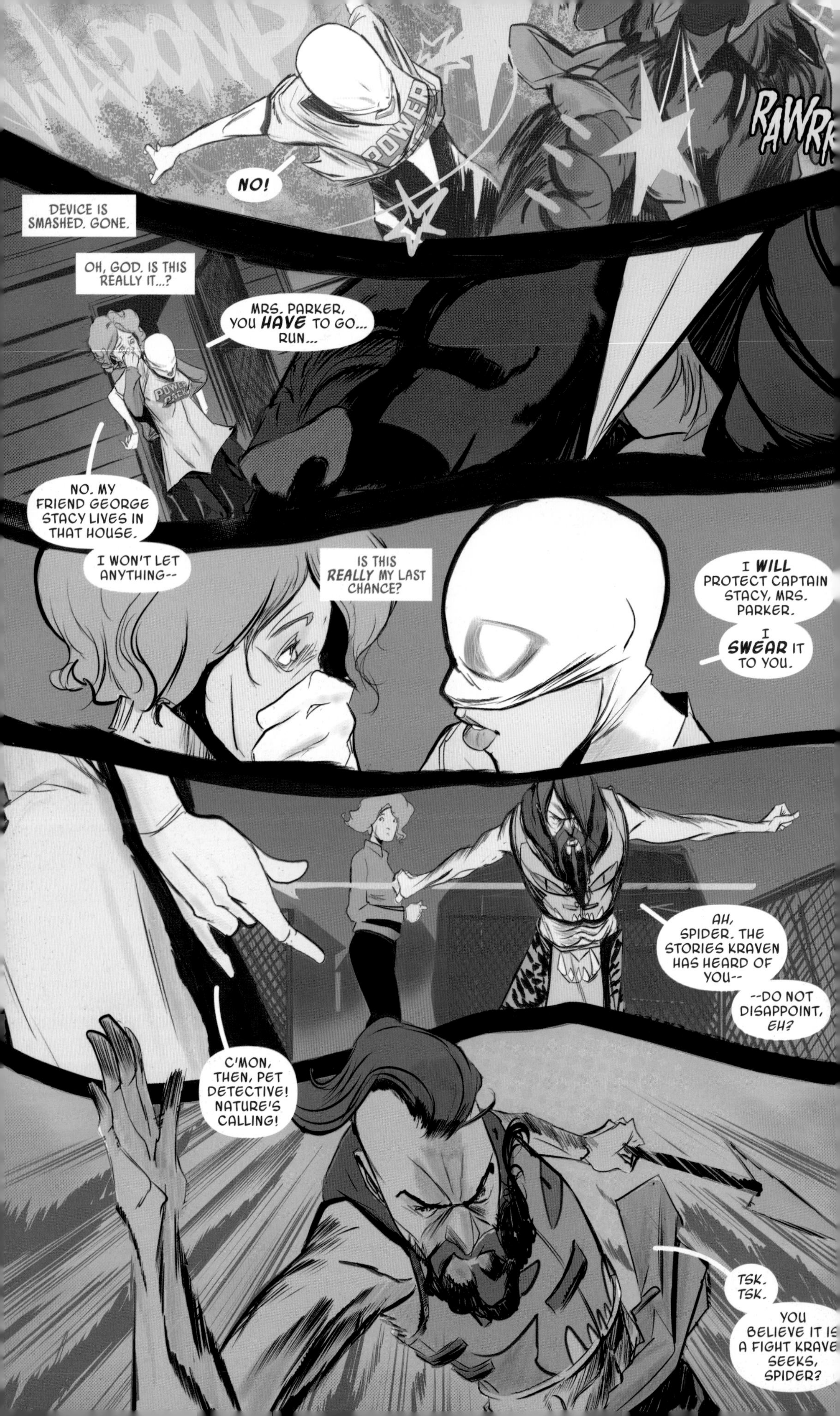
RAWRR
NO!
DEVICE IS SMASHED. GONE.
OH, GOD. IS THIS REALLY IT...?
MRS. PARKER, YOU HAVE TO GO... RUN...
NO. MY FRIEND GEORGE STACY LIVES IN THAT HOUSE.
I WON'T LET ANYTHING--
IS THIS REALLY MY LAST CHANCE?
I WILL PROTECT CAPTAIN STACY, MRS. PARKER.
I SWEAR IT TO YOU.
AH, SPIDER. THE STORIES KRAVEN HAS HEARD OF YOU--
--DO NOT DISAPPOINT, EH?
C'MON, THEN, PET DETECTIVE! NATURE'S CALLING!
TSK. TSK.
YOU BELIEVE IT IS A FIGHT KRAVEN SEEKS, SPIDER?

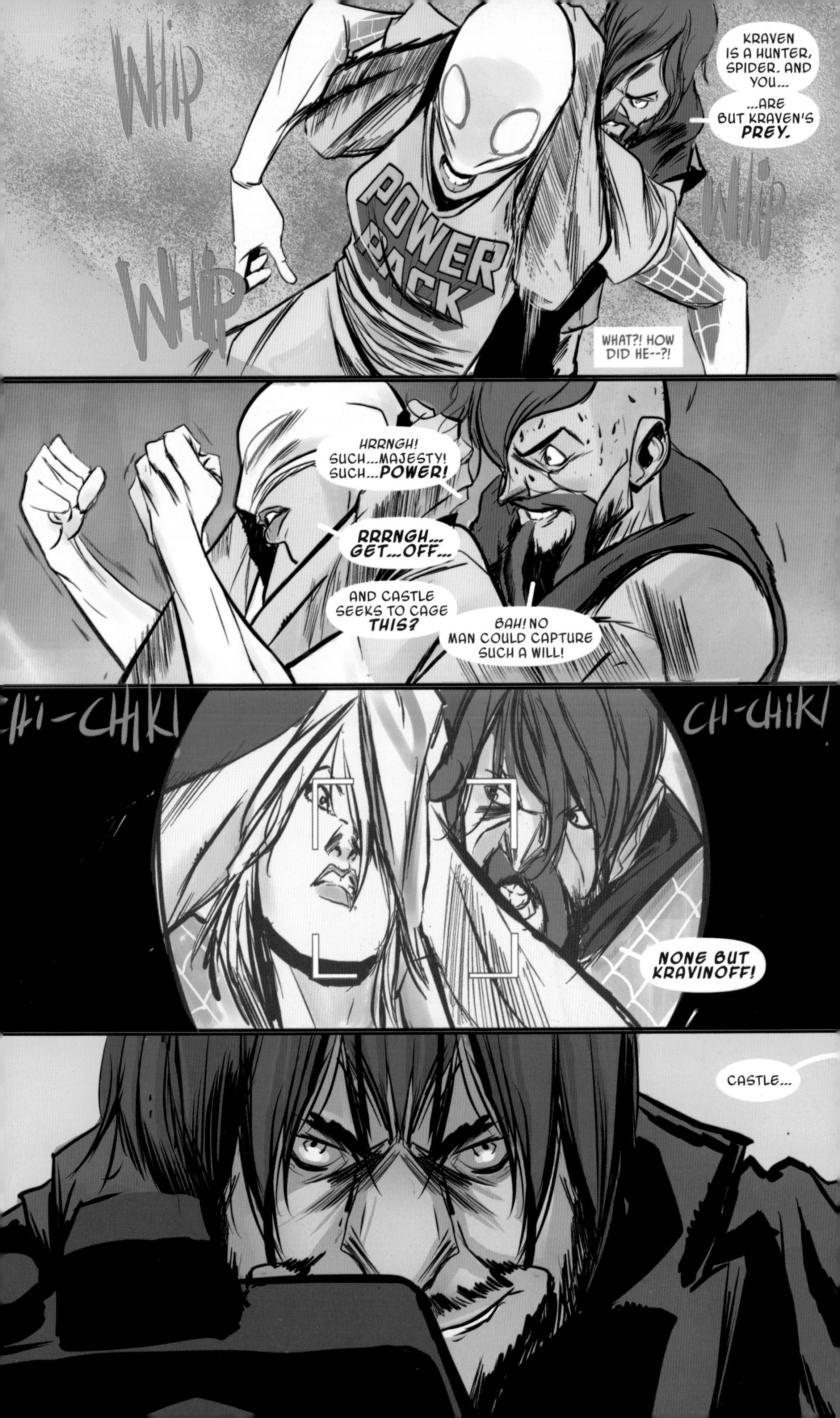
WHIP
KRAVEN IS A HUNTER, SPIDER. AND YOU...
...ARE BUT KRAVEN'S PREY.
WHIP
WHIP
WHAT?! HOW DID HE--?!
HRRNGH! SUCH...MAJESTY! SUCH...POWER!
RRRNGH... GET...OFF...
AND CASTLE SEEKS TO CAGE THIS?
BAH! NO MAN COULD CAPTURE SUCH A WILL!
CHI-CHIK!
CH-CHIK!
NONE BUT KRAVINOFF!
CASTLE...

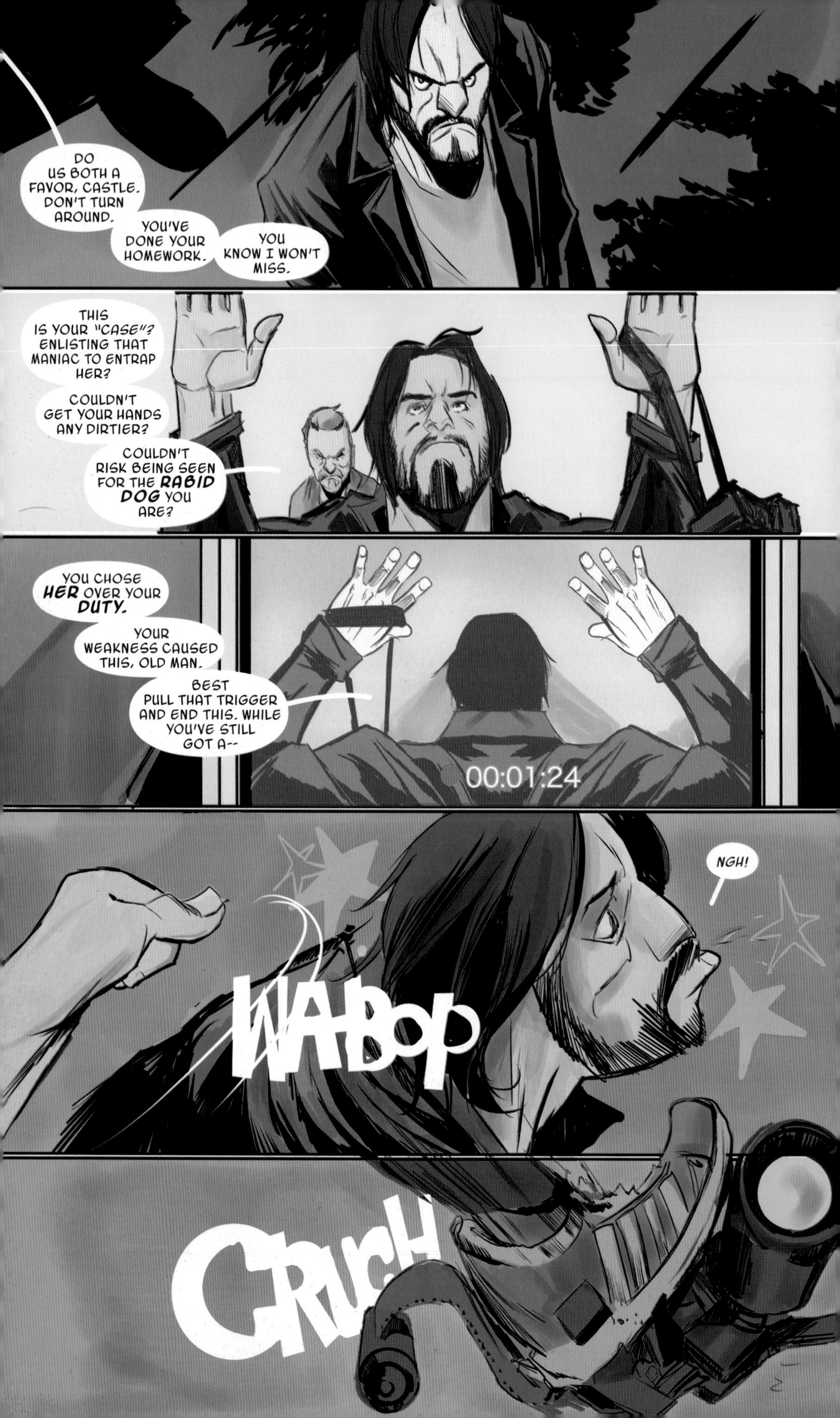
DO US BOTH A FAVOR, CASTLE. DON'T TURN AROUND.
YOU'VE DONE YOUR HOMEWORK.
YOU KNOW I WON'T MISS.
THIS IS YOUR "CASE"? ENLISTING THAT MANIAC TO ENTRAP HER?
COULDN'T GET YOUR HANDS ANY DIRTIER?
COULDN'T RISK BEING SEEN FOR THE RABID DOG YOU ARE?
YOU CHOSE HER OVER YOUR DUTY.
YOUR WEAKNESS CAUSED THIS, OLD MAN.
BEST PULL THAT TRIGGER AND END THIS. WHILE YOU'VE STILL GOT A--
00:01:24
NGH!
WABOP
CRUCH

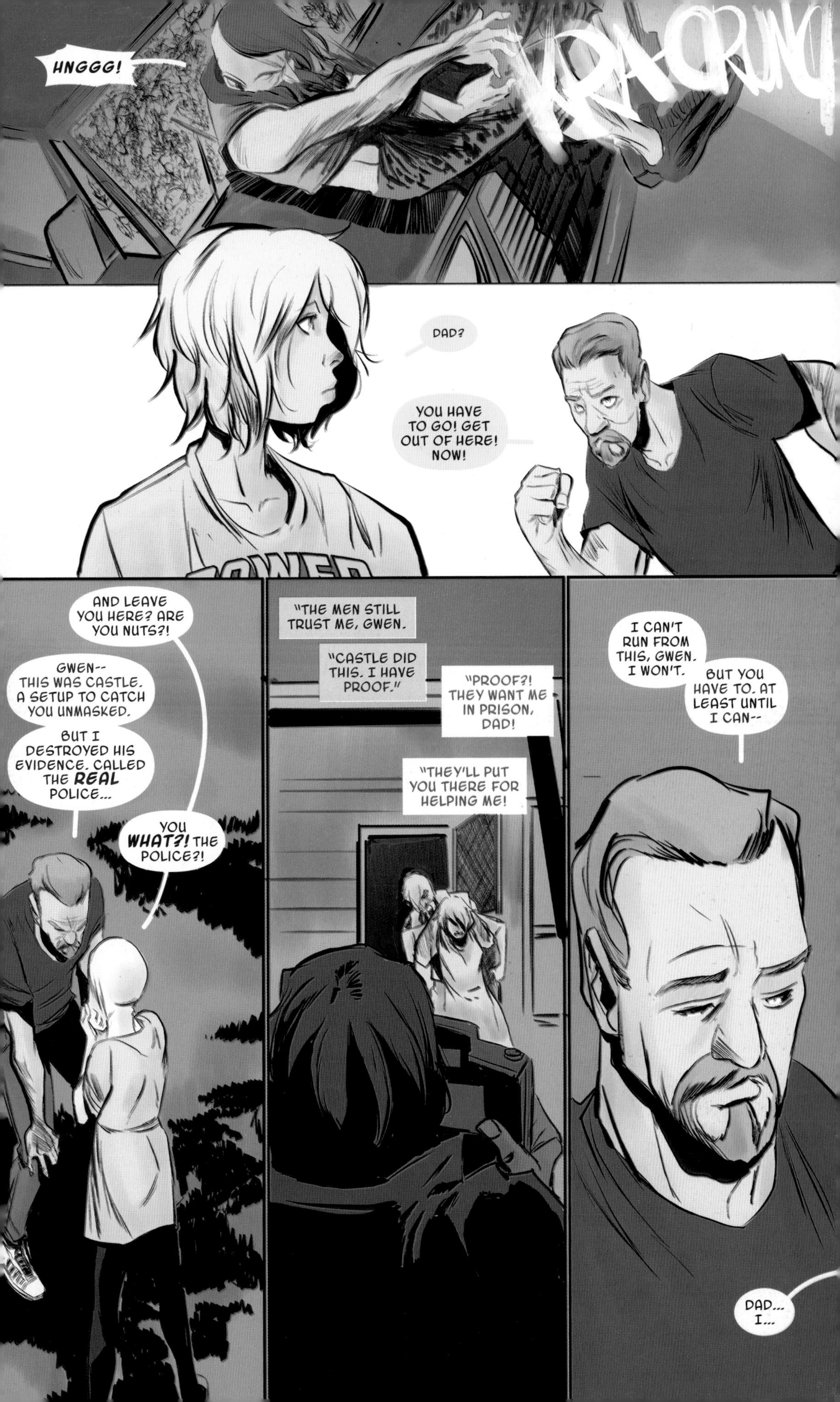

HNGGG!
KRA-CRUNQ
DAD?
YOU HAVE TO GO! GET OUT OF HERE! NOW!
AND LEAVE YOU HERE? ARE YOU NUTS?!
GWEN-- THIS WAS CASTLE. A SETUP TO CATCH YOU UNMASKED.
BUT I DESTROYED HIS EVIDENCE. CALLED THE **REAL** POLICE...
YOU **WHAT?!** THE POLICE?!
"THE MEN STILL TRUST ME, GWEN.
"CASTLE DID THIS. I HAVE PROOF."
"PROOF?! THEY WANT ME IN PRISON, DAD!
"THEY'LL PUT YOU THERE FOR HELPING ME!
I CAN'T RUN FROM THIS, GWEN. I WON'T.
BUT YOU HAVE TO. AT LEAST UNTIL I CAN--
DAD... I...

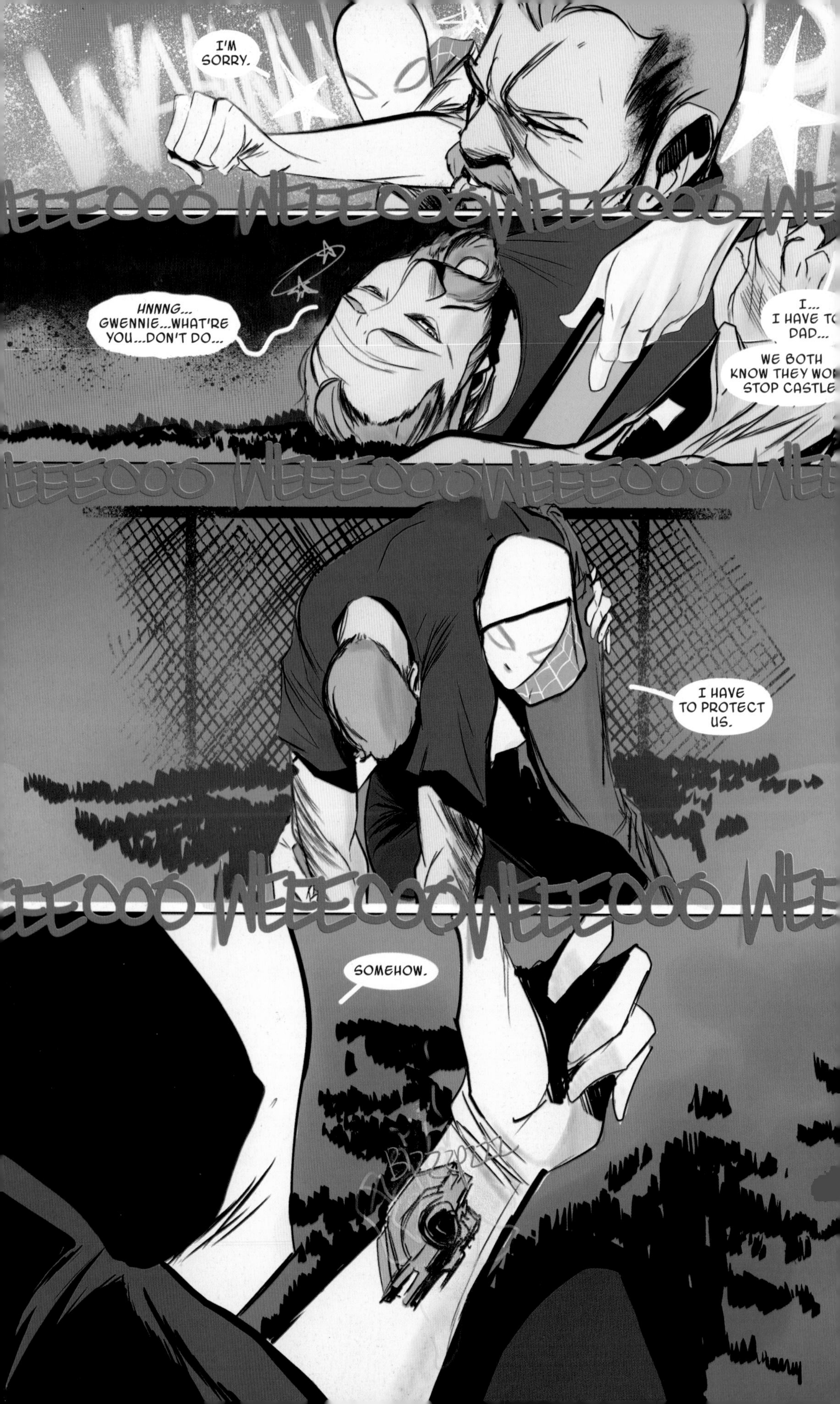
I'M SORRY.
WEEEOOO WEEEOOO WEEEOOO WE
HNNNG... GWENNIE...WHAT'RE YOU...DON'T DO...
I... I HAVE TO DAD...
WE BOTH KNOW THEY WO STOP CASTLE
WEEEOOO WEEEOOO WEEEOOO WEE
I HAVE TO PROTECT US.
WEEEOOO WEEEOOO WEEEOOO WEE
SOMEHOW.

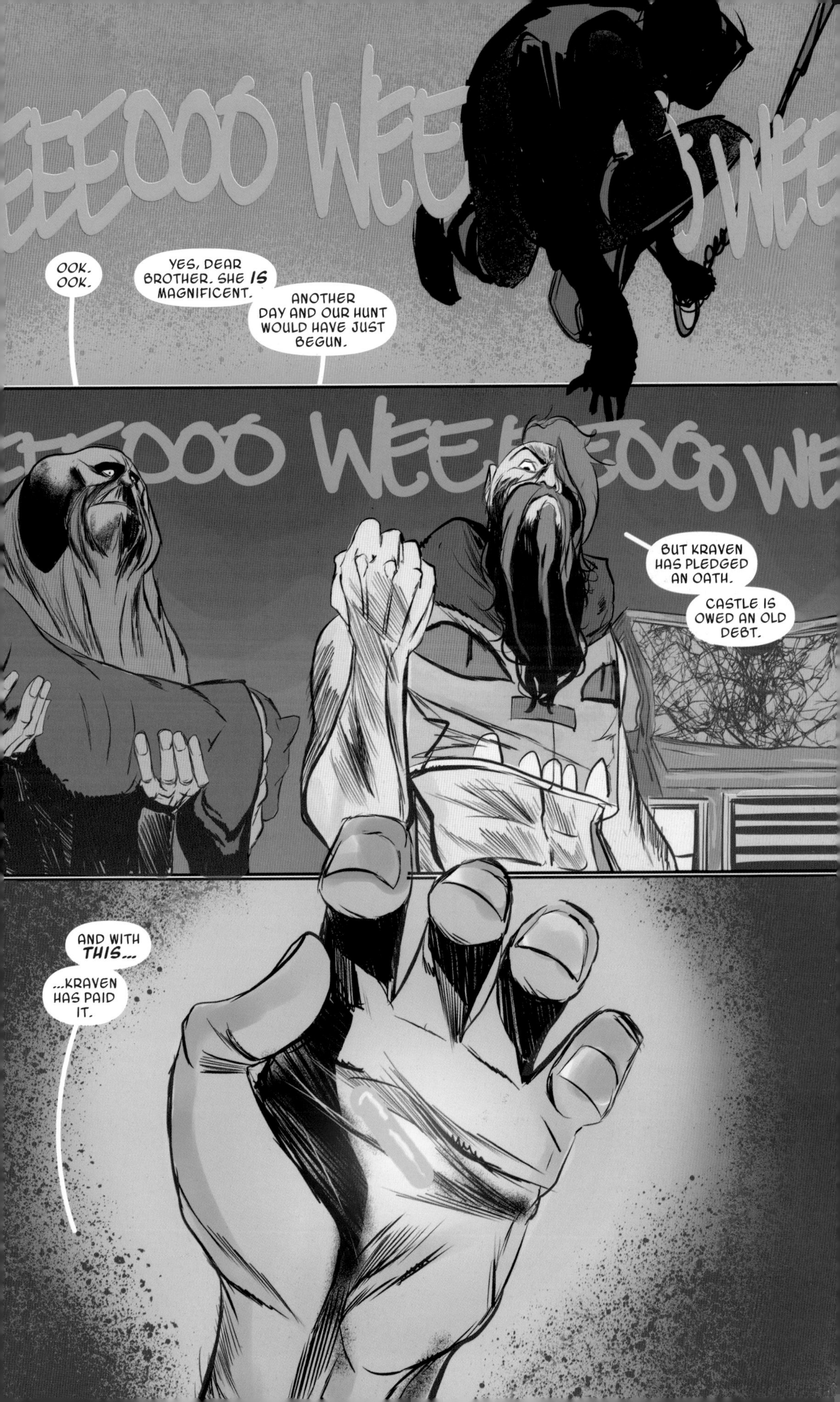

EEOOO WEE WEE
OOK. OOK.
YES, DEAR BROTHER. SHE IS MAGNIFICENT.
ANOTHER DAY AND OUR HUNT WOULD HAVE JUST BEGUN.
EEOOO WEE WEEOOO WE
BUT KRAVEN HAS PLEDGED AN OATH.
CASTLE IS OWED AN OLD DEBT.
AND WITH THIS...
...KRAVEN HAS PAID IT.

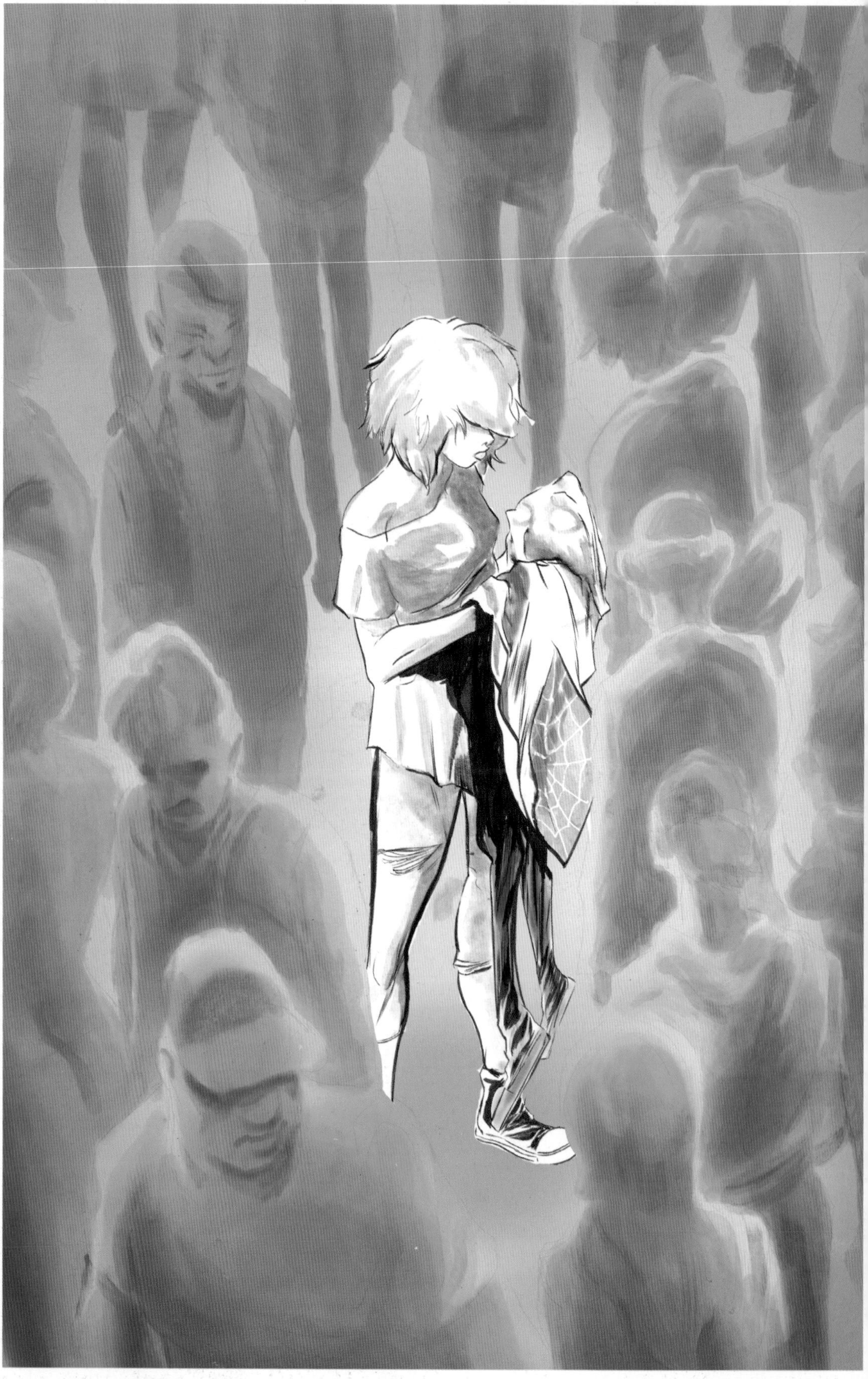

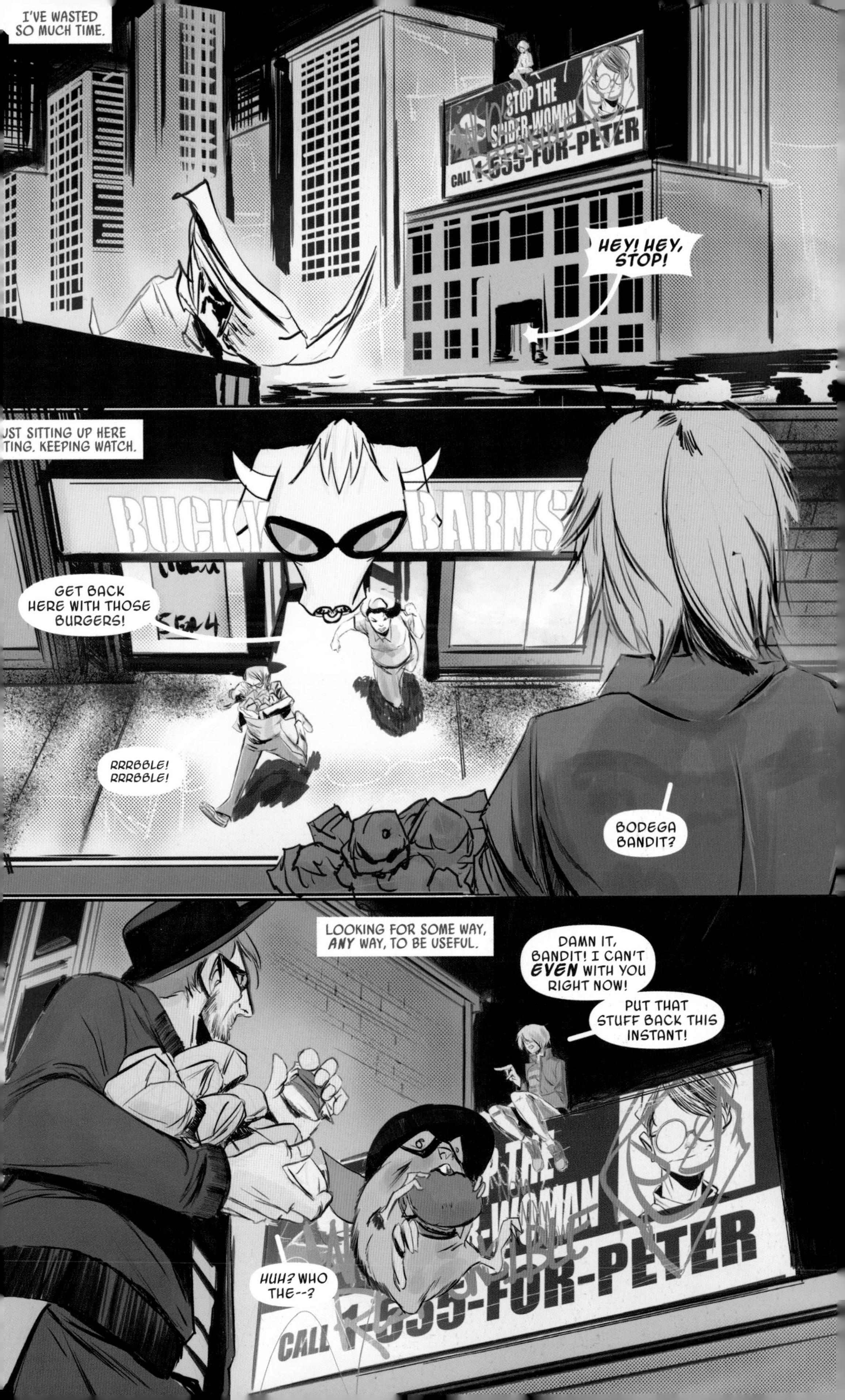
I'VE WASTED SO MUCH TIME.
STOP THE SPIDER-WOMAN
CALL 1-555-FOR-PETER
HEY! HEY, STOP!
UST SITTING UP HERE TING. KEEPING WATCH.
BUCKY BARNS
GET BACK HERE WITH THOSE BURGERS!
RRRBBLE! RRRBBLE!
BODEGA BANDIT?
LOOKING FOR SOME WAY, ANY WAY, TO BE USEFUL.
DAMN IT, BANDIT! I CAN'T EVEN WITH YOU RIGHT NOW!
PUT THAT STUFF BACK THIS INSTANT!
HUH? WHO THE--?
1-555-FOR-PETER

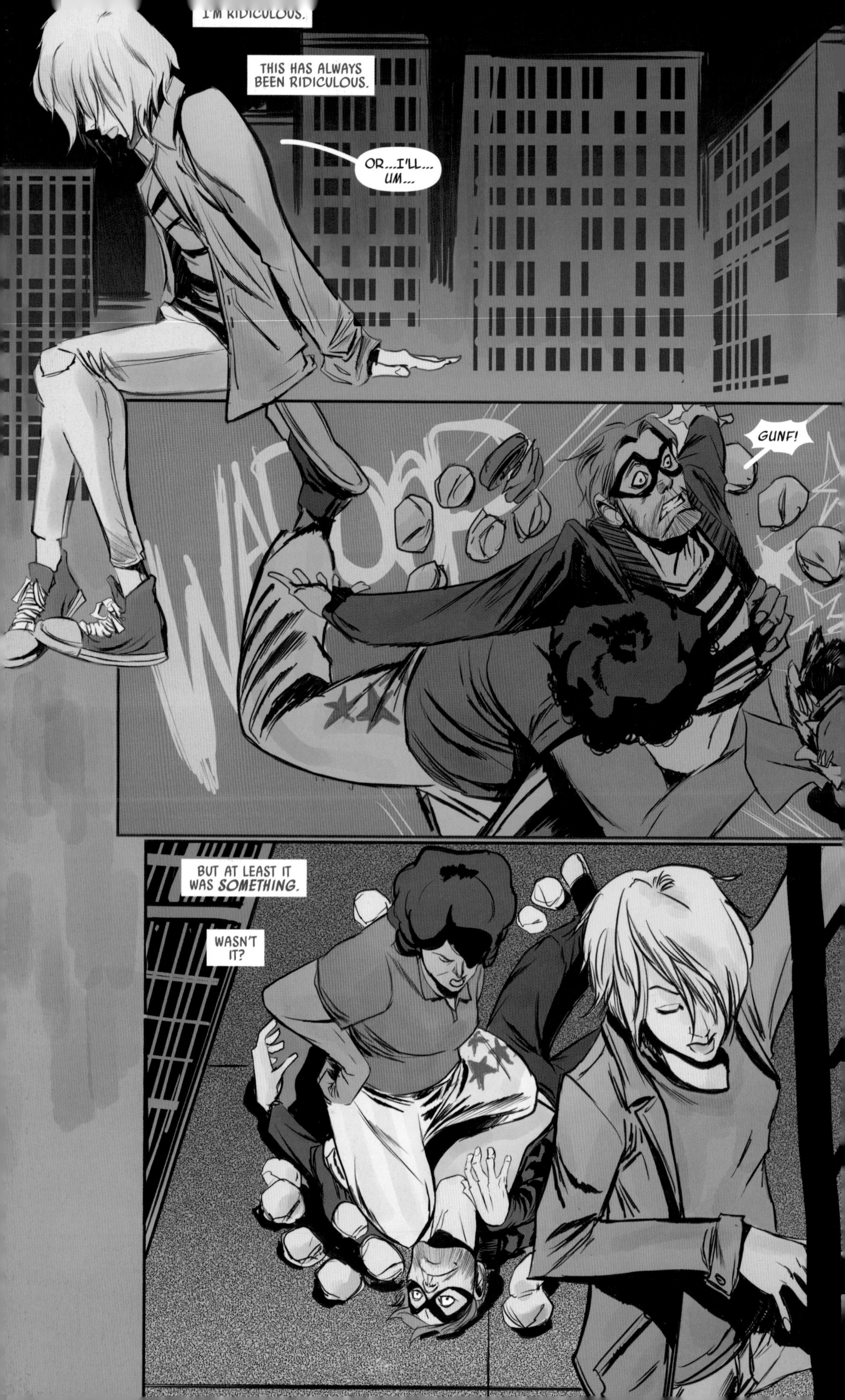
I'M RIDICULOUS.
THIS HAS ALWAYS BEEN RIDICULOUS.
OR...I'LL... UM...
GUNF!
BUT AT LEAST IT WAS *SOMETHING.*
WASN'T IT?

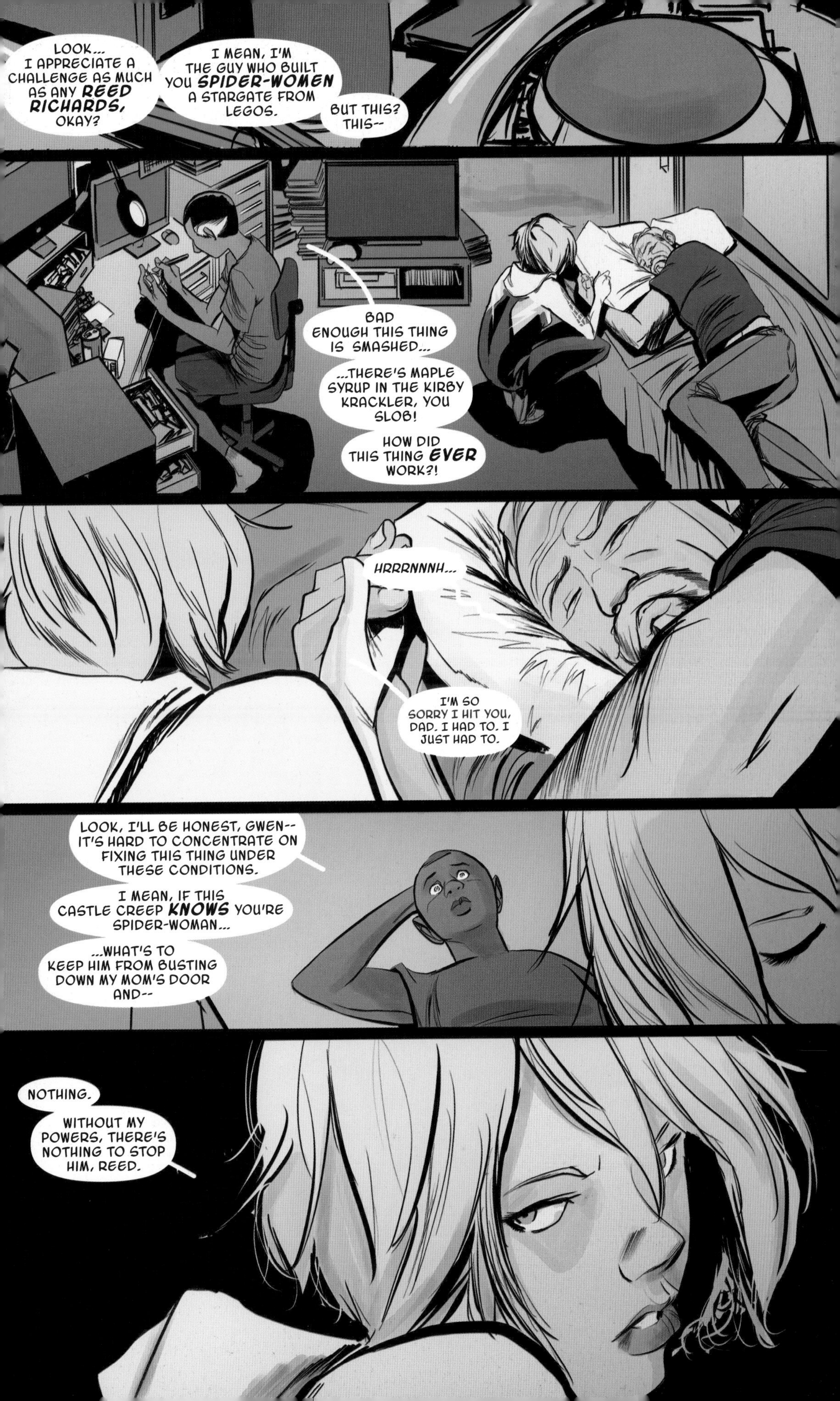
LOOK... I APPRECIATE A CHALLENGE AS MUCH AS ANY REED RICHARDS, OKAY?
I MEAN, I'M THE GUY WHO BUILT YOU SPIDER-WOMEN A STARGATE FROM LEGOS.
BUT THIS? THIS--
BAD ENOUGH THIS THING IS SMASHED...
...THERE'S MAPLE SYRUP IN THE KIRBY KRACKLER, YOU SLOB!
HOW DID THIS THING EVER WORK?!
HRRRNNNH...
I'M SO SORRY I HIT YOU, DAD. I HAD TO. I JUST HAD TO.
LOOK, I'LL BE HONEST, GWEN-- IT'S HARD TO CONCENTRATE ON FIXING THIS THING UNDER THESE CONDITIONS.
I MEAN, IF THIS CASTLE CREEP KNOWS YOU'RE SPIDER-WOMAN...
...WHAT'S TO KEEP HIM FROM BUSTING DOWN MY MOM'S DOOR AND--
NOTHING.
WITHOUT MY POWERS, THERE'S NOTHING TO STOP HIM, REED.

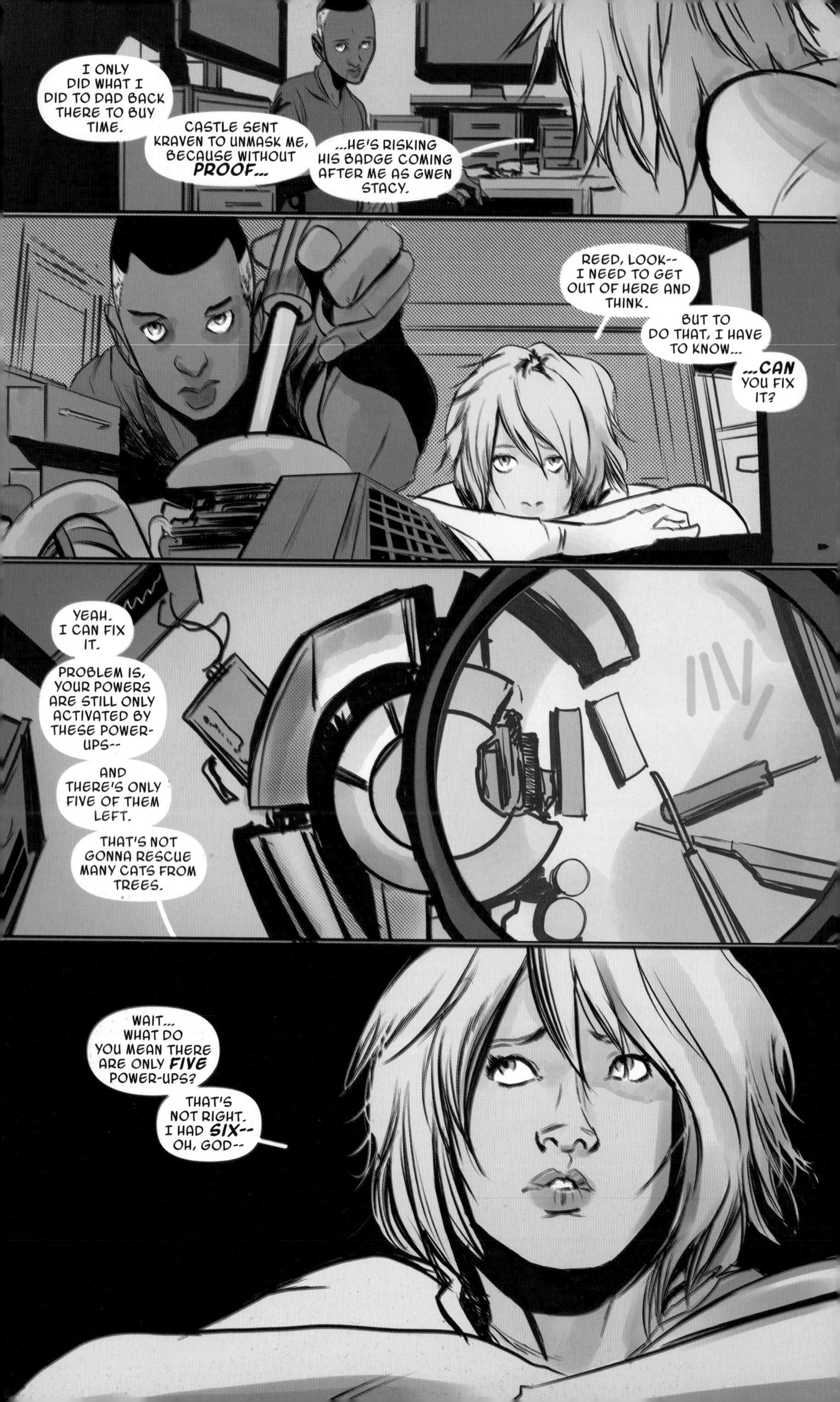
I ONLY DID WHAT I DID TO DAD BACK THERE TO BUY TIME.
CASTLE SENT KRAVEN TO UNMASK ME, BECAUSE WITHOUT **PROOF...**
...HE'S RISKING HIS BADGE COMING AFTER ME AS GWEN STACY.
REED, LOOK-- I NEED TO GET OUT OF HERE AND THINK.
BUT TO DO THAT, I HAVE TO KNOW...
**...CAN** YOU FIX IT?
YEAH. I CAN FIX IT.
PROBLEM IS, YOUR POWERS ARE STILL ONLY ACTIVATED BY THESE POWER-UPS--
AND THERE'S ONLY FIVE OF THEM LEFT.
THAT'S NOT GONNA RESCUE MANY CATS FROM TREES.
WAIT... WHAT DO YOU MEAN THERE ARE ONLY ***FIVE*** POWER-UPS?
THAT'S NOT RIGHT. I HAD ***SIX***-- OH, GOD--

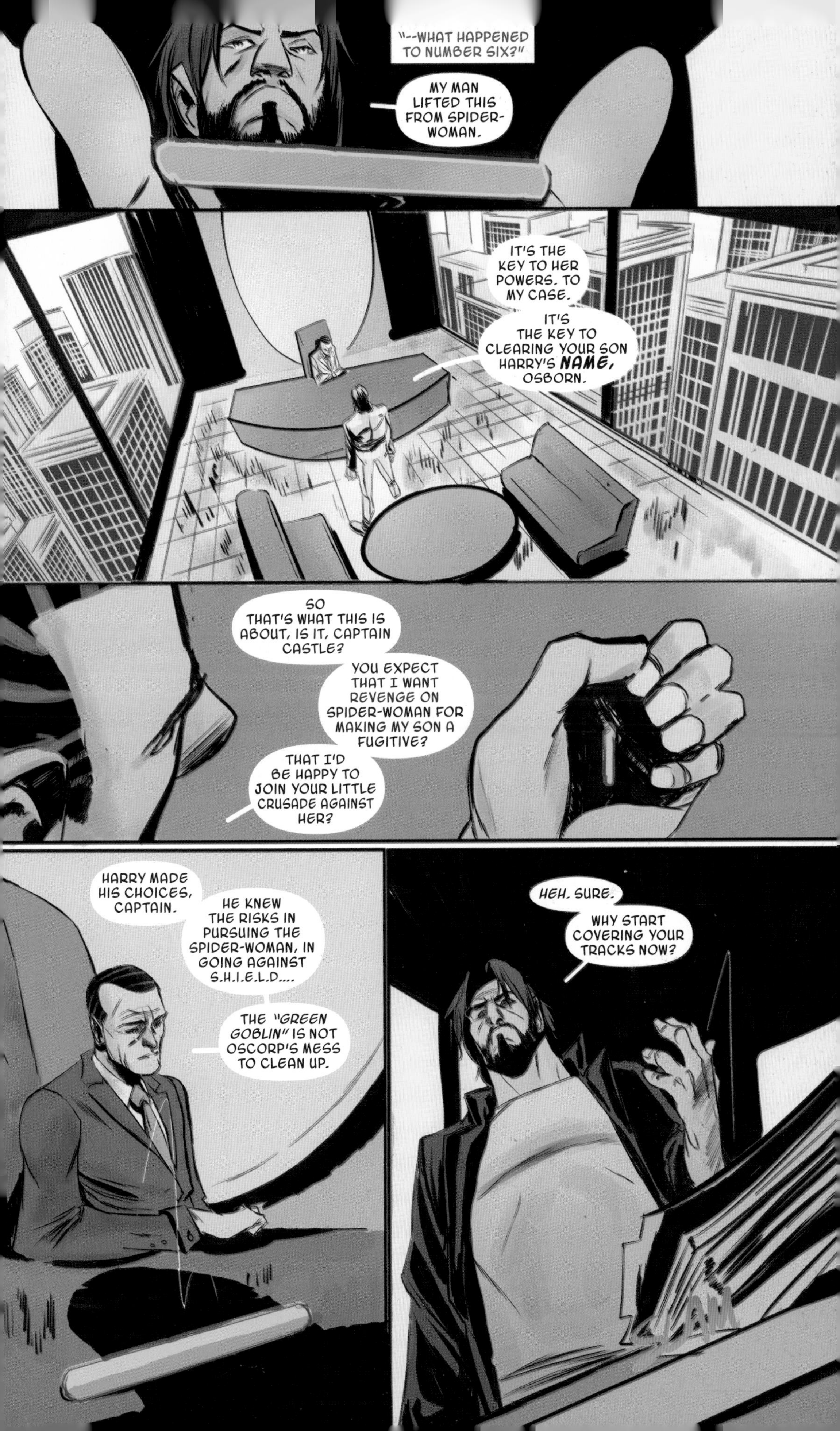
"--WHAT HAPPENED TO NUMBER SIX?"
MY MAN LIFTED THIS FROM SPIDER-WOMAN.
IT'S THE KEY TO HER POWERS. TO MY CASE.
IT'S THE KEY TO CLEARING YOUR SON HARRY'S NAME, OSBORN.
SO THAT'S WHAT THIS IS ABOUT, IS IT, CAPTAIN CASTLE?
YOU EXPECT THAT I WANT REVENGE ON SPIDER-WOMAN FOR MAKING MY SON A FUGITIVE?
THAT I'D BE HAPPY TO JOIN YOUR LITTLE CRUSADE AGAINST HER?
HARRY MADE HIS CHOICES, CAPTAIN.
HE KNEW THE RISKS IN PURSUING THE SPIDER-WOMAN, IN GOING AGAINST S.H.I.E.L.D....
THE "GREEN GOBLIN" IS NOT OSCORP'S MESS TO CLEAN UP.
HEH. SURE.
WHY START COVERING YOUR TRACKS NOW?

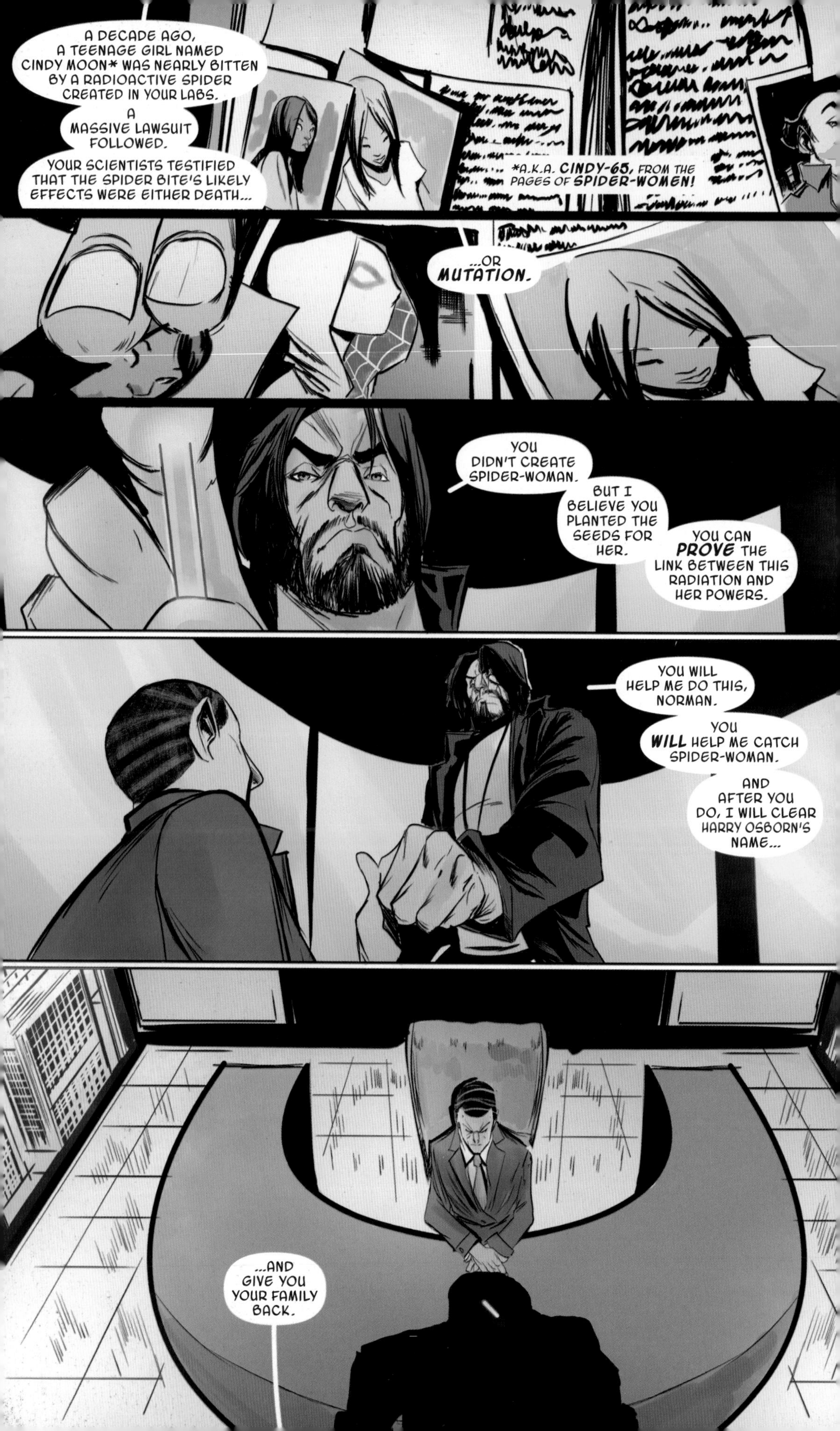
A DECADE AGO, A TEENAGE GIRL NAMED CINDY MOON* WAS NEARLY BITTEN BY A RADIOACTIVE SPIDER CREATED IN YOUR LABS.
A MASSIVE LAWSUIT FOLLOWED.
YOUR SCIENTISTS TESTIFIED THAT THE SPIDER BITE'S LIKELY EFFECTS WERE EITHER DEATH...
*A.K.A. CINDY-65, FROM THE PAGES OF SPIDER-WOMEN!
...OR MUTATION.
YOU DIDN'T CREATE SPIDER-WOMAN.
BUT I BELIEVE YOU PLANTED THE SEEDS FOR HER.
YOU CAN PROVE THE LINK BETWEEN THIS RADIATION AND HER POWERS.
YOU WILL HELP ME DO THIS, NORMAN.
YOU WILL HELP ME CATCH SPIDER-WOMAN.
AND AFTER YOU DO, I WILL CLEAR HARRY OSBORN'S NAME...
...AND GIVE YOU YOUR FAMILY BACK.

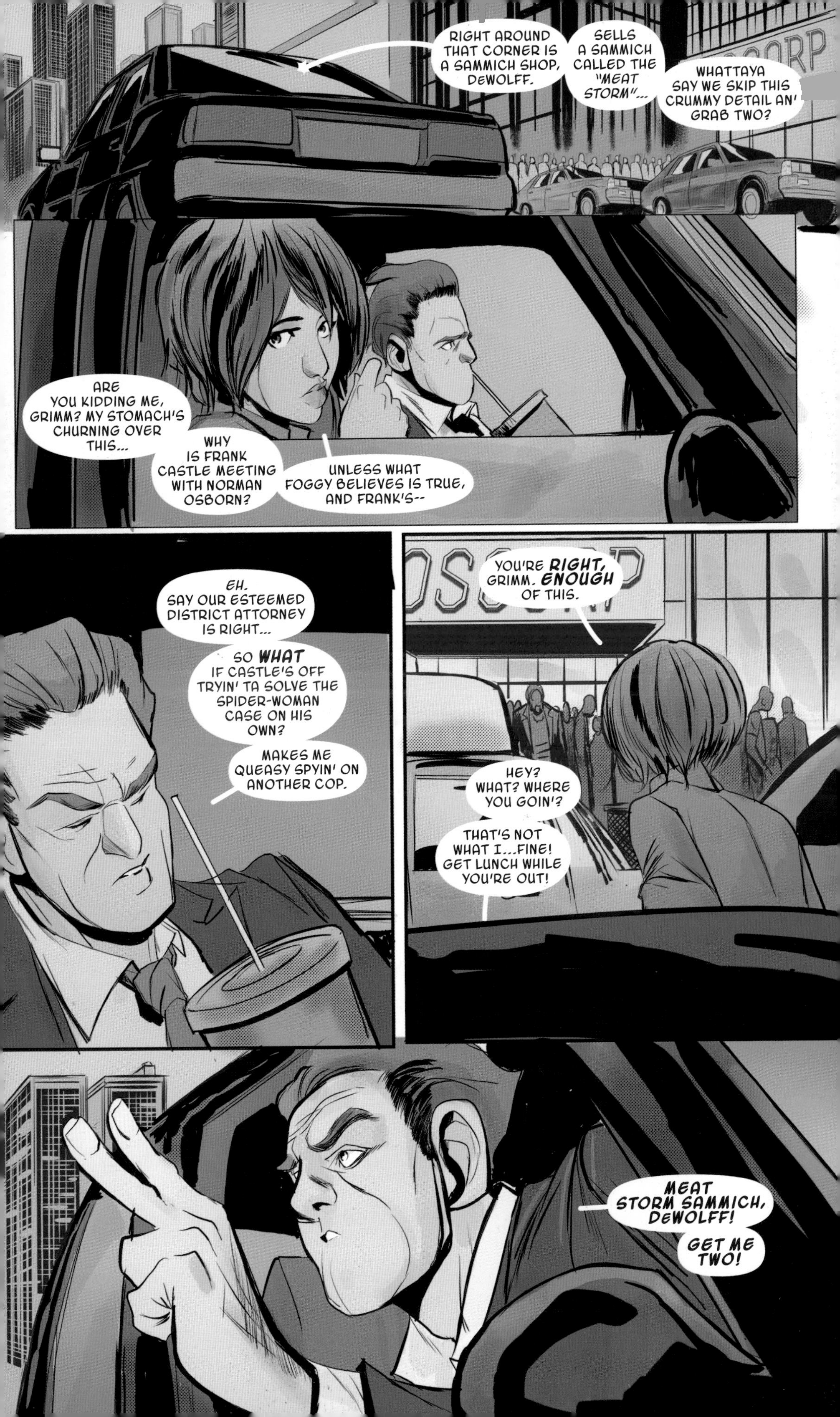
RIGHT AROUND THAT CORNER IS A SAMMICH SHOP, DEWOLFF.
SELLS A SAMMICH CALLED THE "MEAT STORM"...
WHATTAYA SAY WE SKIP THIS CRUMMY DETAIL AN' GRAB TWO?
ARE YOU KIDDING ME, GRIMM? MY STOMACH'S CHURNING OVER THIS...
WHY IS FRANK CASTLE MEETING WITH NORMAN OSBORN?
UNLESS WHAT FOGGY BELIEVES IS TRUE, AND FRANK'S--
EH. SAY OUR ESTEEMED DISTRICT ATTORNEY IS RIGHT...
SO WHAT IF CASTLE'S OFF TRYIN' TA SOLVE THE SPIDER-WOMAN CASE ON HIS OWN?
MAKES ME QUEASY SPYIN' ON ANOTHER COP.
YOU'RE RIGHT, GRIMM. ENOUGH OF THIS.
HEY? WHAT? WHERE YOU GOIN'?
THAT'S NOT WHAT I...FINE! GET LUNCH WHILE YOU'RE OUT!
MEAT STORM SAMMICH, DEWOLFF!
GET ME TWO!

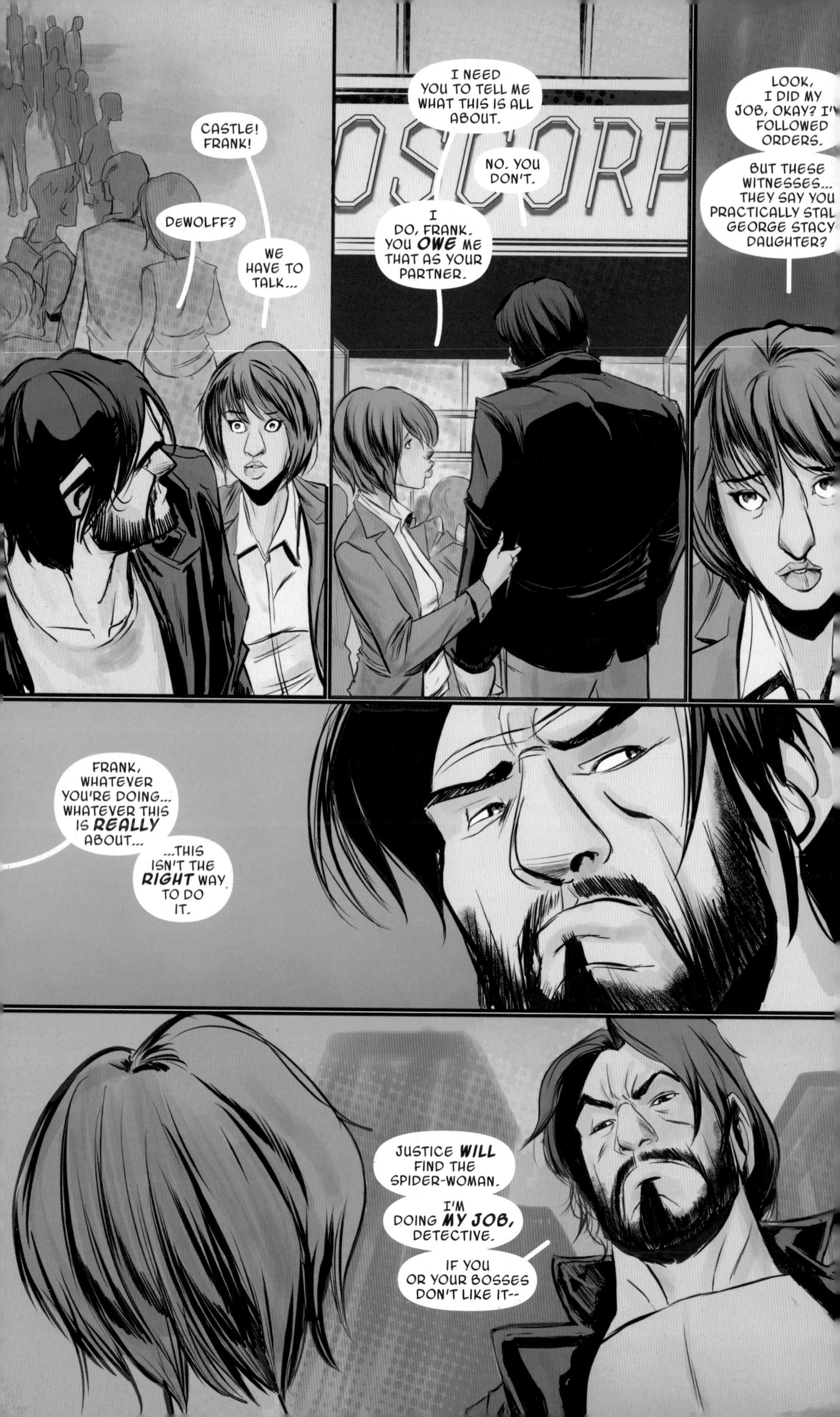
CASTLE! FRANK!
DEWOLFF?
WE HAVE TO TALK...
I NEED YOU TO TELL ME WHAT THIS IS ALL ABOUT.
NO. YOU DON'T.
I DO, FRANK. YOU OWE ME THAT AS YOUR PARTNER.
OSCORP
LOOK, I DID MY JOB, OKAY? I'
FOLLOWED ORDERS.
BUT THESE WITNESSES... THEY SAY YOU PRACTICALLY STAL
GEORGE STACY
DAUGHTER?
FRANK, WHATEVER YOU'RE DOING... WHATEVER THIS IS REALLY ABOUT...
...THIS ISN'T THE RIGHT WAY TO DO IT.
JUSTICE WILL FIND THE SPIDER-WOMAN.
I'M DOING MY JOB, DETECTIVE.
IF YOU OR YOUR BOSSES DON'T LIKE IT--

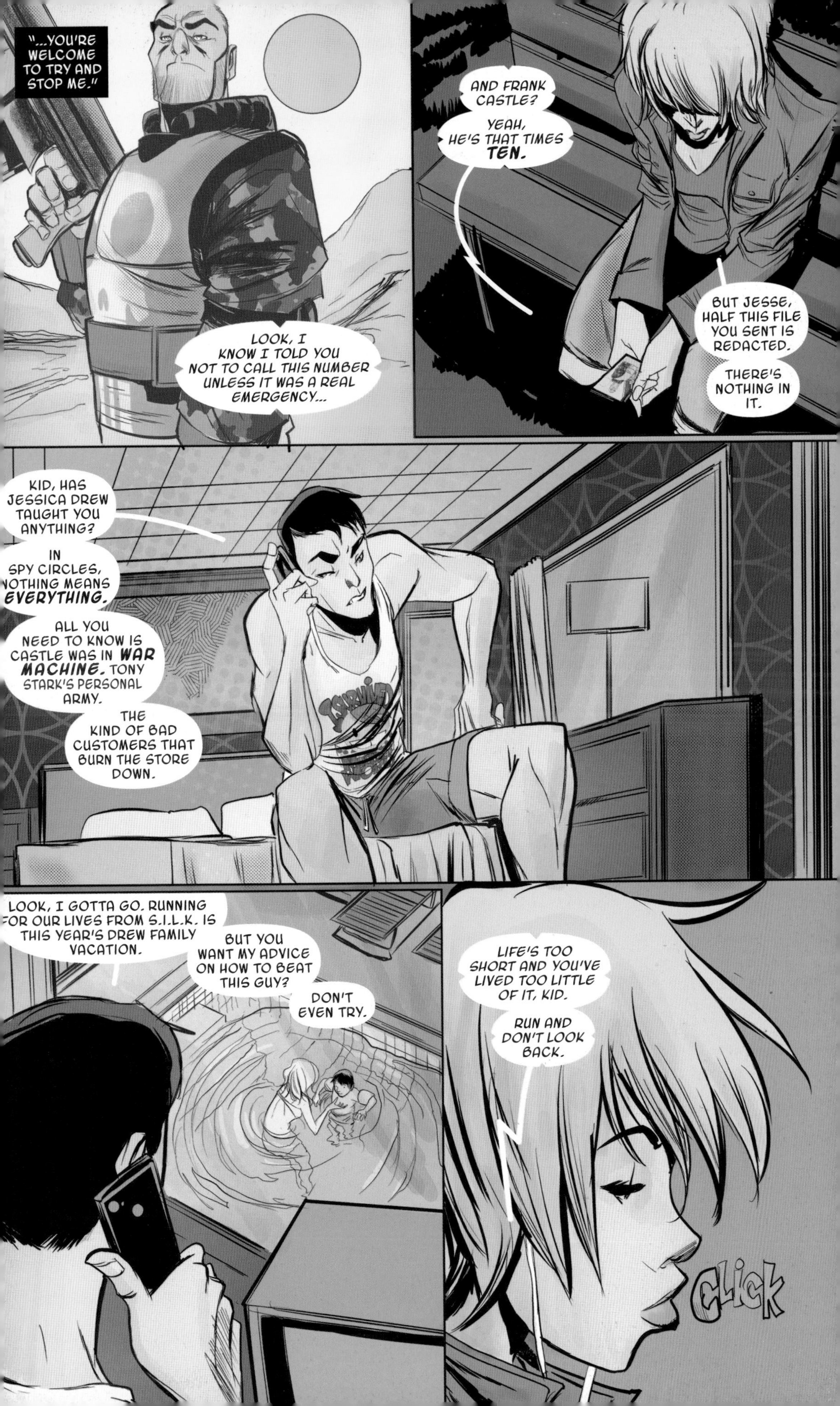
"...YOU'RE WELCOME TO TRY AND STOP ME."
AND FRANK CASTLE?
YEAH, HE'S THAT TIMES TEN.
LOOK, I KNOW I TOLD YOU NOT TO CALL THIS NUMBER UNLESS IT WAS A REAL EMERGENCY...
BUT JESSE, HALF THIS FILE YOU SENT IS REDACTED.
THERE'S NOTHING IN IT.
KID, HAS JESSICA DREW TAUGHT YOU ANYTHING?
IN SPY CIRCLES, NOTHING MEANS EVERYTHING.
ALL YOU NEED TO KNOW IS CASTLE WAS IN WAR MACHINE. TONY STARK'S PERSONAL ARMY.
THE KIND OF BAD CUSTOMERS THAT BURN THE STORE DOWN.
LOOK, I GOTTA GO. RUNNING FOR OUR LIVES FROM S.I.L.K. IS THIS YEAR'S DREW FAMILY VACATION.
BUT YOU WANT MY ADVICE ON HOW TO BEAT THIS GUY?
DON'T EVEN TRY.
LIFE'S TOO SHORT AND YOU'VE LIVED TOO LITTLE OF IT, KID.
RUN AND DON'T LOOK BACK.
CLICK

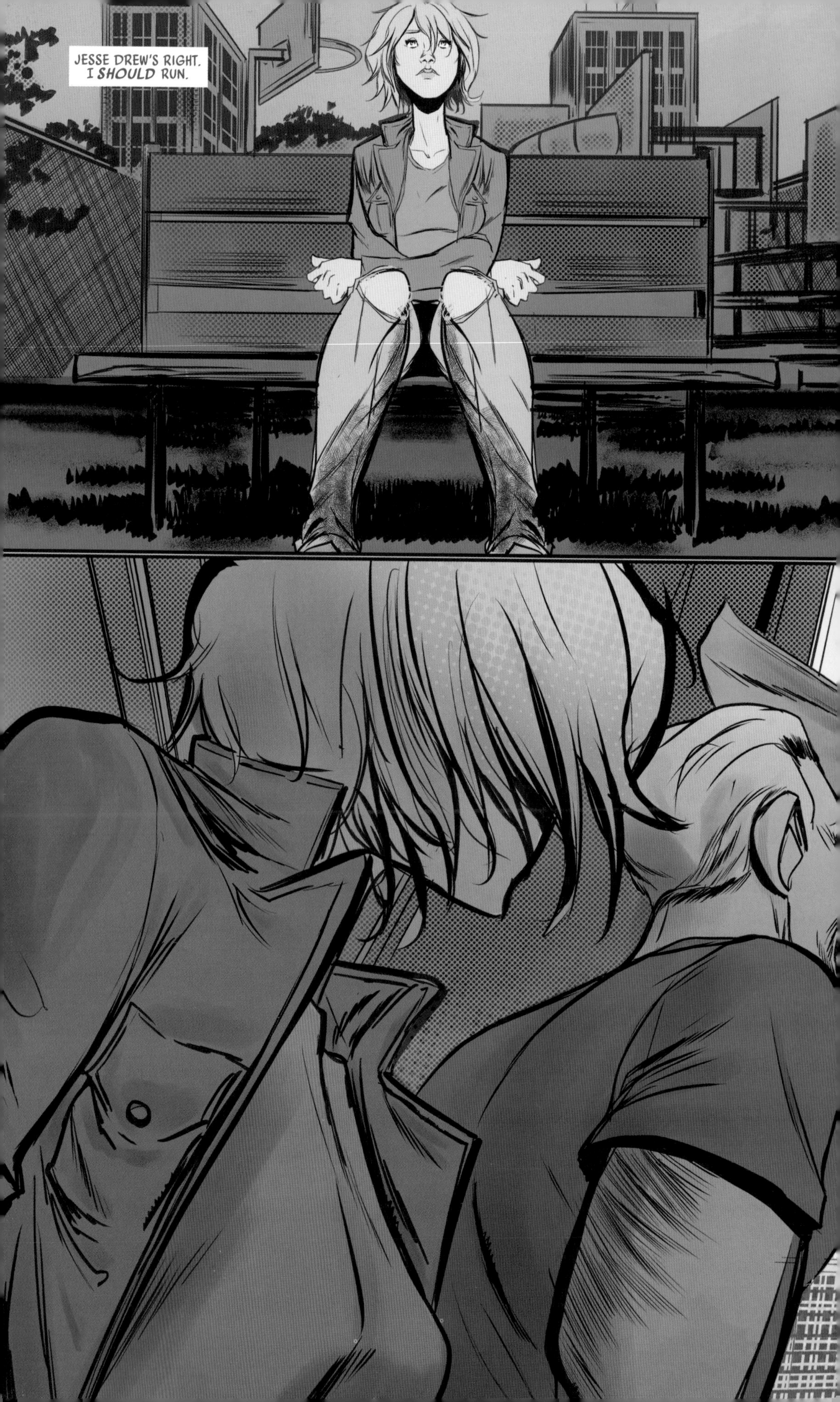
JESSE DREW'S RIGHT. I SHOULD RUN.

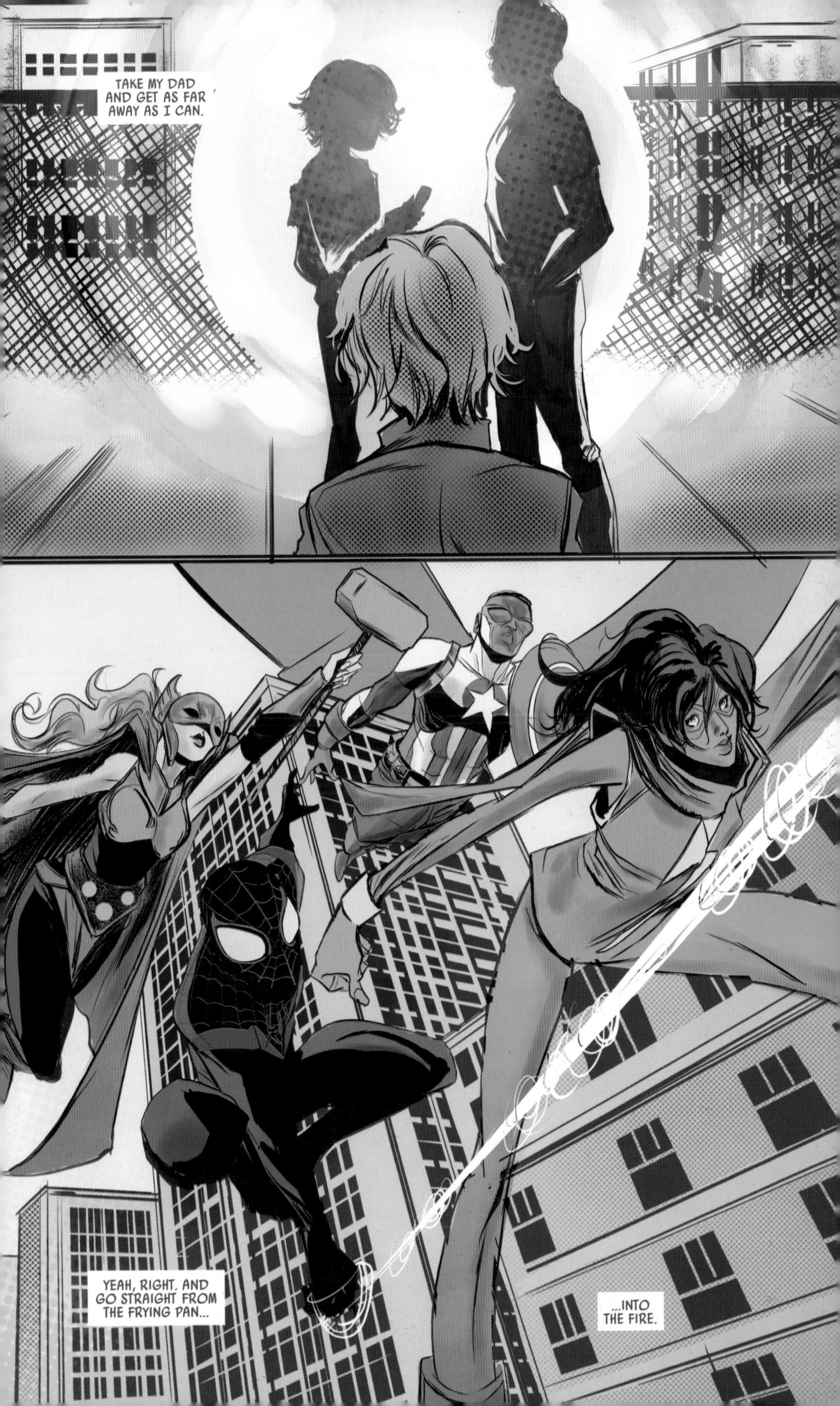
TAKE MY DAD AND GET AS FAR AWAY AS I CAN.
YEAH, RIGHT. AND GO STRAIGHT FROM THE FRYING PAN...
...INTO THE FIRE.

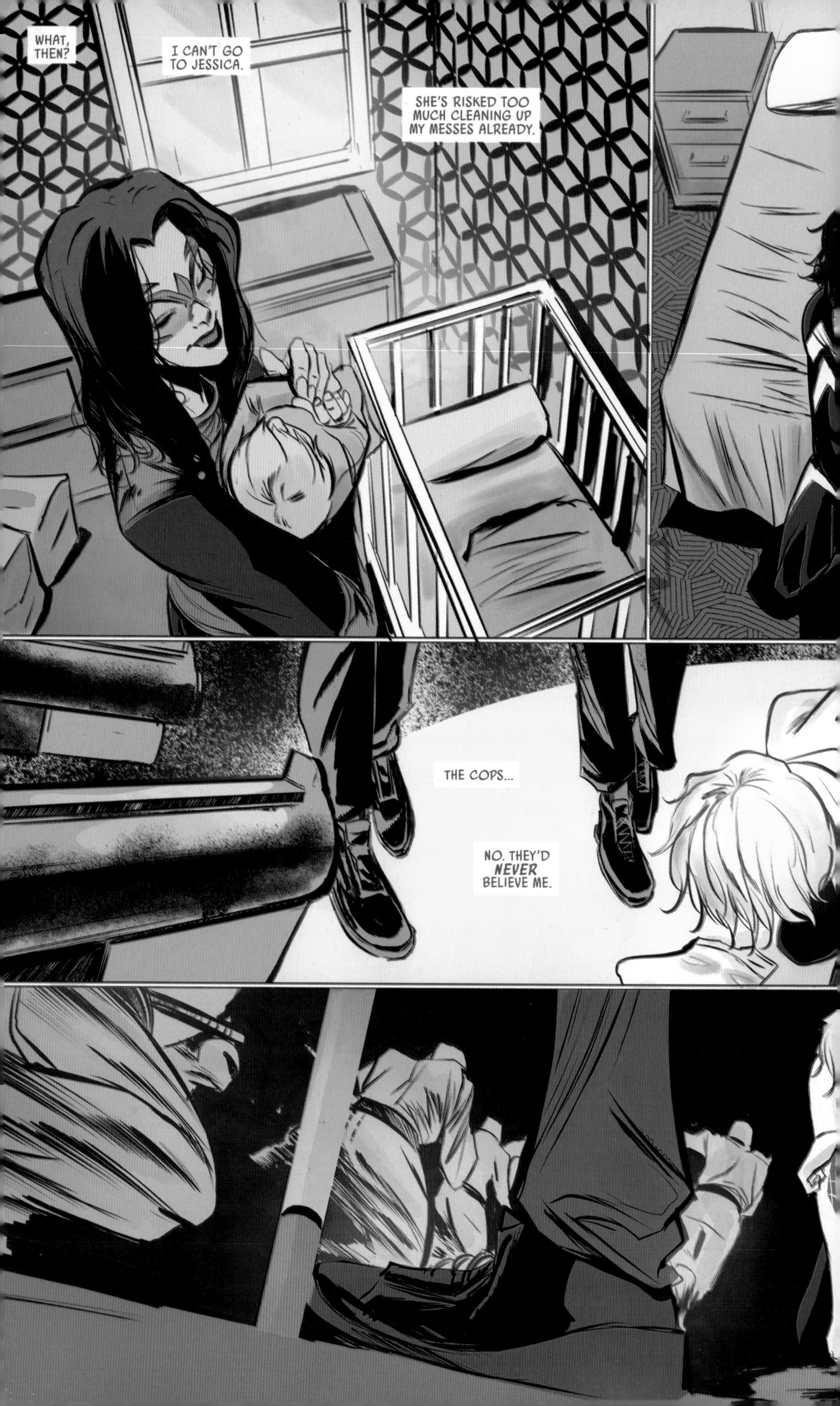
WHAT, THEN?
I CAN'T GO TO JESSICA.
SHE'S RISKED TOO MUCH CLEANING UP MY MESSES ALREADY.
THE COPS...
NO. THEY'D *NEVER* BELIEVE ME.

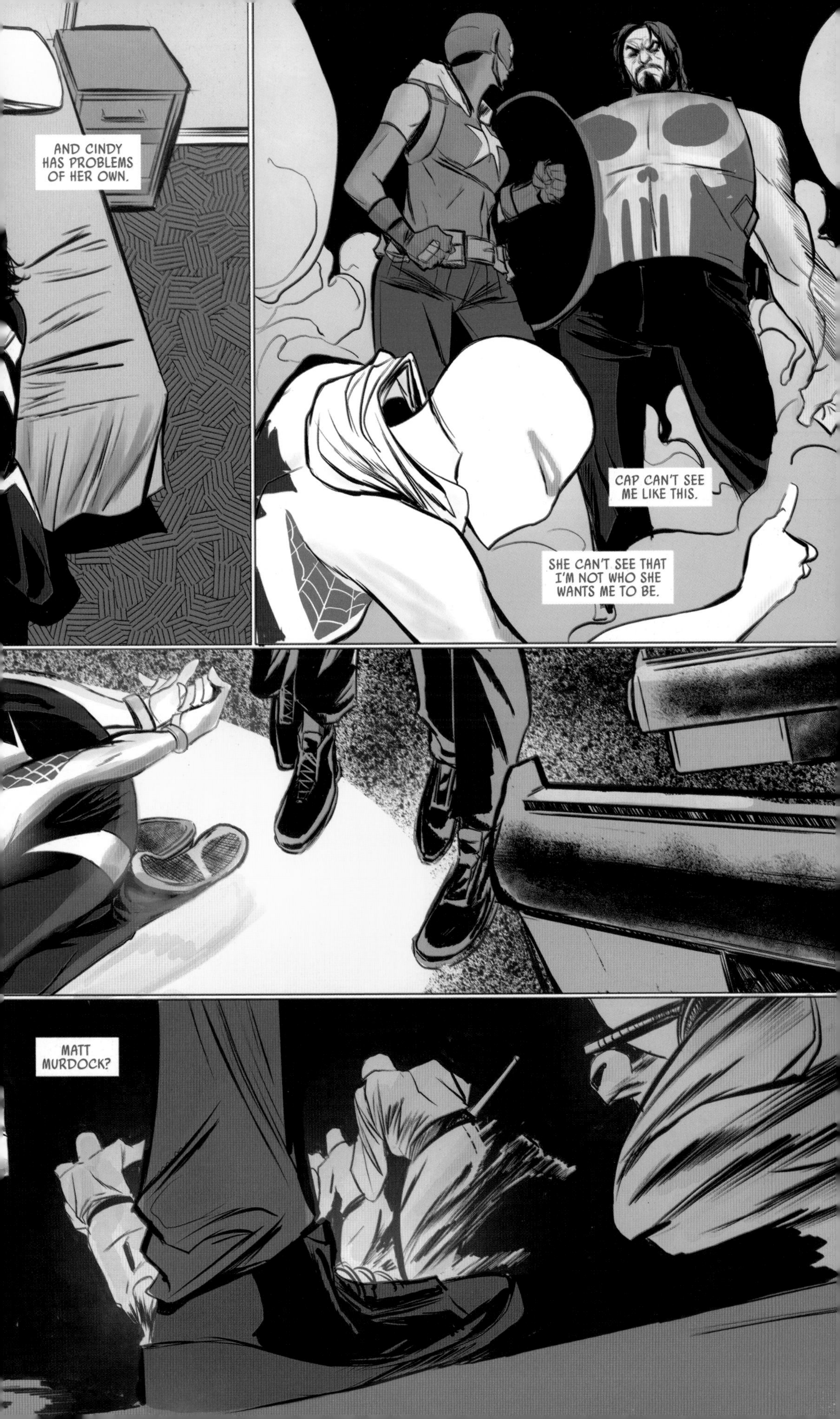
AND CINDY HAS PROBLEMS OF HER OWN.
CAP CAN'T SEE ME LIKE THIS.
SHE CAN'T SEE THAT I'M NOT WHO SHE WANTS ME TO BE.
MATT MURDOCK?

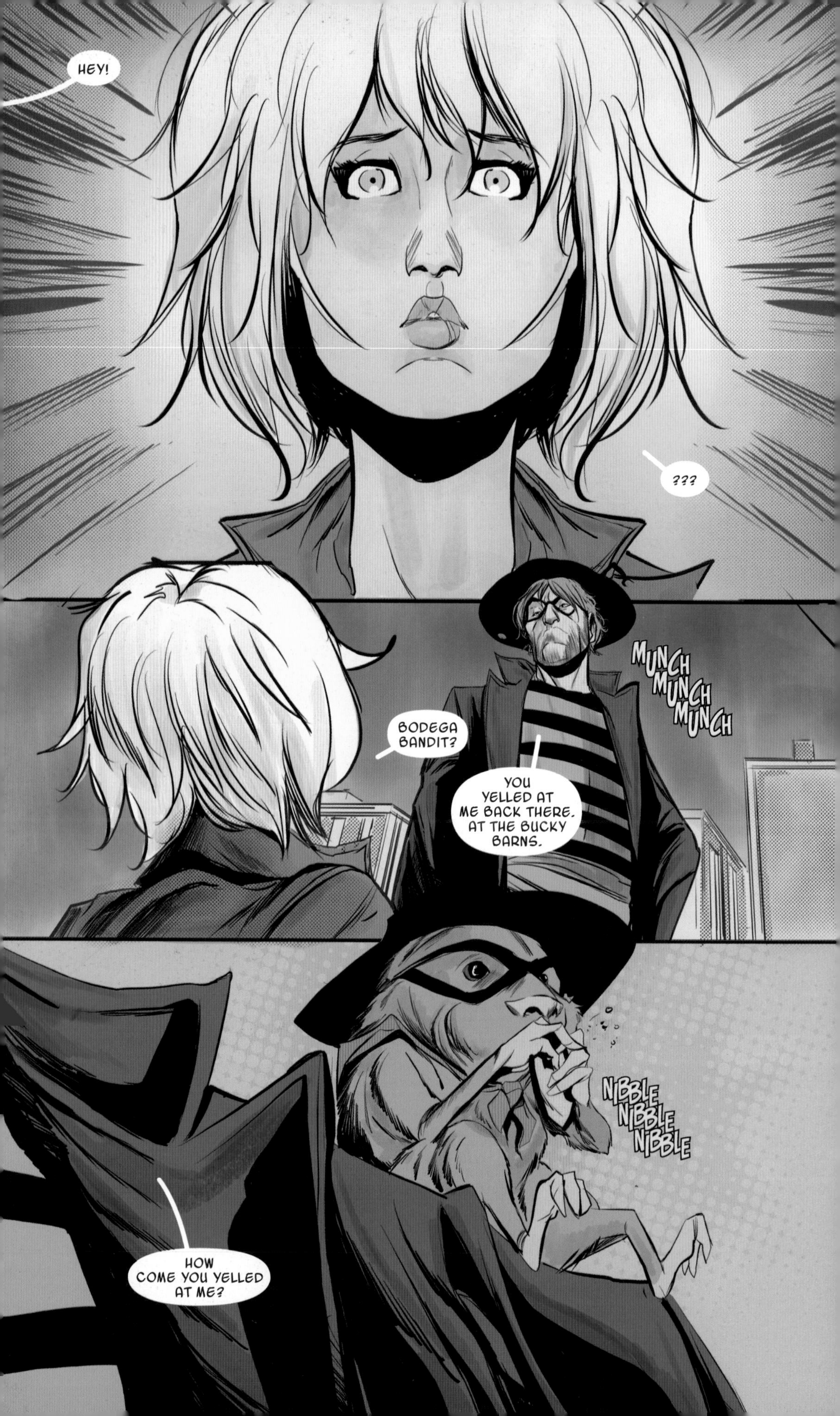
HEY!
???
BODEGA BANDIT?
YOU YELLED AT ME BACK THERE. AT THE BUCKY BARNS.
MUNCH MUNCH MUNCH
NIBBLE NIBBLE NIBBLE
HOW COME YOU YELLED AT ME?

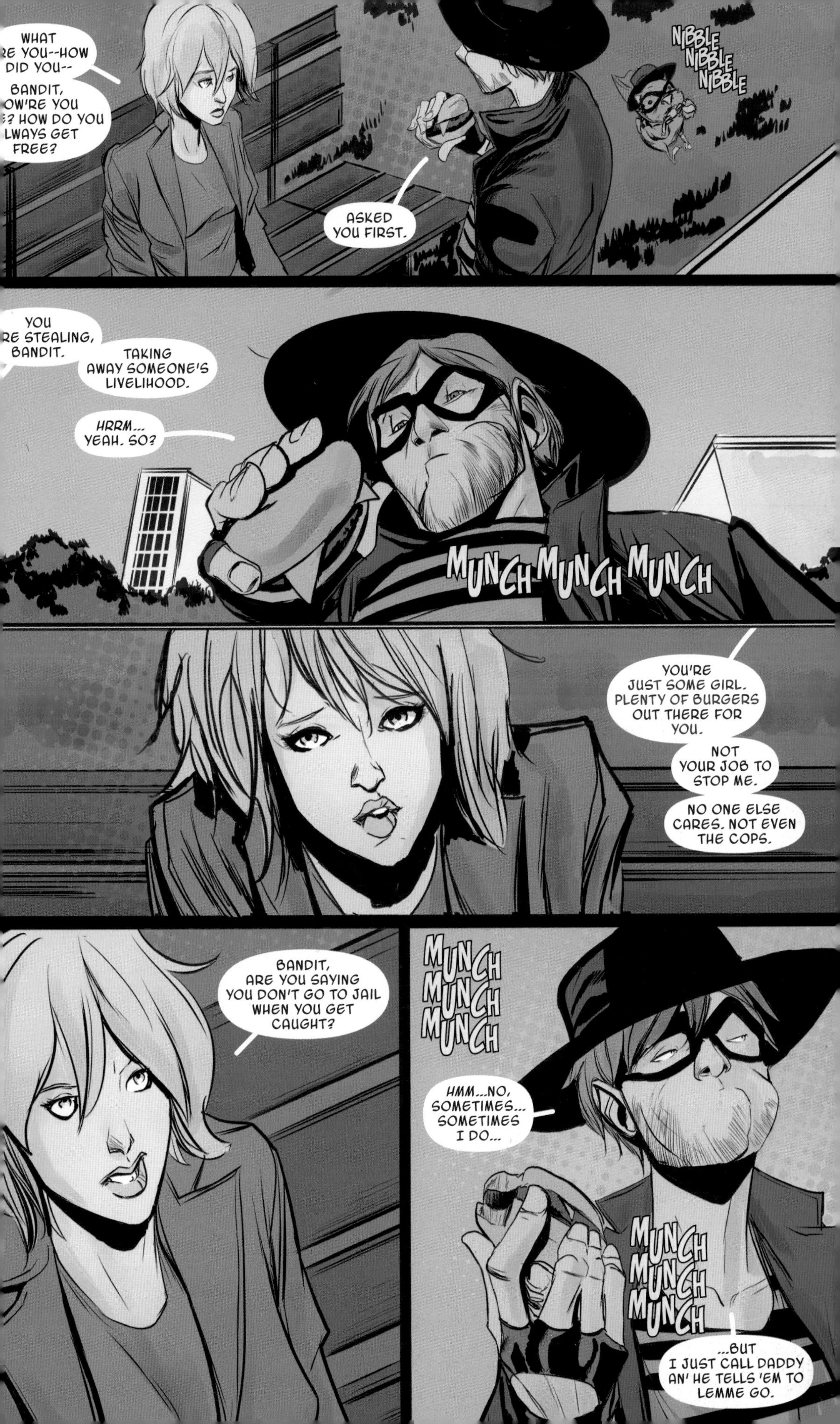

WHAT RE YOU--HOW DID YOU--
BANDIT, OW'RE YOU E? HOW DO YOU LWAYS GET FREE?
NIBBLE NIBBLE NIBBLE
ASKED YOU FIRST.
YOU RE STEALING, BANDIT.
TAKING AWAY SOMEONE'S LIVELIHOOD.
HRRM... YEAH. SO?
MUNCH MUNCH MUNCH
YOU'RE JUST SOME GIRL. PLENTY OF BURGERS OUT THERE FOR YOU.
NOT YOUR JOB TO STOP ME.
NO ONE ELSE CARES. NOT EVEN THE COPS.
BANDIT, ARE YOU SAYING YOU DON'T GO TO JAIL WHEN YOU GET CAUGHT?
MUNCH MUNCH MUNCH
HMM...NO, SOMETIMES... SOMETIMES I DO...
MUNCH MUNCH MUNCH
...BUT I JUST CALL DADDY AN' HE TELLS 'EM TO LEMME GO.

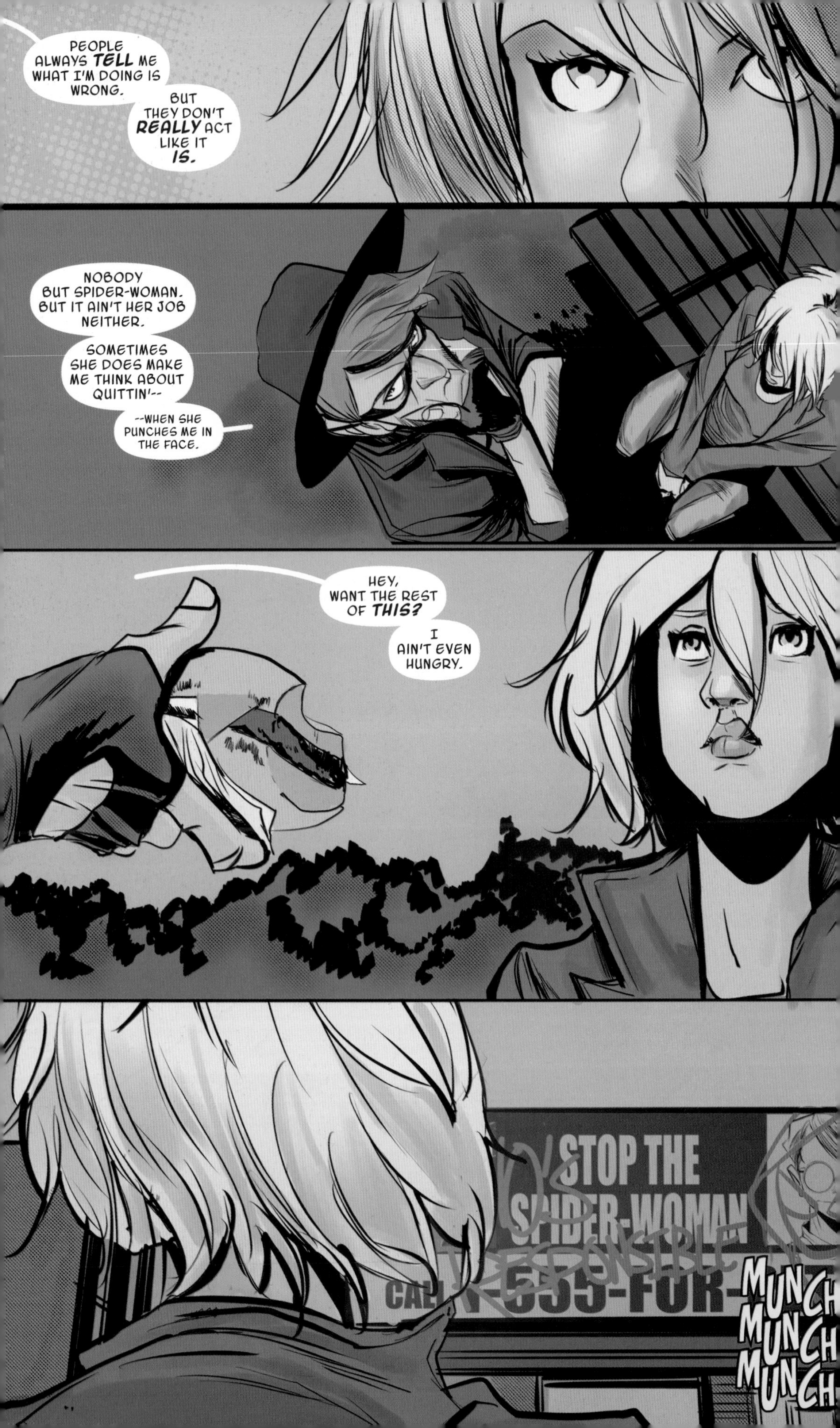
PEOPLE ALWAYS TELL ME WHAT I'M DOING IS WRONG.
BUT THEY DON'T REALLY ACT LIKE IT IS.
NOBODY BUT SPIDER-WOMAN. BUT IT AIN'T HER JOB NEITHER.
SOMETIMES SHE DOES MAKE ME THINK ABOUT QUITTIN'--
--WHEN SHE PUNCHES ME IN THE FACE.
HEY, WANT THE REST OF THIS?
I AIN'T EVEN HUNGRY.
STOP THE SPIDER-WOMAN
RESPONSIBLE
CALL 1-555-FOR-
MUNCH MUNCH MUNCH

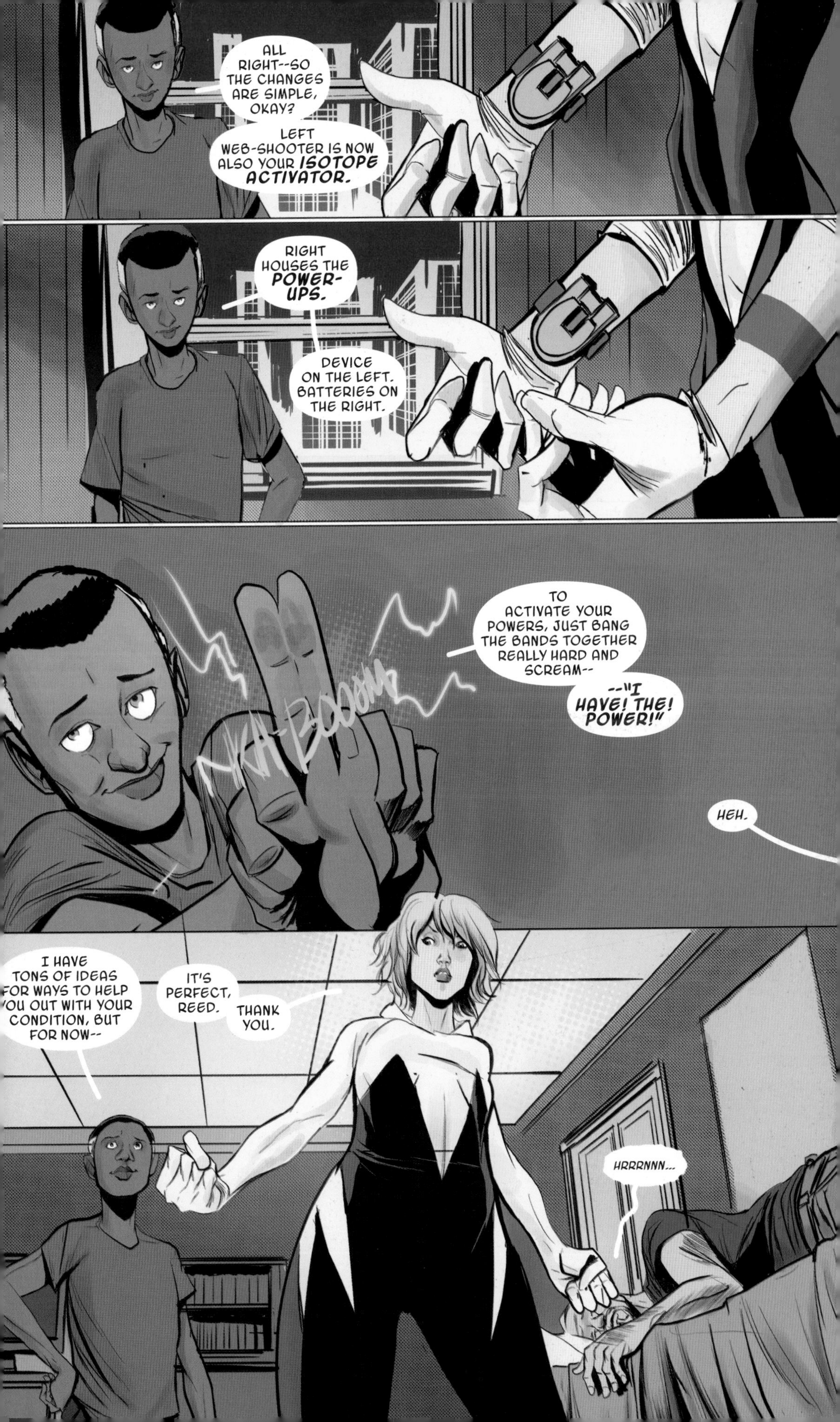
ALL RIGHT--SO THE CHANGES ARE SIMPLE, OKAY?
LEFT WEB-SHOOTER IS NOW ALSO YOUR ISOTOPE ACTIVATOR.
RIGHT HOUSES THE POWER-UPS.
DEVICE ON THE LEFT. BATTERIES ON THE RIGHT.
TO ACTIVATE YOUR POWERS, JUST BANG THE BANDS TOGETHER REALLY HARD AND SCREAM--
--"I HAVE! THE! POWER!"
HEH.
I HAVE TONS OF IDEAS FOR WAYS TO HELP YOU OUT WITH YOUR CONDITION, BUT FOR NOW--
IT'S PERFECT, REED.
THANK YOU.
HRRRNNN...

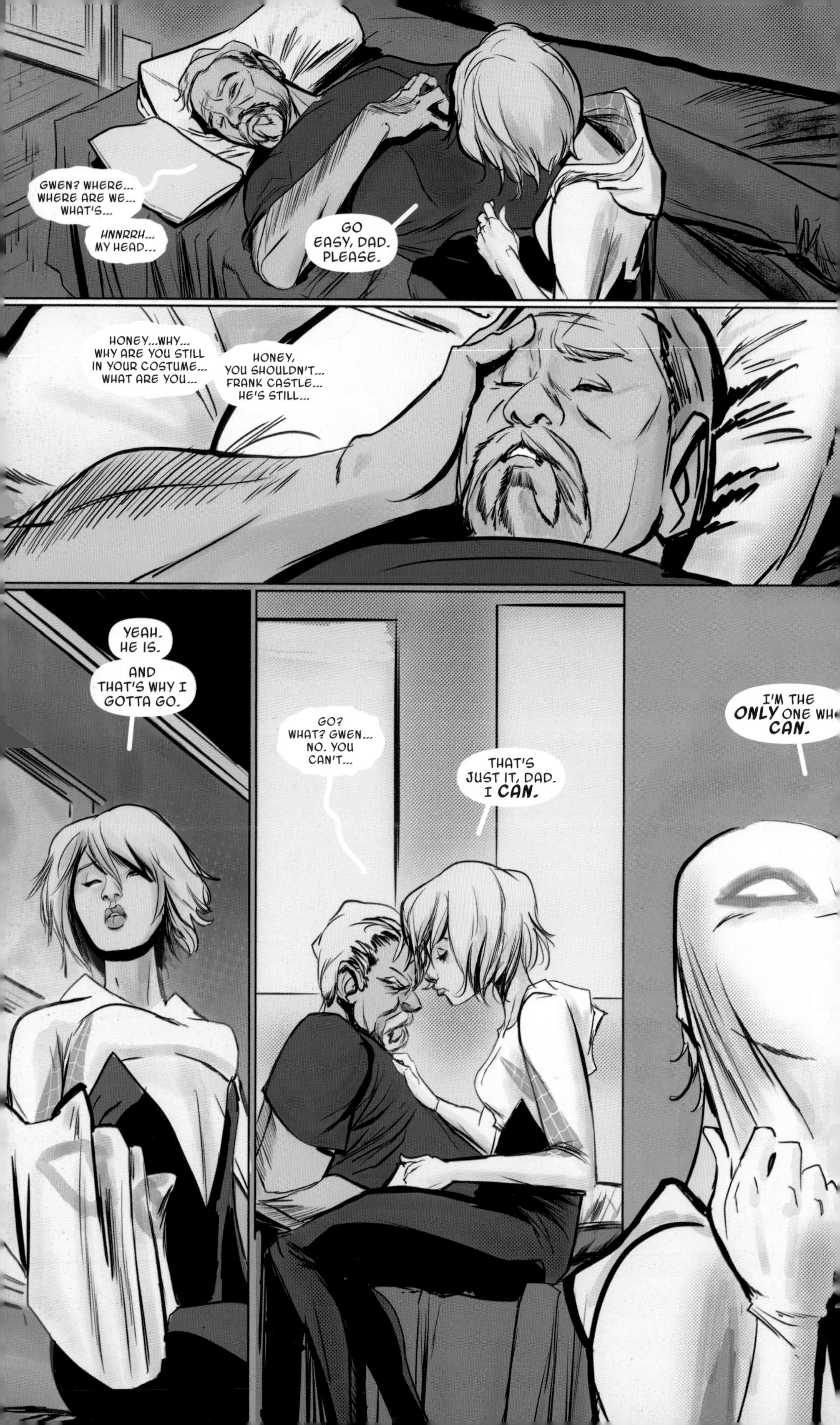
GWEN? WHERE... WHERE ARE WE... WHAT'S...
HNNRRH... MY HEAD...
GO EASY, DAD. PLEASE.
HONEY...WHY... WHY ARE YOU STILL IN YOUR COSTUME... WHAT ARE YOU...
HONEY, YOU SHOULDN'T... FRANK CASTLE... HE'S STILL...
YEAH. HE IS.
AND THAT'S WHY I GOTTA GO.
GO? WHAT? GWEN... NO. YOU CAN'T...
THAT'S JUST IT, DAD. I CAN.
I'M THE ONLY ONE WH CAN.

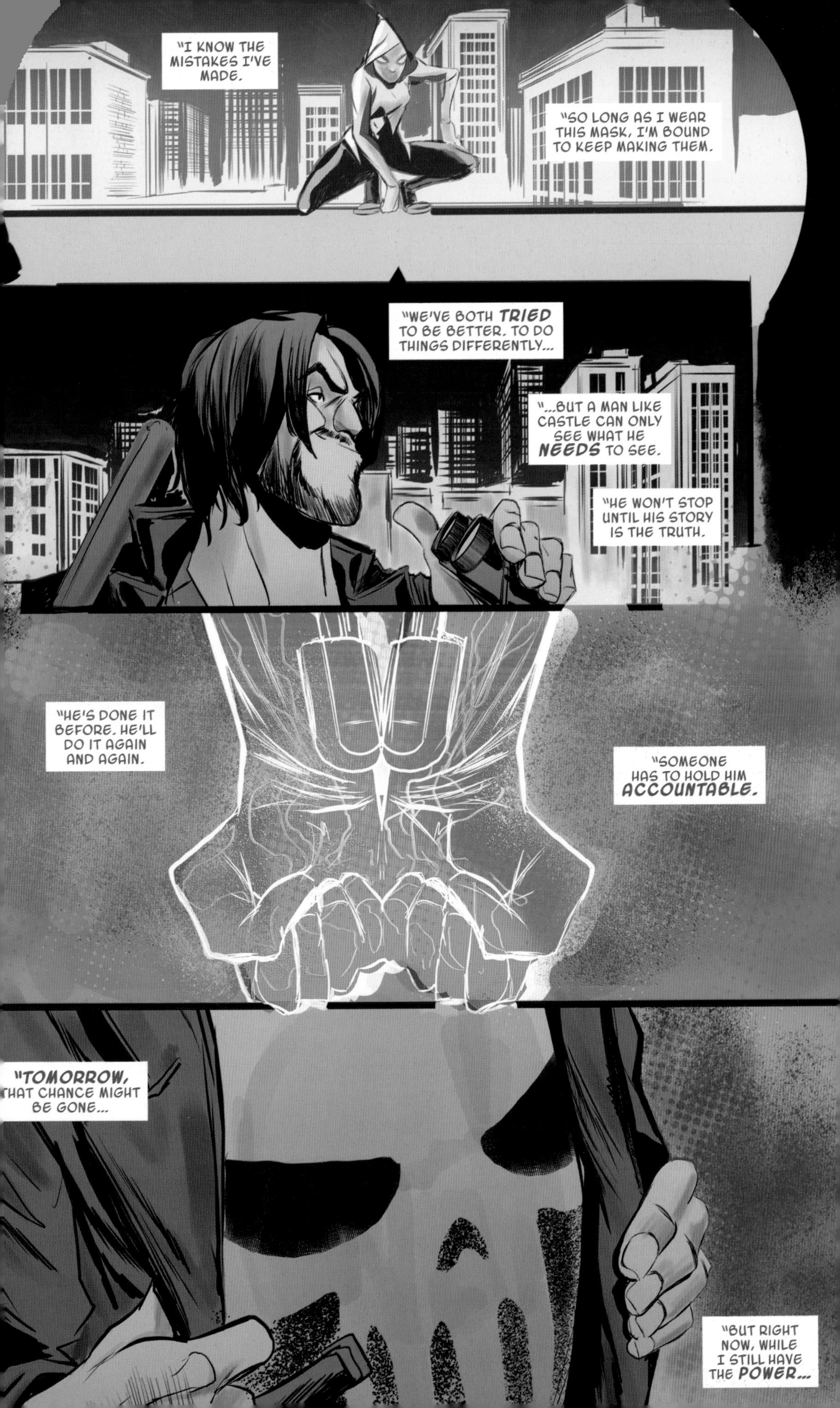
"I KNOW THE MISTAKES I'VE MADE.
"SO LONG AS I WEAR THIS MASK, I'M BOUND TO KEEP MAKING THEM.
"WE'VE BOTH TRIED TO BE BETTER. TO DO THINGS DIFFERENTLY...
"...BUT A MAN LIKE CASTLE CAN ONLY SEE WHAT HE NEEDS TO SEE.
"HE WON'T STOP UNTIL HIS STORY IS THE TRUTH.
"HE'S DONE IT BEFORE. HE'LL DO IT AGAIN AND AGAIN.
"SOMEONE HAS TO HOLD HIM ACCOUNTABLE.
"TOMORROW, THAT CHANCE MIGHT BE GONE...
"BUT RIGHT NOW, WHILE I STILL HAVE THE POWER...

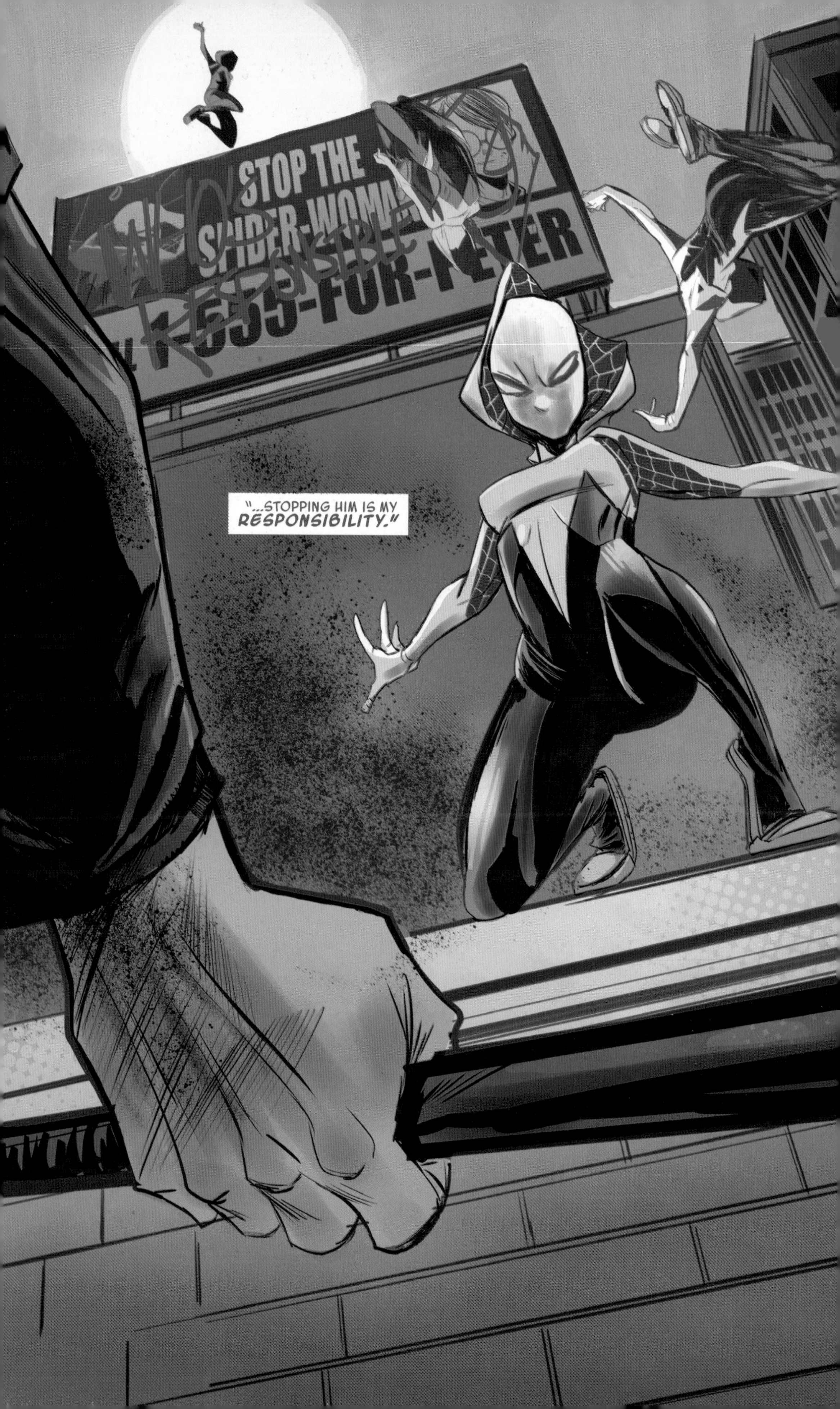
STOP THE
"...STOPPING HIM IS MY RESPONSIBILITY."

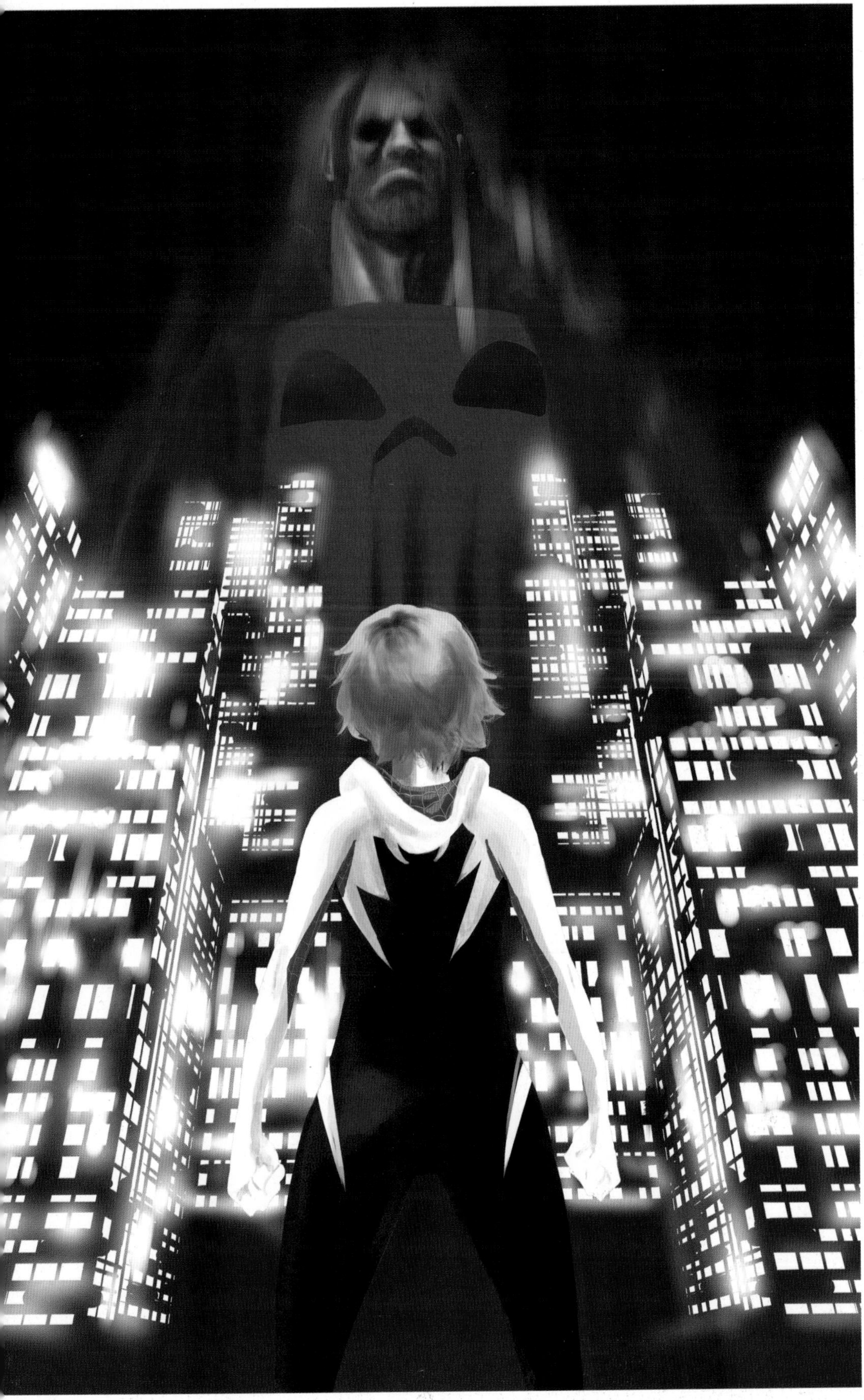

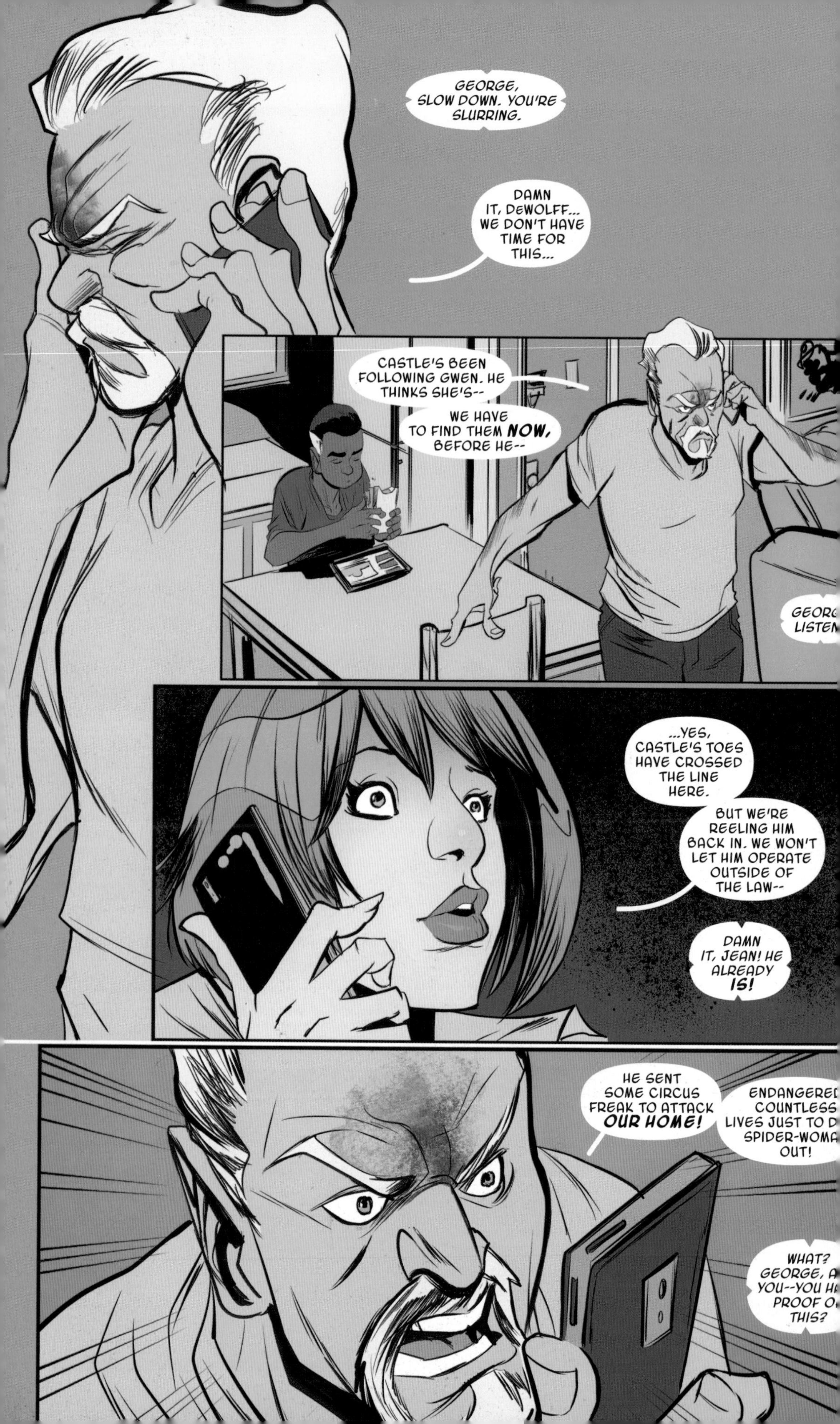
GEORGE, SLOW DOWN. YOU'RE SLURRING.
DAMN IT, DEWOLFF... WE DON'T HAVE TIME FOR THIS...
CASTLE'S BEEN FOLLOWING GWEN. HE THINKS SHE'S--
WE HAVE TO FIND THEM NOW, BEFORE HE--
...YES, CASTLE'S TOES HAVE CROSSED THE LINE HERE.
BUT WE'RE REELING HIM BACK IN. WE WON'T LET HIM OPERATE OUTSIDE OF THE LAW--
DAMN IT, JEAN! HE ALREADY IS!
HE SENT SOME CIRCUS FREAK TO ATTACK OUR HOME!

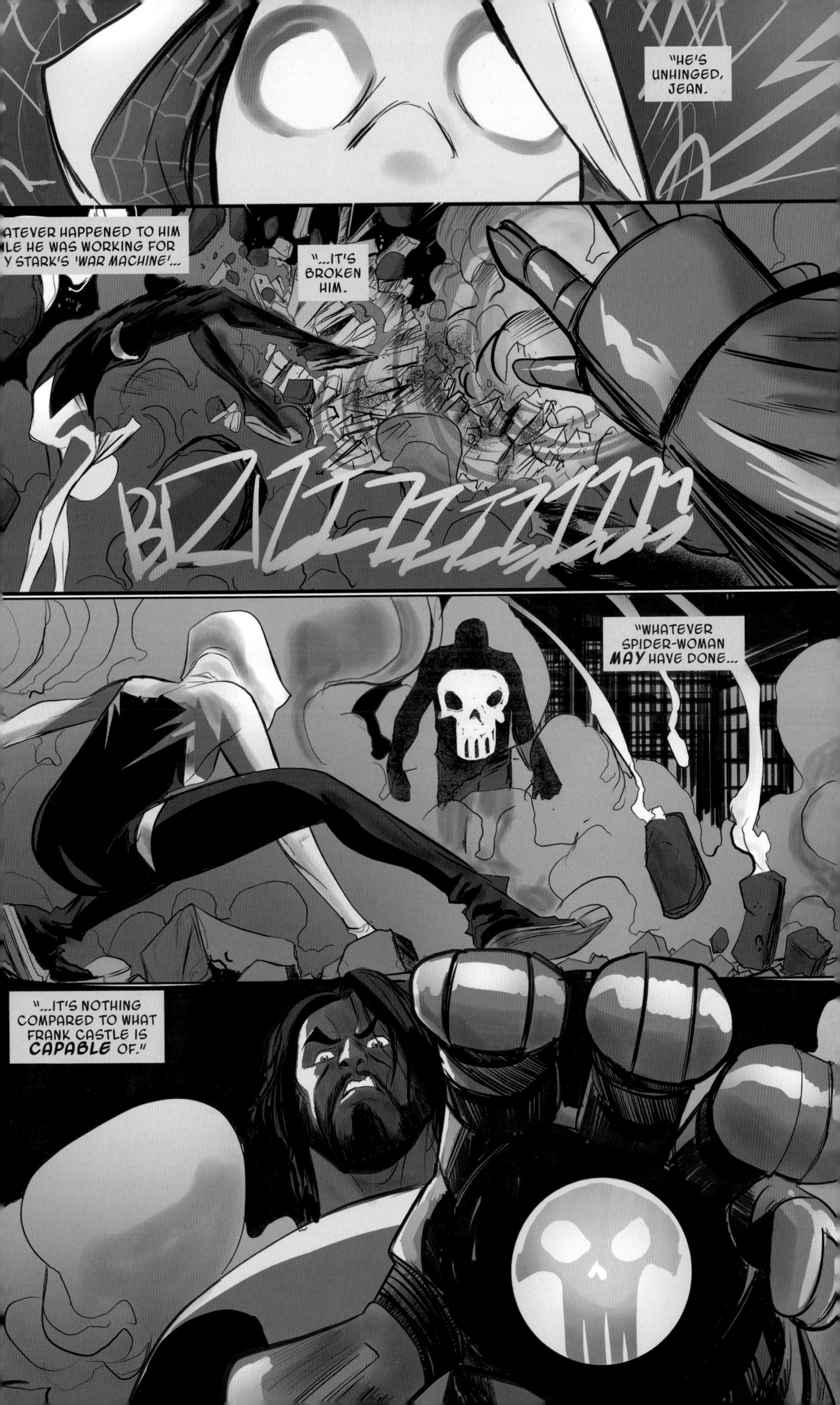
"HE'S UNHINGED, JEAN.
ATEVER HAPPENED TO HIM LE HE WAS WORKING FOR Y STARK'S 'WAR MACHINE'...
"...IT'S BROKEN HIM.
BZZZZZZZZZZ
"WHATEVER SPIDER-WOMAN MAY HAVE DONE...
"...IT'S NOTHING COMPARED TO WHAT FRANK CASTLE IS CAPABLE OF."

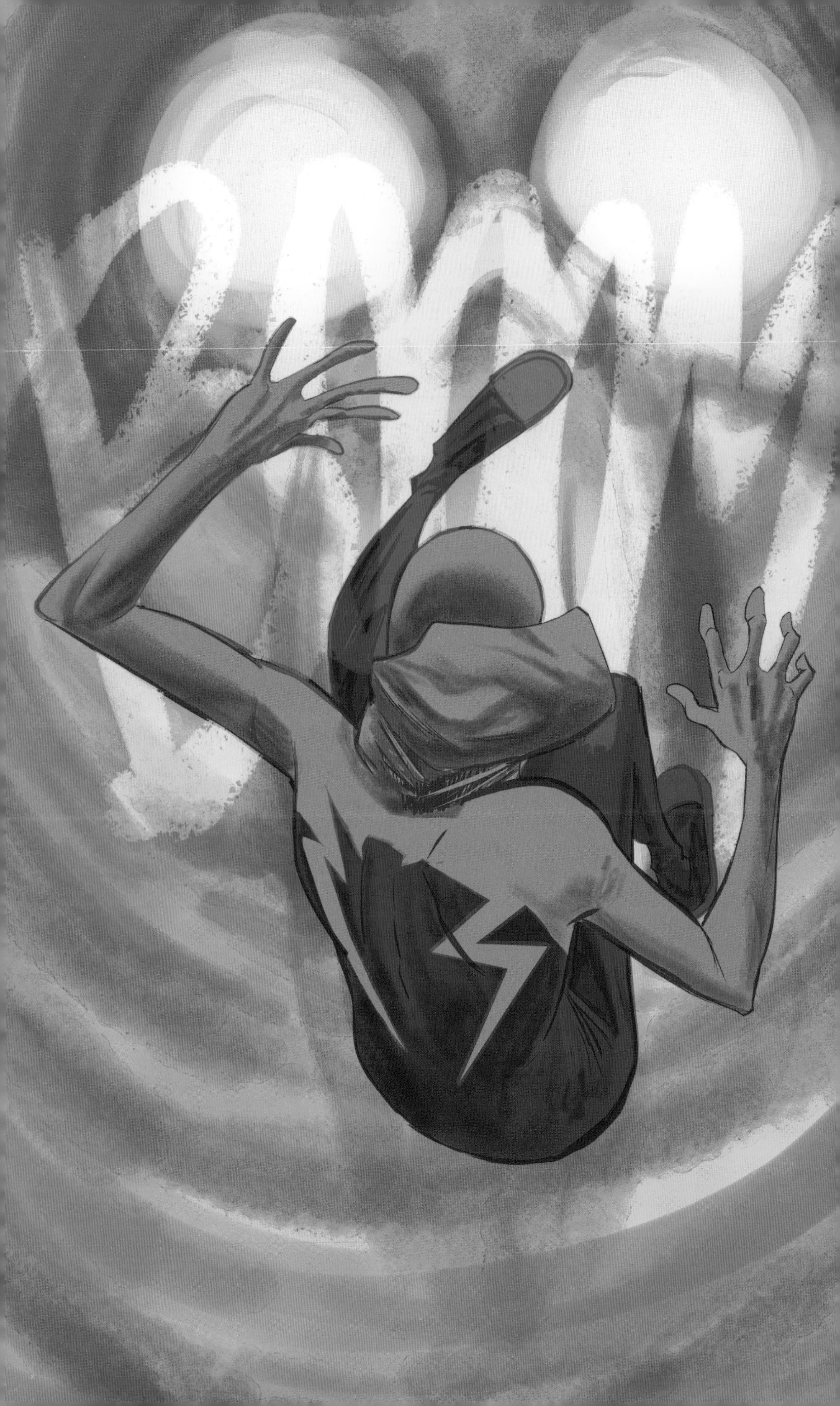

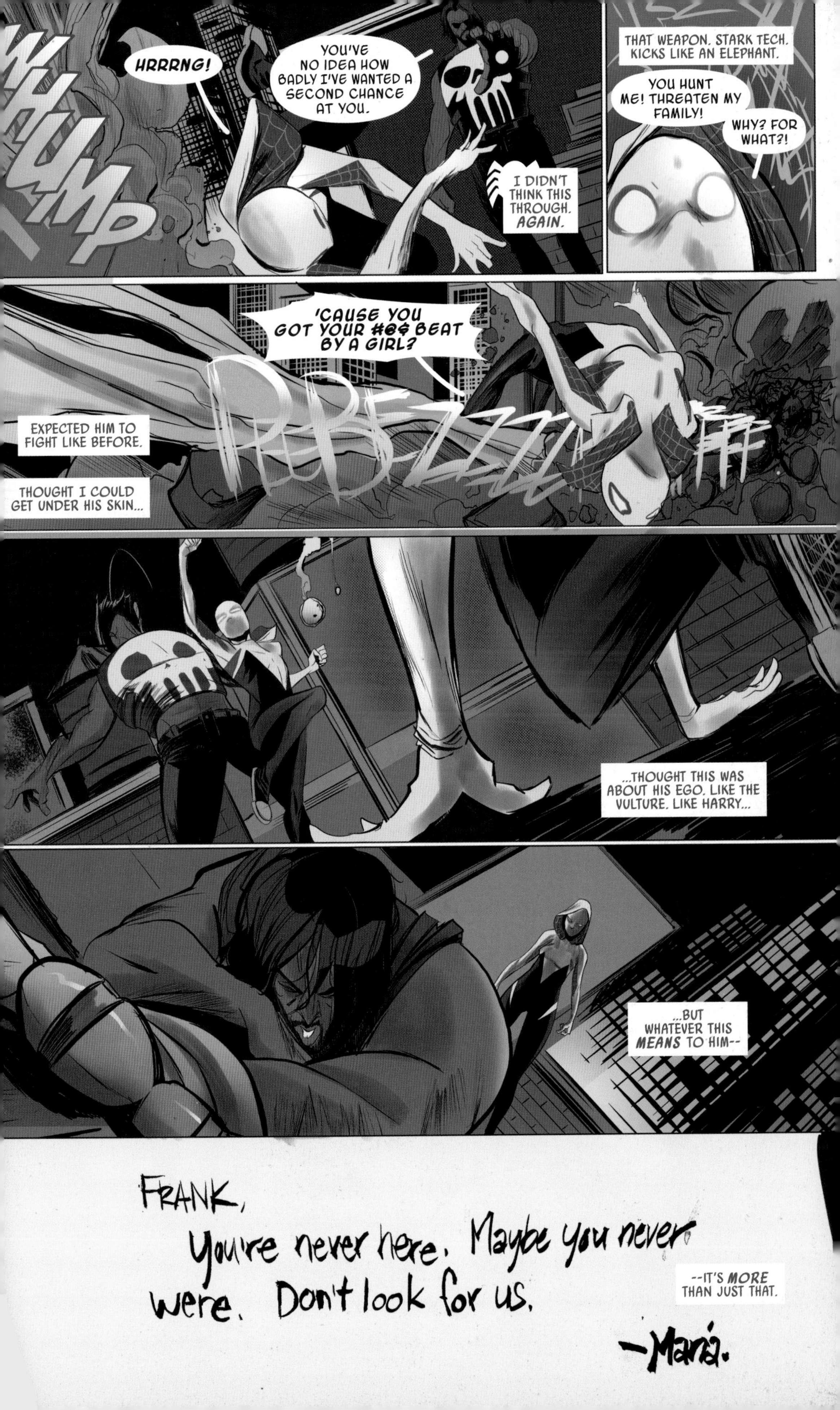
WHUMP
HRRRNG!
YOU'VE NO IDEA HOW BADLY I'VE WANTED A SECOND CHANCE AT YOU.
I DIDN'T THINK THIS THROUGH. AGAIN.
THAT WEAPON. STARK TECH. KICKS LIKE AN ELEPHANT.
YOU HUNT ME! THREATEN MY FAMILY!
WHY? FOR WHAT?!
'CAUSE YOU GOT YOUR #@$ BEAT BY A GIRL?
EXPECTED HIM TO FIGHT LIKE BEFORE.
THOUGHT I COULD GET UNDER HIS SKIN...
...THOUGHT THIS WAS ABOUT HIS EGO. LIKE THE VULTURE. LIKE HARRY...
...BUT WHATEVER THIS MEANS TO HIM--
FRANK,
You're never here. Maybe you never were. Don't look for us.
--IT'S MORE THAN JUST THAT.
-María.

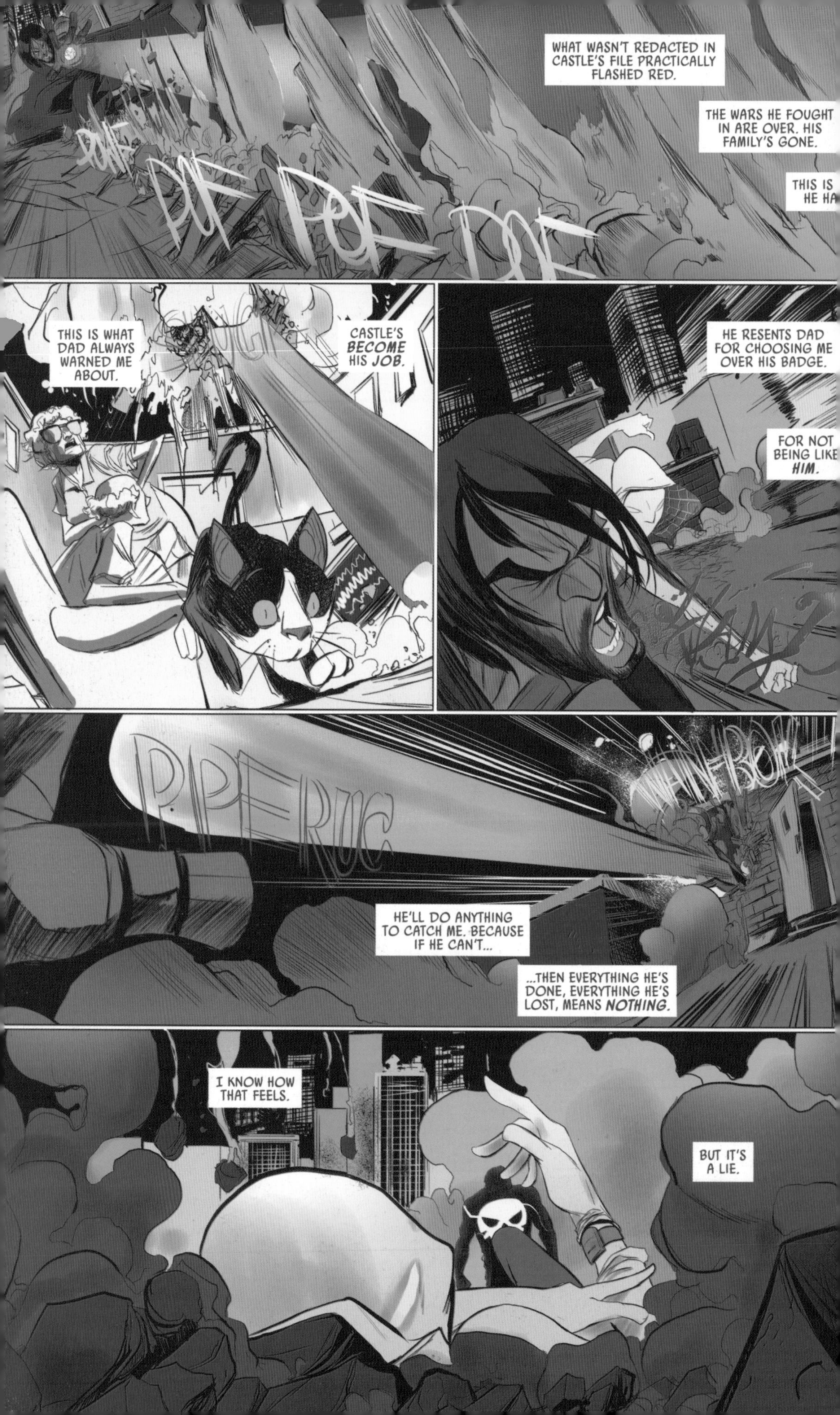
WHAT WASN'T REDACTED IN CASTLE'S FILE PRACTICALLY FLASHED RED.
THE WARS HE FOUGHT IN ARE OVER. HIS FAMILY'S GONE.
THIS IS HE HA
THIS IS WHAT DAD ALWAYS WARNED ME ABOUT.
CASTLE'S *BECOME* HIS *JOB*.
HE RESENTS DAD FOR CHOOSING ME OVER HIS BADGE.
FOR NOT BEING LIKE *HIM*.
HE'LL DO ANYTHING TO CATCH ME. BECAUSE IF HE CAN'T...
...THEN EVERYTHING HE'S DONE, EVERYTHING HE'S LOST, MEANS *NOTHING*.
I KNOW HOW THAT FEELS.
BUT IT'S A LIE.

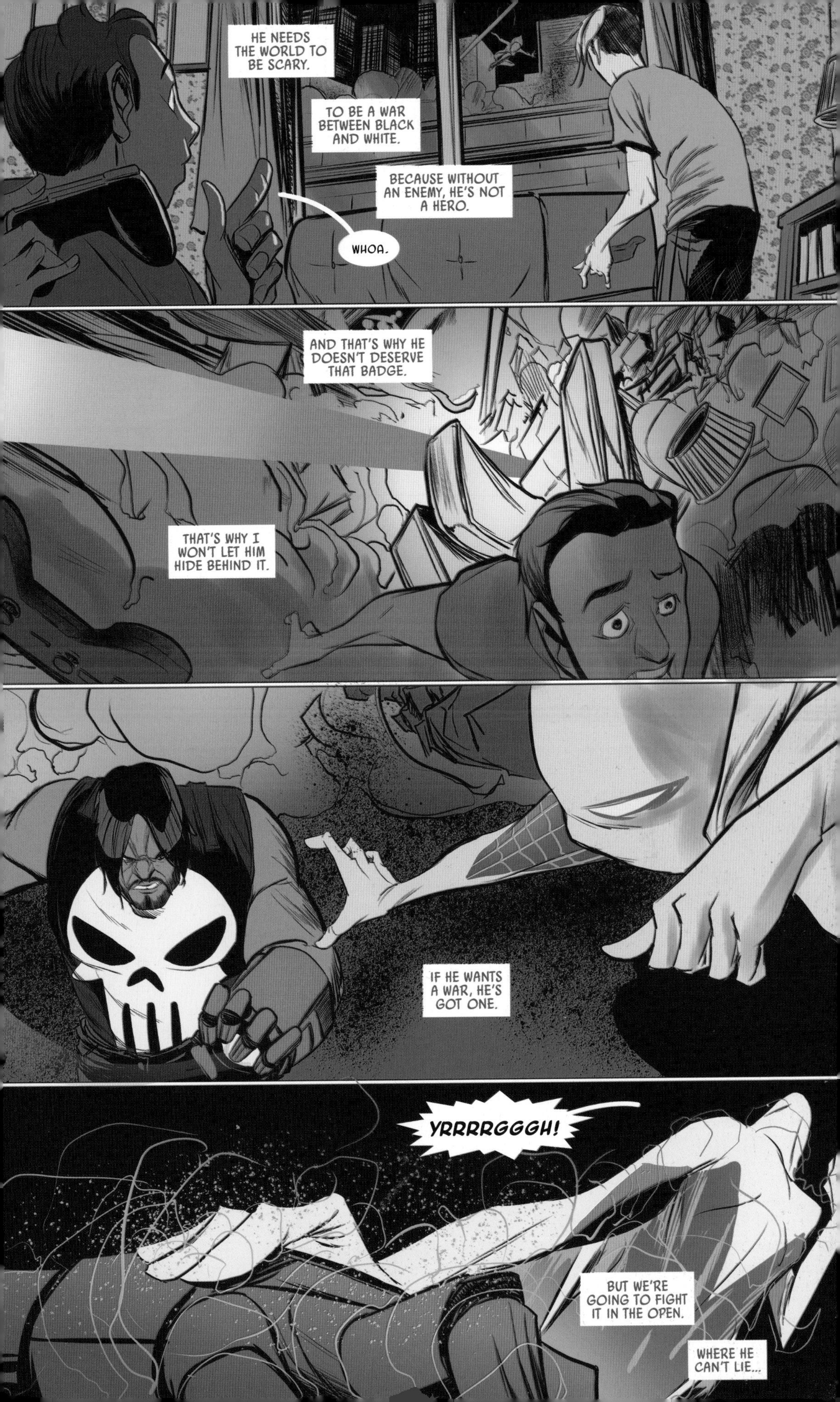
HE NEEDS THE WORLD TO BE SCARY.
TO BE A WAR BETWEEN BLACK AND WHITE.
BECAUSE WITHOUT AN ENEMY, HE'S NOT A HERO.
WHOA.
AND THAT'S WHY HE DOESN'T DESERVE THAT BADGE.
THAT'S WHY I WON'T LET HIM HIDE BEHIND IT.
IF HE WANTS A WAR, HE'S GOT ONE.
YRRRRGGGH!
BUT WE'RE GOING TO FIGHT IT IN THE OPEN.
WHERE HE CAN'T LIE...

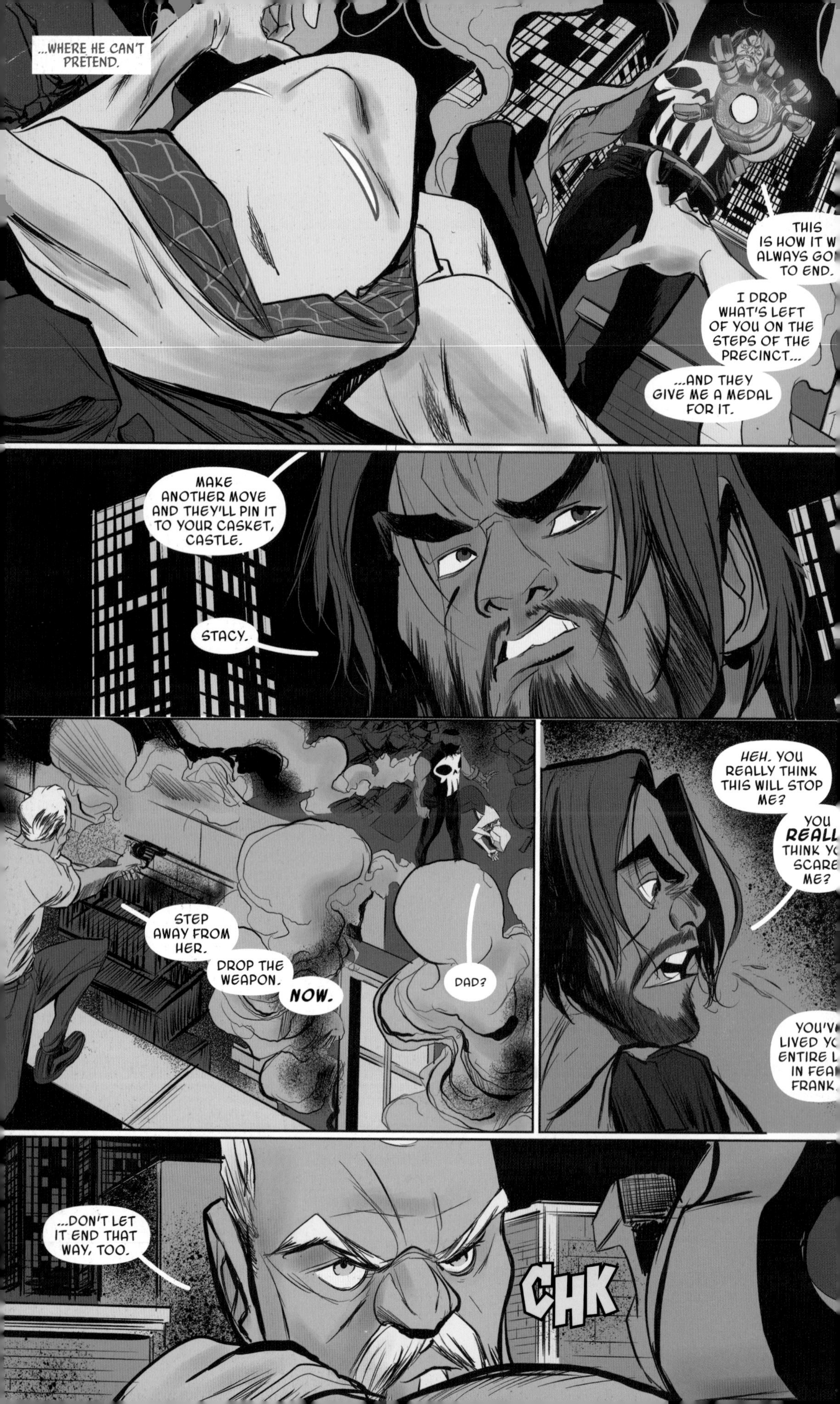
...WHERE HE CAN'T PRETEND.
THIS IS HOW IT W ALWAYS GO TO END.
I DROP WHAT'S LEFT OF YOU ON THE STEPS OF THE PRECINCT...
...AND THEY GIVE ME A MEDAL FOR IT.
MAKE ANOTHER MOVE AND THEY'LL PIN IT TO YOUR CASKET, CASTLE.
STACY.
STEP AWAY FROM HER.
DROP THE WEAPON.
NOW.
DAD?
HEH. YOU REALLY THINK THIS WILL STOP ME?
YOU REALL THINK Y SCARE ME?
YOU'V LIVED Y ENTIRE L IN FEA FRANK.
...DON'T LET IT END THAT WAY, TOO.
CHK

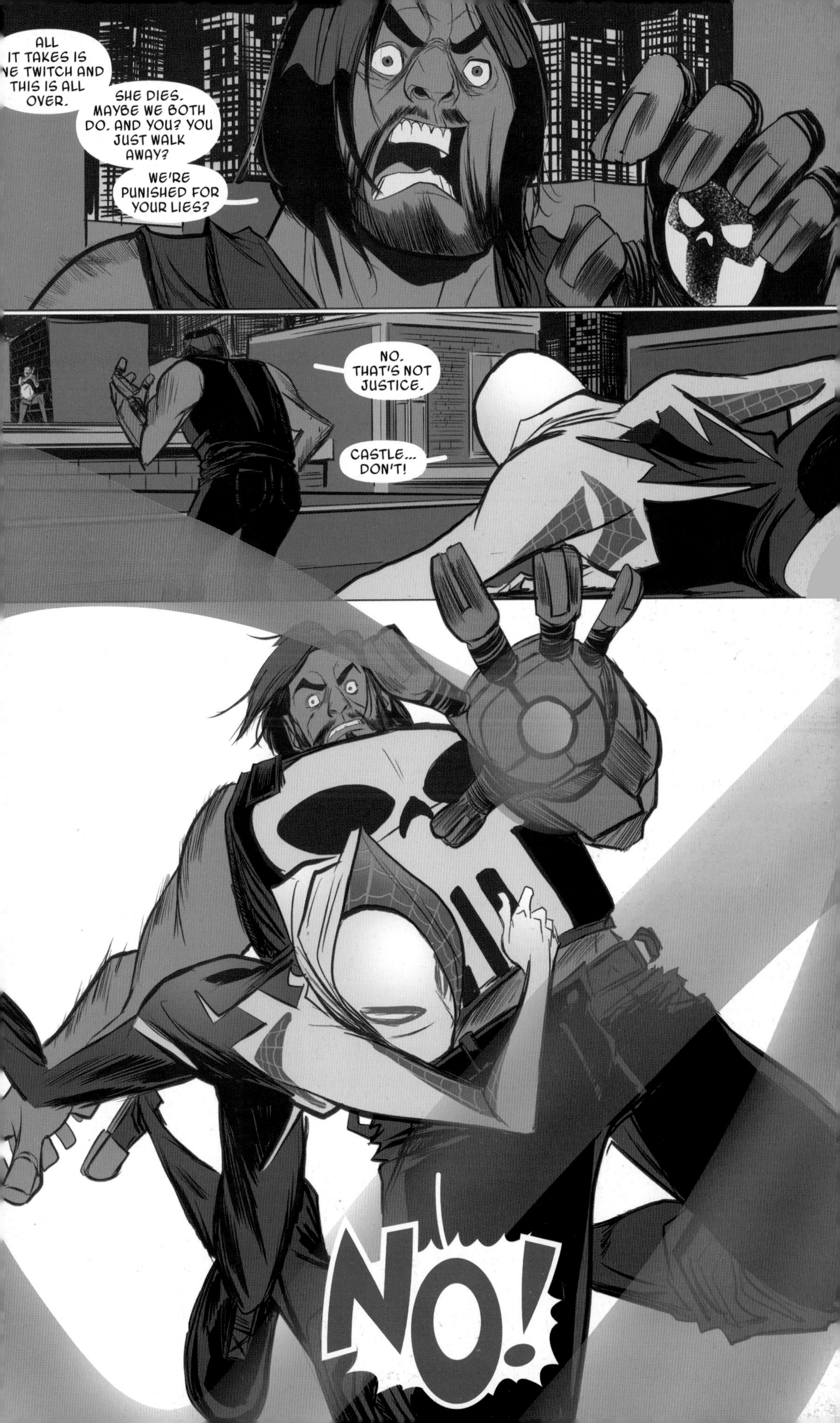

ALL IT TAKES IS NE TWITCH AND THIS IS ALL OVER.
SHE DIES. MAYBE WE BOTH DO. AND YOU? YOU JUST WALK AWAY?
WE'RE PUNISHED FOR YOUR LIES?
NO. THAT'S NOT JUSTICE.
CASTLE... DON'T!
NO!

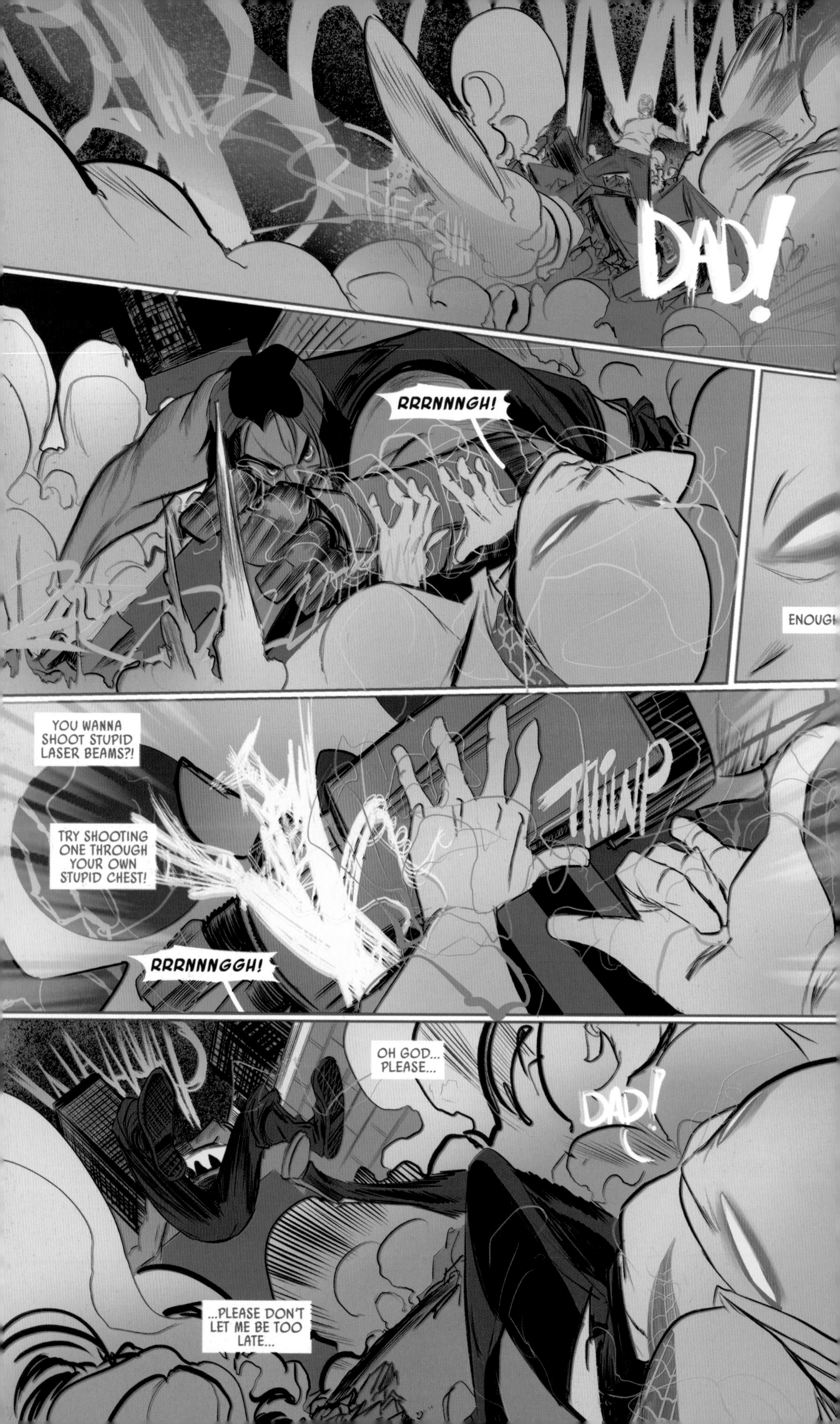
DAD!
RRRNNNGH!
ENOUG
YOU WANNA SHOOT STUPID LASER BEAMS?!
TRY SHOOTING ONE THROUGH YOUR OWN STUPID CHEST!
THWP
RRRNNNGGH!
OH GOD... PLEASE...
DAD!
...PLEASE DON'T LET ME BE TOO LATE...

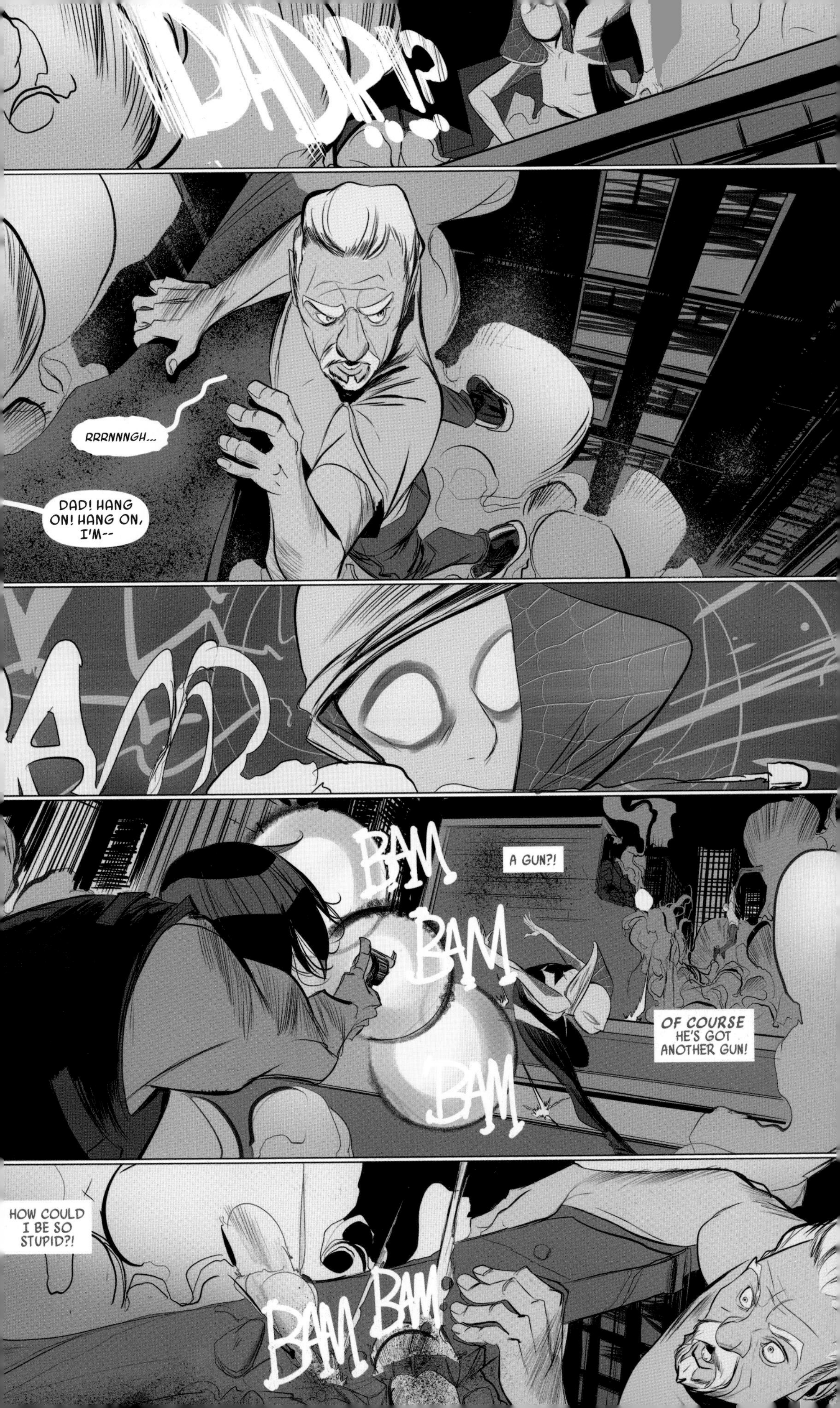
DAD?!
RRRNNNGH...
DAD! HANG ON! HANG ON, I'M--
BAM
BAM
A GUN?!
BAM
OF COURSE HE'S GOT ANOTHER GUN!
HOW COULD I BE SO STUPID?!
BAM BAM

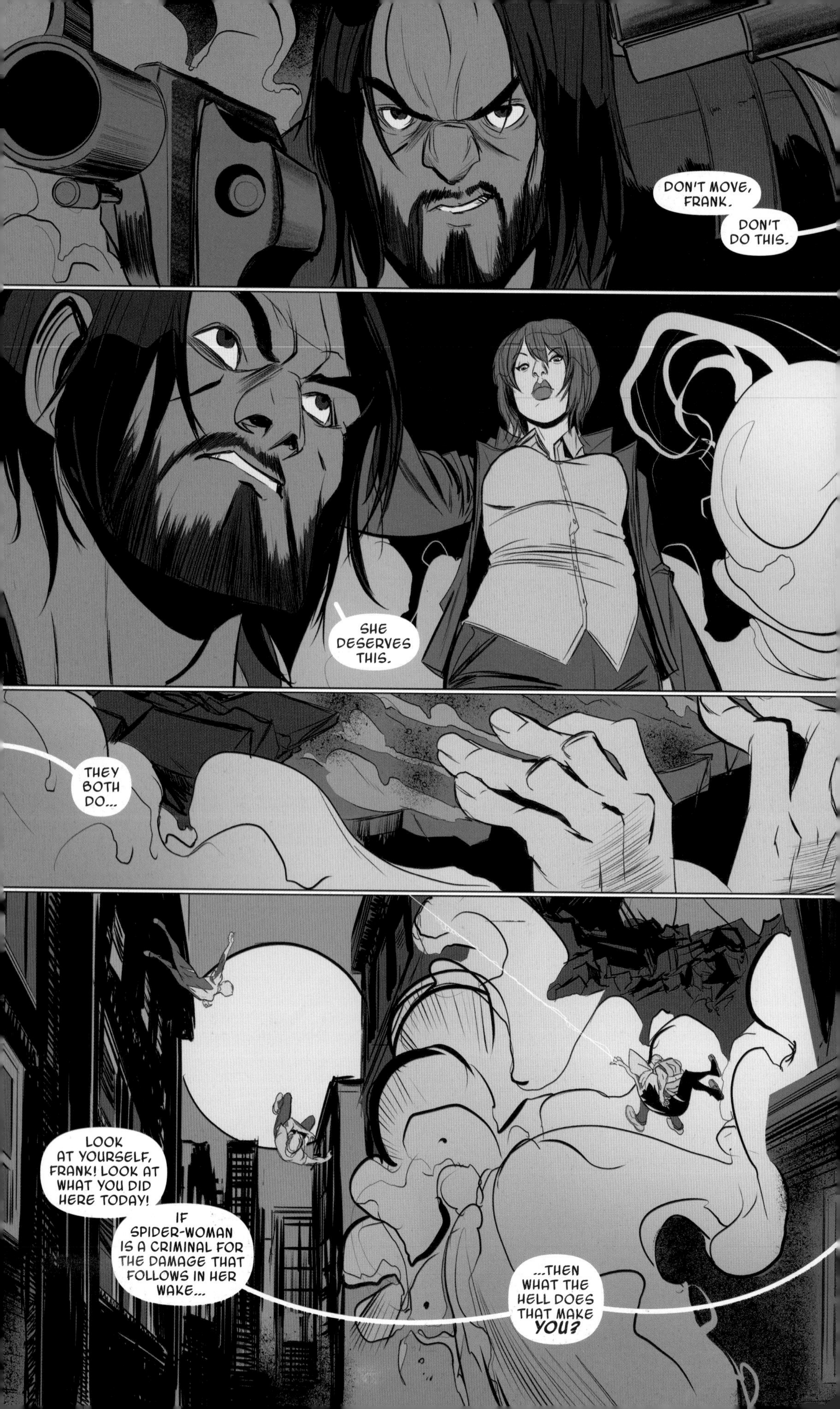
DON'T MOVE, FRANK.
DON'T DO THIS.
SHE DESERVES THIS.
THEY BOTH DO...
LOOK AT YOURSELF, FRANK! LOOK AT WHAT YOU DID HERE TODAY!
IF SPIDER-WOMAN IS A CRIMINAL FOR THE DAMAGE THAT FOLLOWS IN HER WAKE...
...THEN WHAT THE HELL DOES THAT MAKE YOU?

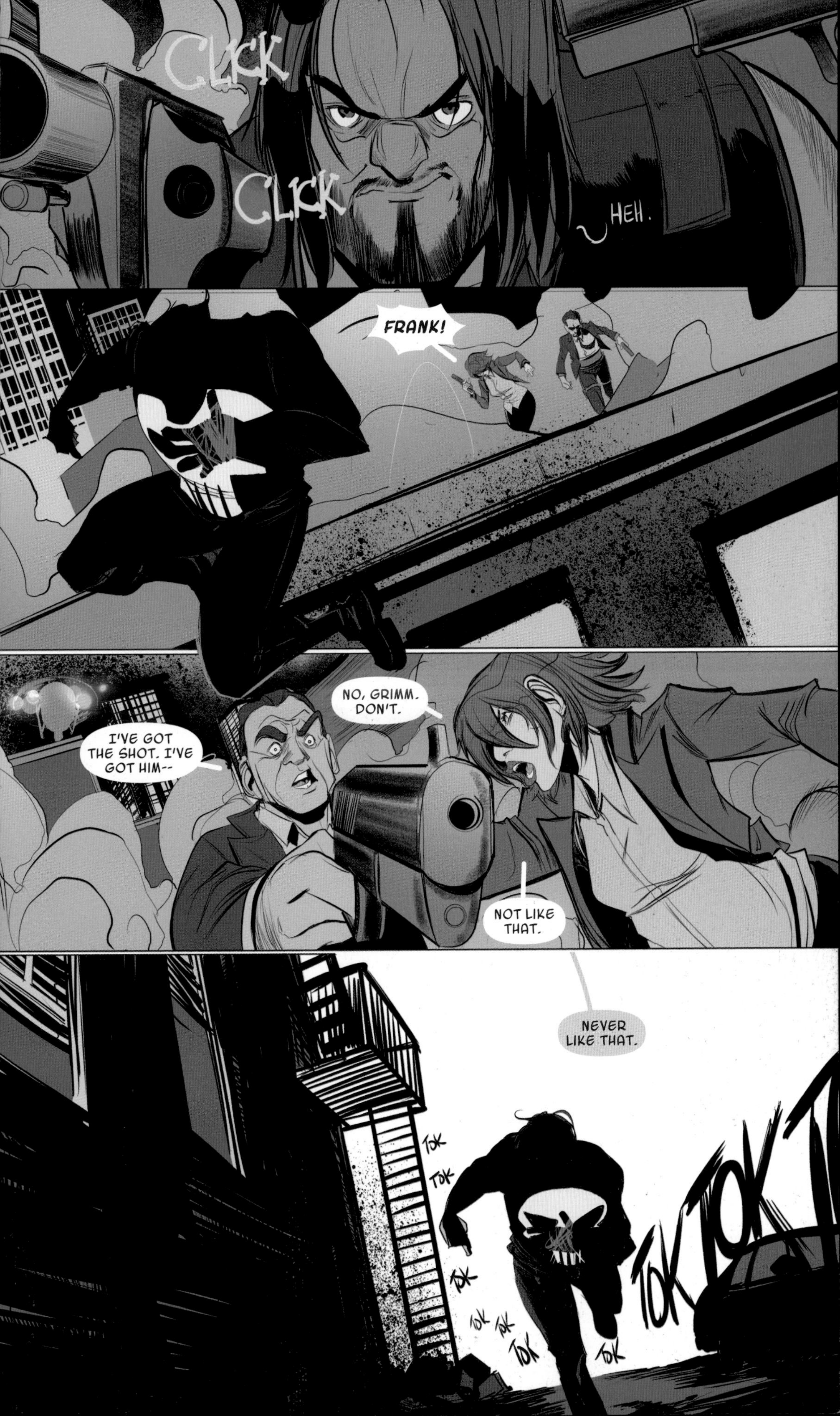
CLICK
CLICK
HEH.
FRANK!
NO, GRIMM. DON'T.
I'VE GOT THE SHOT. I'VE GOT HIM--
NOT LIKE THAT.
NEVER LIKE THAT.
TOK
TOK
TOK
TOK TOK
TOK
TOK
TOK TOK TOK

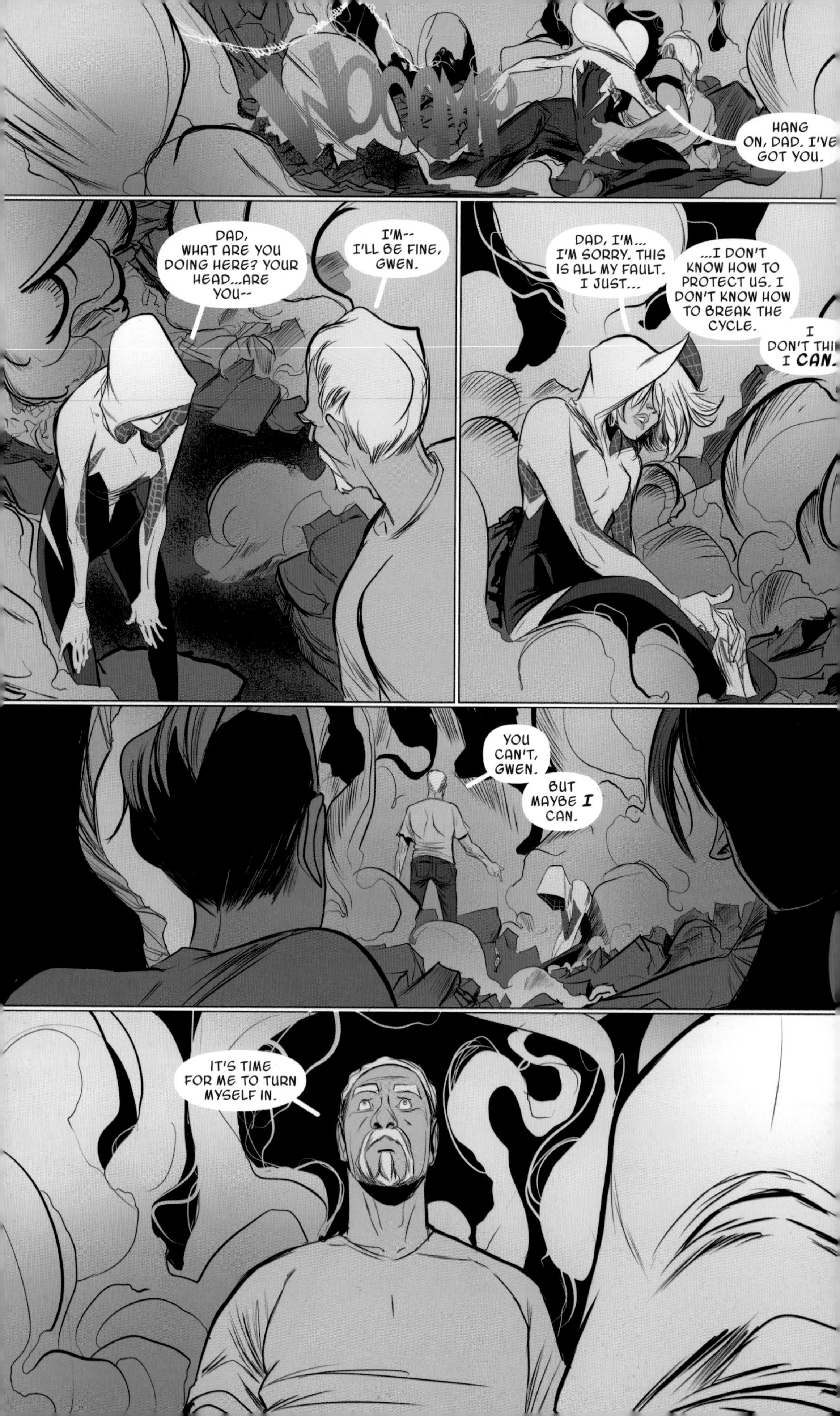
WOOMP
HANG ON, DAD. I'VE GOT YOU.
DAD, WHAT ARE YOU DOING HERE? YOUR HEAD...ARE YOU--
I'M-- I'LL BE FINE, GWEN.
DAD, I'M... I'M SORRY. THIS IS ALL MY FAULT. I JUST...
...I DON'T KNOW HOW TO PROTECT US. I DON'T KNOW HOW TO BREAK THE CYCLE.
YOU CAN'T, GWEN.
BUT MAYBE I CAN.
IT'S TIME FOR ME TO TURN MYSELF IN.

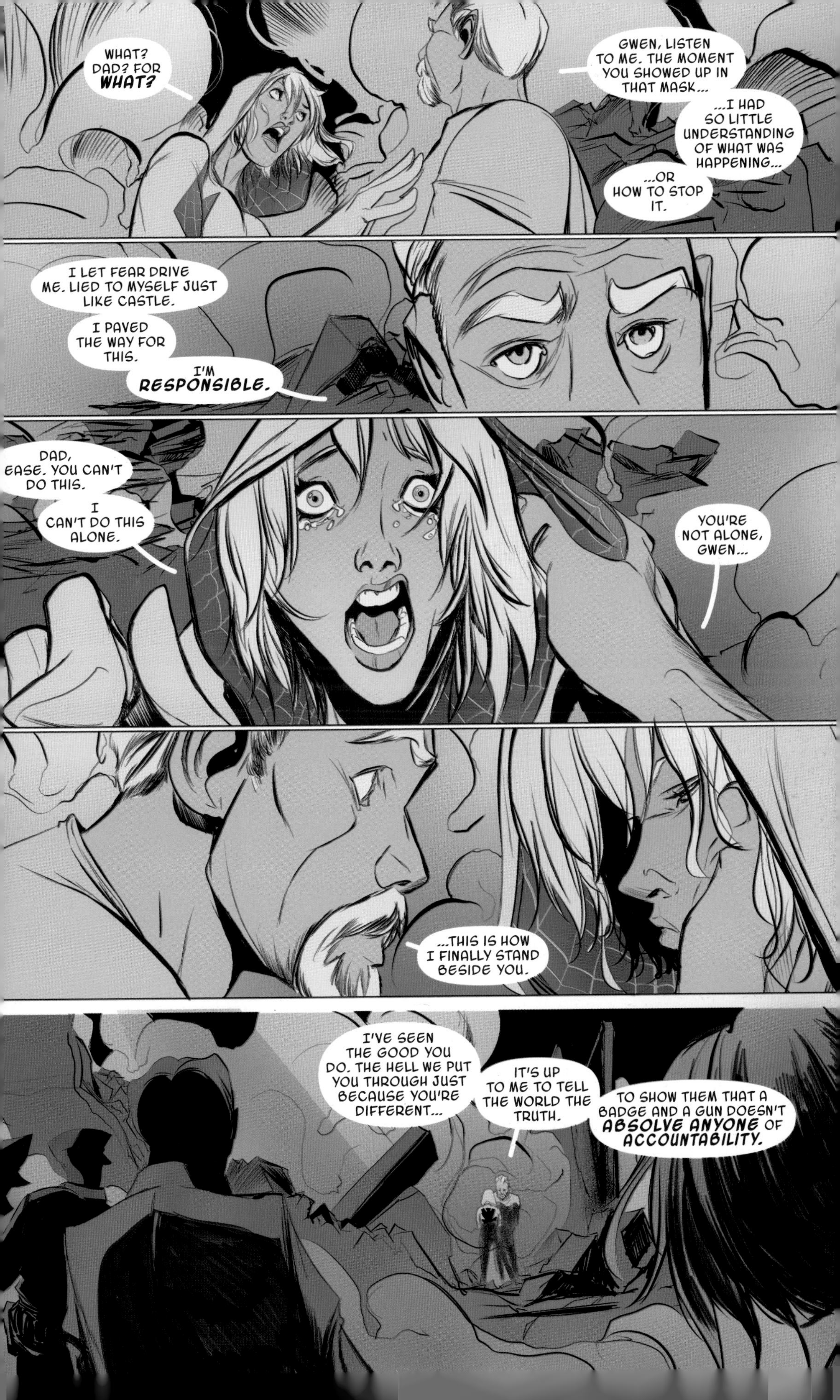
WHAT? DAD? FOR WHAT?
GWEN, LISTEN TO ME. THE MOMENT YOU SHOWED UP IN THAT MASK...
...I HAD SO LITTLE UNDERSTANDING OF WHAT WAS HAPPENING...
...OR HOW TO STOP IT.
I LET FEAR DRIVE ME. LIED TO MYSELF JUST LIKE CASTLE.
I PAVED THE WAY FOR THIS.
I'M RESPONSIBLE.
DAD, EASE. YOU CAN'T DO THIS.
I CAN'T DO THIS ALONE.
YOU'RE NOT ALONE, GWEN...
...THIS IS HOW I FINALLY STAND BESIDE YOU.
I'VE SEEN THE GOOD YOU DO. THE HELL WE PUT YOU THROUGH JUST BECAUSE YOU'RE DIFFERENT...
IT'S UP TO ME TO TELL THE WORLD THE TRUTH.
TO SHOW THEM THAT A BADGE AND A GUN DOESN'T ABSOLVE ANYONE OF ACCOUNTABILITY.

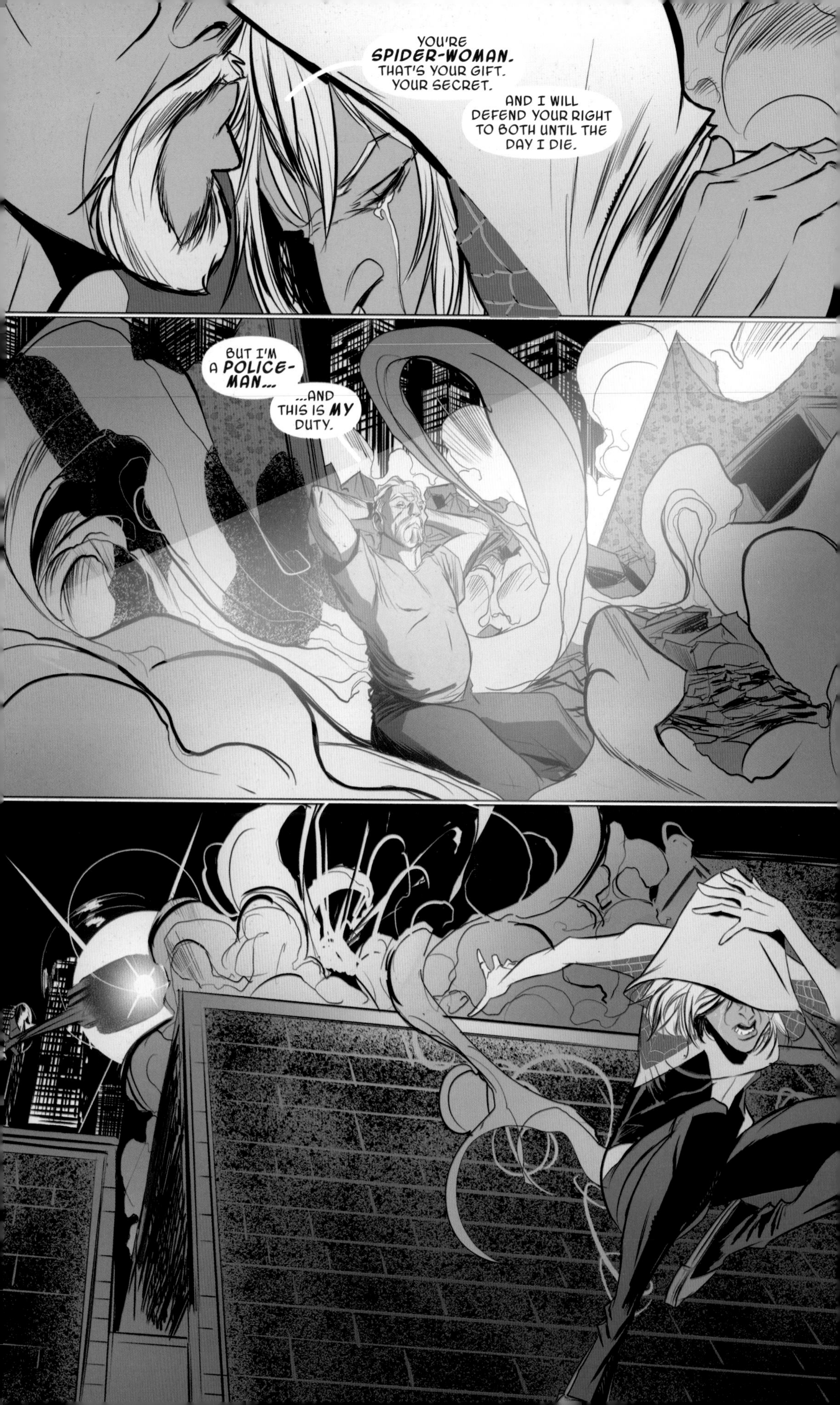
YOU'RE SPIDER-WOMAN. THAT'S YOUR GIFT. YOUR SECRET.
AND I WILL DEFEND YOUR RIGHT TO BOTH UNTIL THE DAY I DIE.
BUT I'M A POLICE-MAN...
...AND THIS IS MY DUTY.

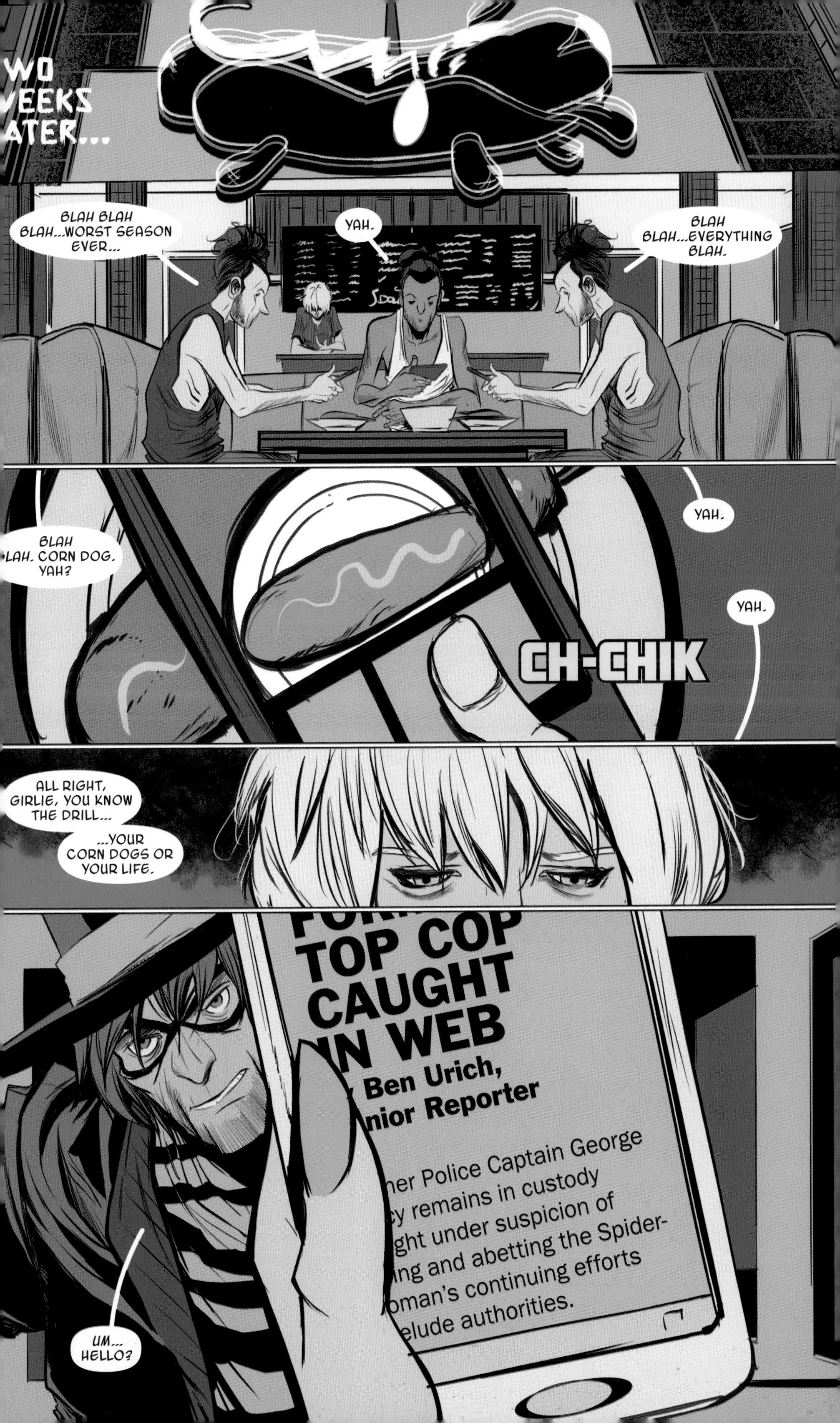

WO
VEEKS
ATER...
BLAH BLAH BLAH...WORST SEASON EVER...
YAH.
BLAH BLAH...EVERYTHING BLAH.
BLAH
LAH. CORN DOG. YAH?
YAH.
YAH.
CH-CHIK
ALL RIGHT, GIRLIE, YOU KNOW THE DRILL...
...YOUR CORN DOGS OR YOUR LIFE.
TOP COP
CAUGHT
IN WEB
Ben Urich,
nior Reporter
her Police Captain George
cy remains in custody
ght under suspicion of
ing and abetting the Spider-
oman's continuing efforts
elude authorities.
UM... HELLO?

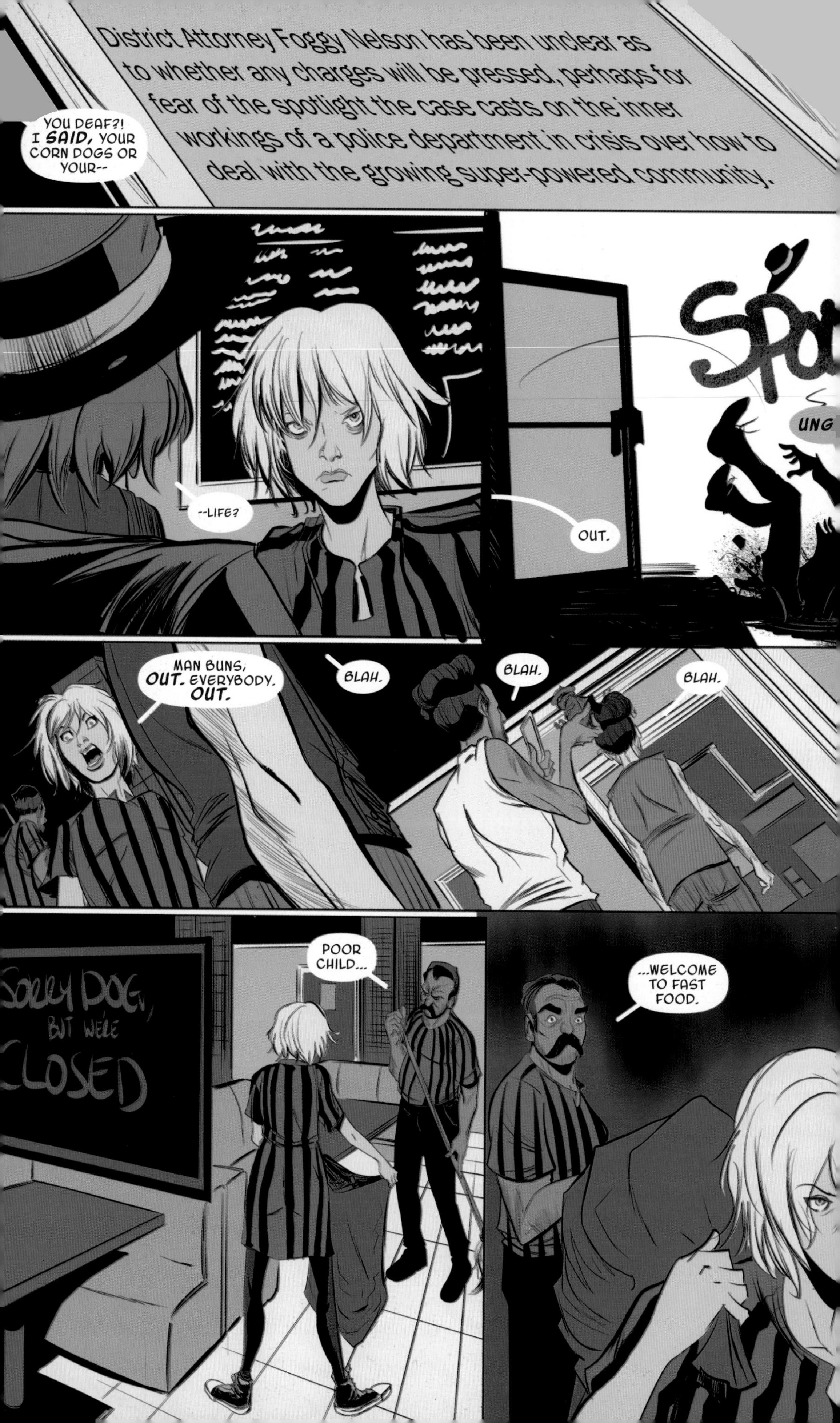
District Attorney Foggy Nelson has been unclear as to whether any charges will be pressed, perhaps for fear of the spotlight the case casts on the inner workings of a police department in crisis over how to deal with the growing super-powered community.
YOU DEAF?! I SAID, YOUR CORN DOGS OR YOUR--
--LIFE?
OUT.
SPO
UNG
MAN BUNS, OUT. EVERYBODY. OUT.
BLAH.
BLAH.
BLAH.
SORRY DOG, BUT WE'RE CLOSED
POOR CHILD...
...WELCOME TO FAST FOOD.

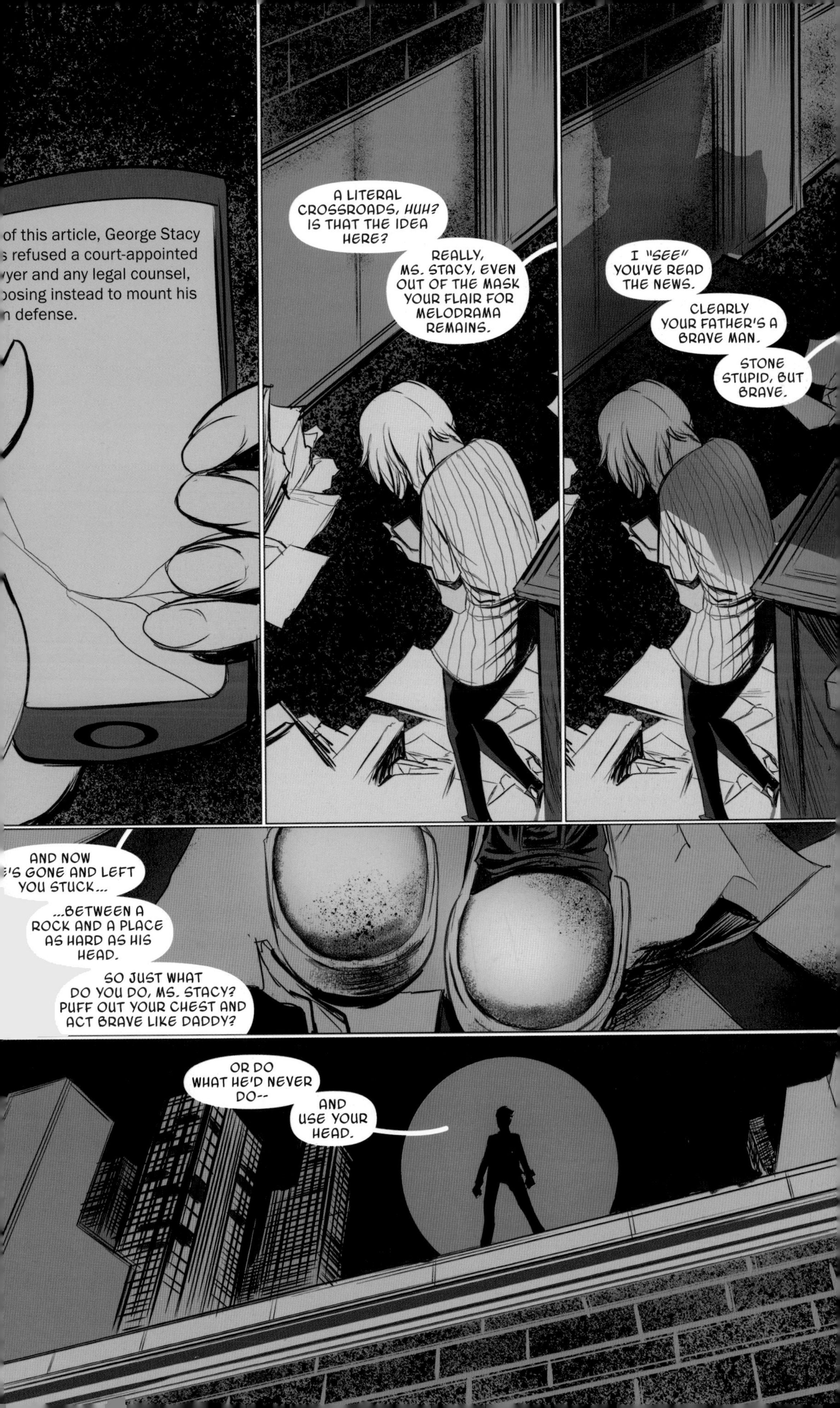
of this article, George Stacy
s refused a court-appointed
wyer and any legal counsel,
posing instead to mount his
n defense.
A LITERAL CROSSROADS, HUH? IS THAT THE IDEA HERE?
REALLY, MS. STACY, EVEN OUT OF THE MASK YOUR FLAIR FOR MELODRAMA REMAINS.
I "SEE" YOU'VE READ THE NEWS.
CLEARLY YOUR FATHER'S A BRAVE MAN.
STONE STUPID, BUT BRAVE.
AND NOW 'S GONE AND LEFT YOU STUCK...
...BETWEEN A ROCK AND A PLACE AS HARD AS HIS HEAD.
SO JUST WHAT DO YOU DO, MS. STACY? PUFF OUT YOUR CHEST AND ACT BRAVE LIKE DADDY?
OR DO WHAT HE'D NEVER DO--
AND USE YOUR HEAD.

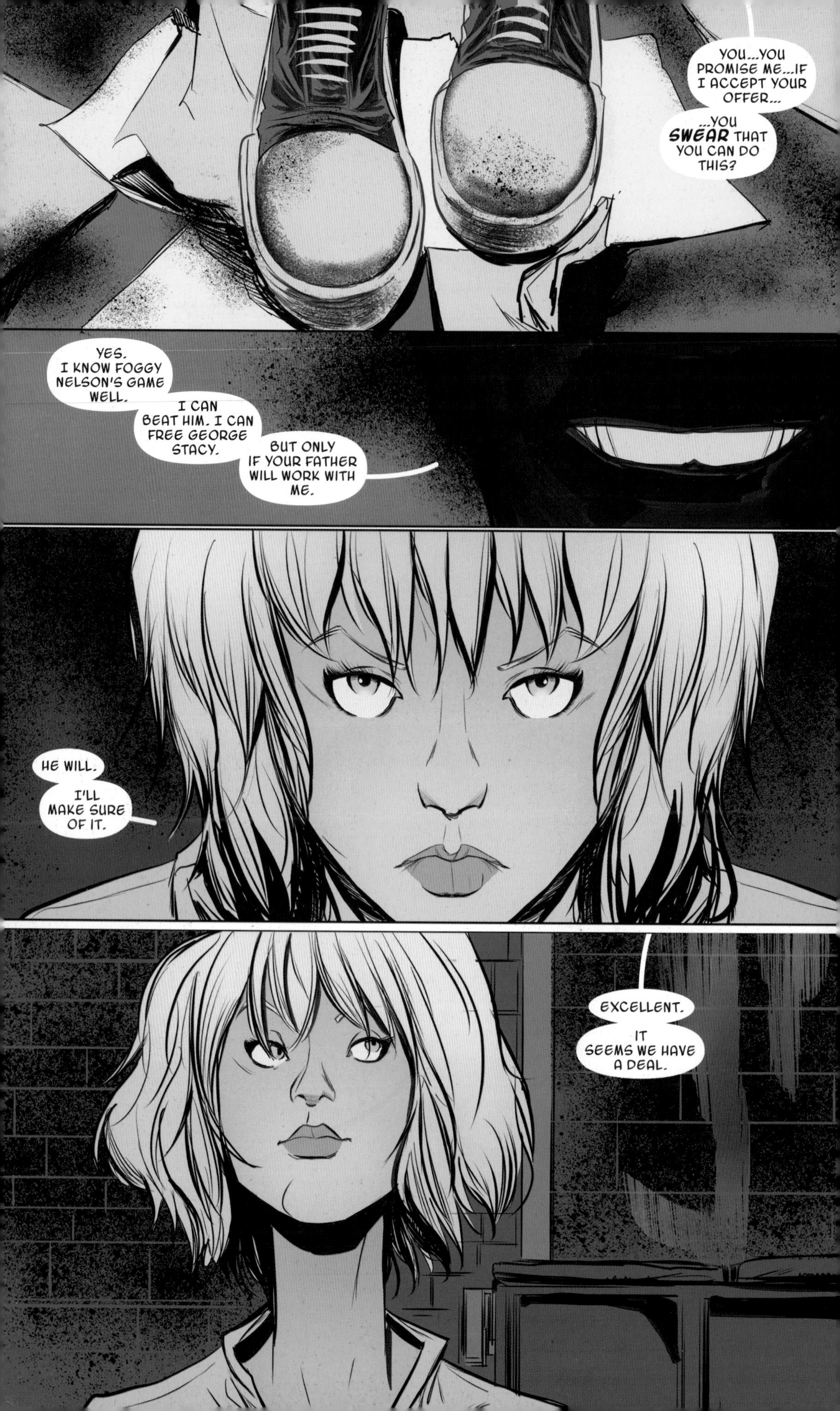
YOU...YOU PROMISE ME...IF I ACCEPT YOUR OFFER...
...YOU SWEAR THAT YOU CAN DO THIS?
YES. I KNOW FOGGY NELSON'S GAME WELL.
I CAN BEAT HIM. I CAN FREE GEORGE STACY.
BUT ONLY IF YOUR FATHER WILL WORK WITH ME.
HE WILL.
I'LL MAKE SURE OF IT.
EXCELLENT.
IT SEEMS WE HAVE A DEAL.

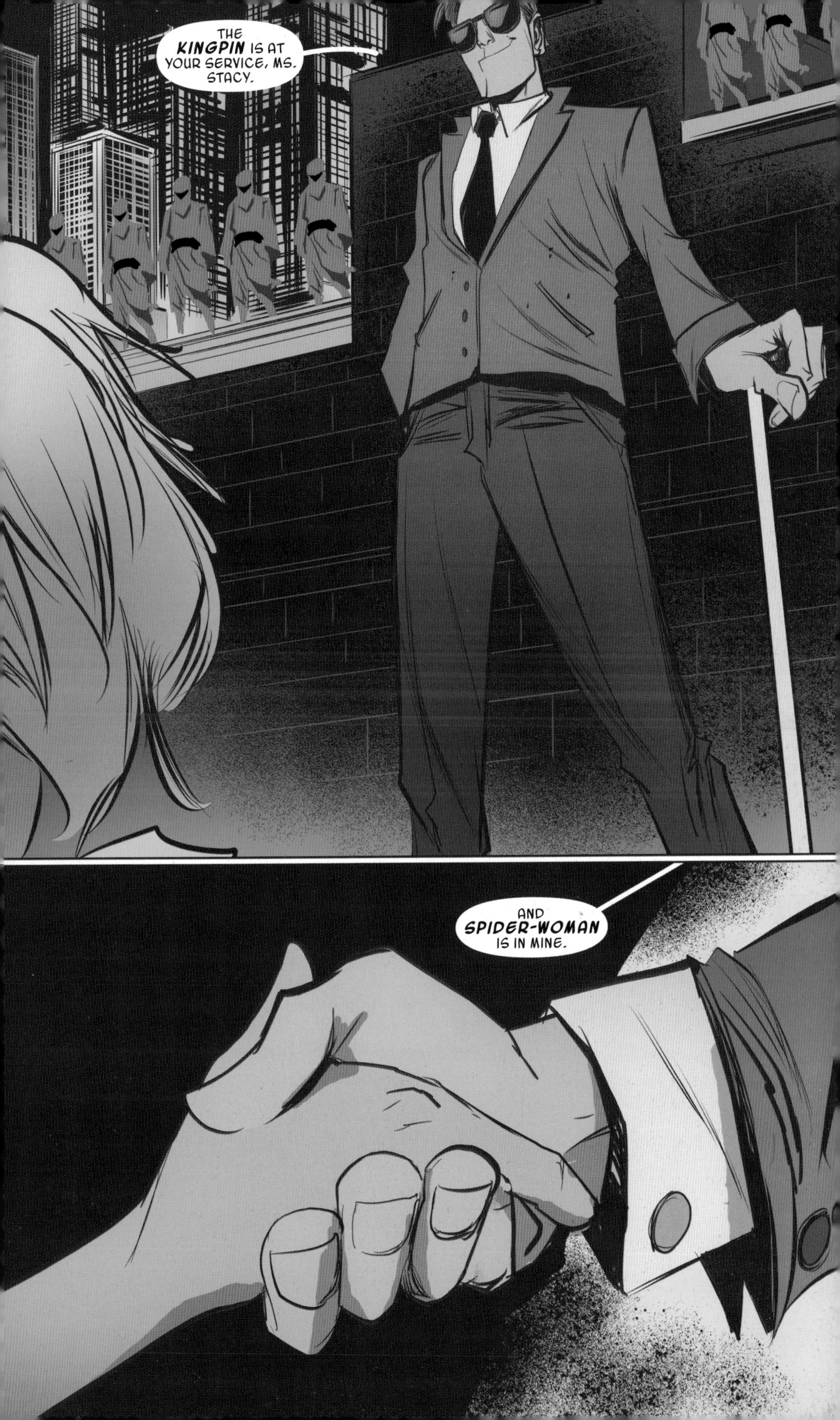
THE KINGPIN IS AT YOUR SERVICE, MS. STACY.
AND SPIDER-WOMAN IS IN MINE.

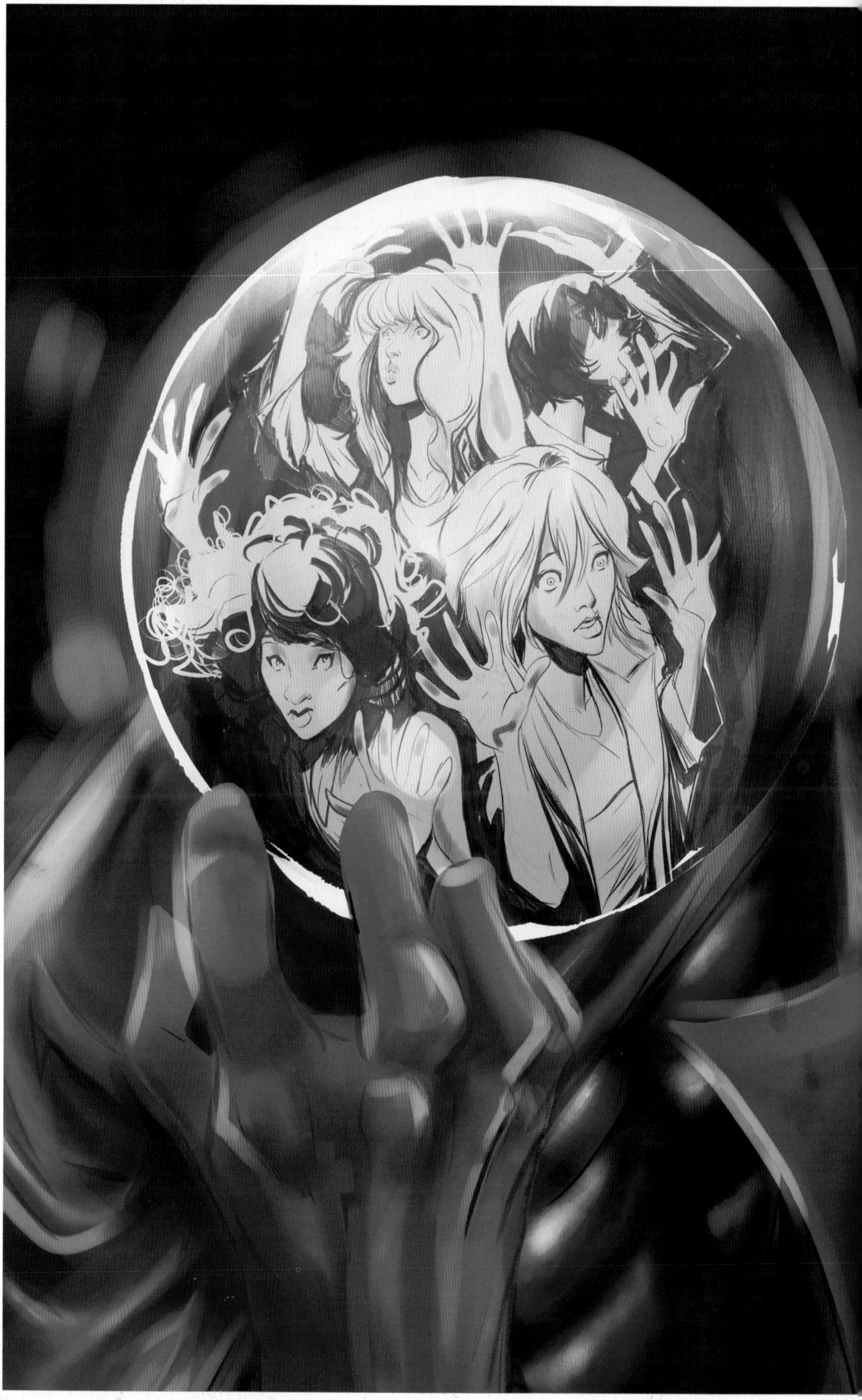

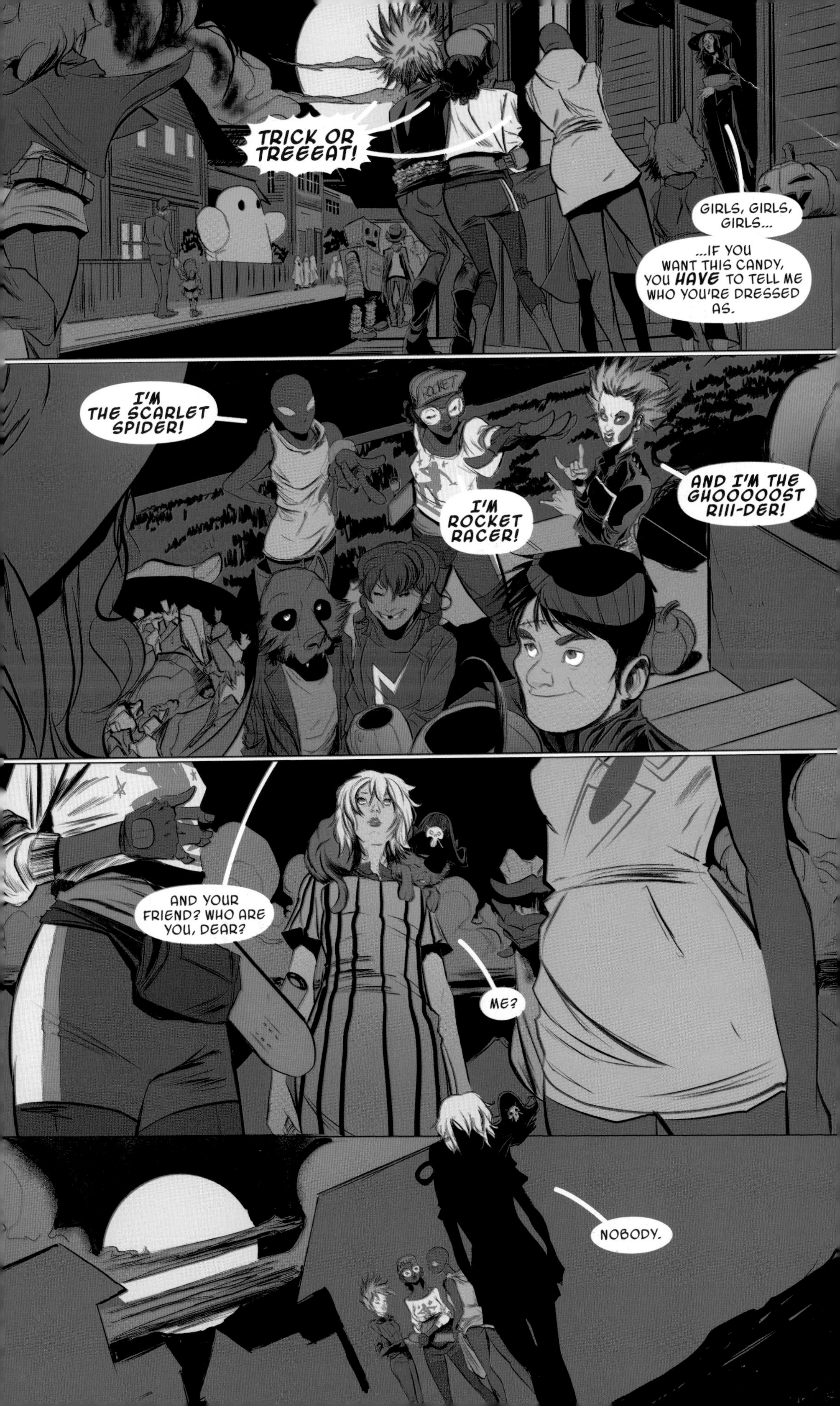
TRICK OR TREEEAT!
GIRLS, GIRLS, GIRLS...
...IF YOU WANT THIS CANDY, YOU HAVE TO TELL ME WHO YOU'RE DRESSED AS.
I'M THE SCARLET SPIDER!
I'M ROCKET RACER!
AND I'M THE GHOOOOOST RIII-DER!
AND YOUR FRIEND? WHO ARE YOU, DEAR?
ME?
NOBODY.

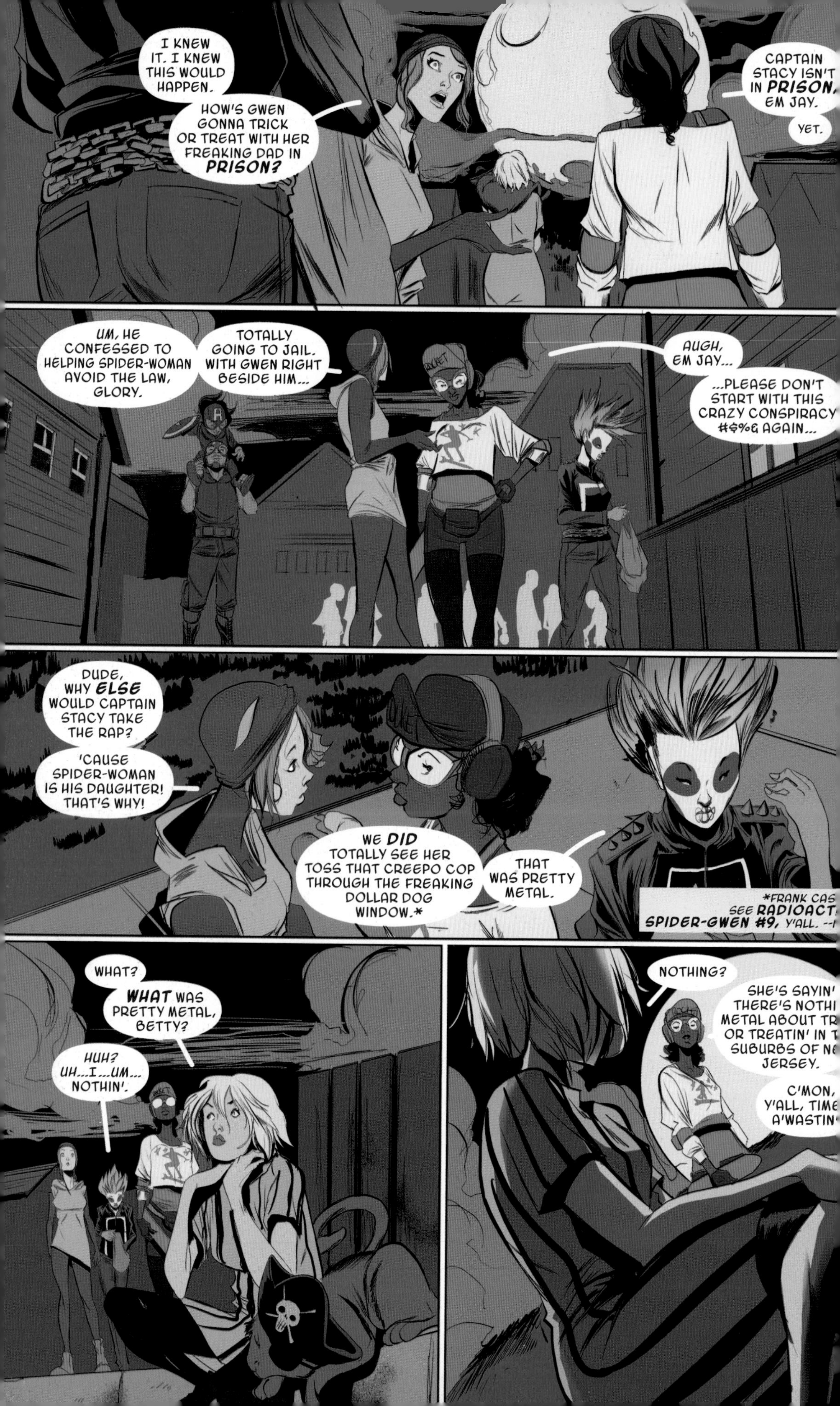
I KNEW IT. I KNEW THIS WOULD HAPPEN.
HOW'S GWEN GONNA TRICK OR TREAT WITH HER FREAKING DAD IN PRISON?
CAPTAIN STACY ISN'T IN PRISON, EM JAY.
YET.
UM, HE CONFESSED TO HELPING SPIDER-WOMAN AVOID THE LAW, GLORY.
TOTALLY GOING TO JAIL. WITH GWEN RIGHT BESIDE HIM...
AUGH, EM JAY...
...PLEASE DON'T START WITH THIS CRAZY CONSPIRACY #$%& AGAIN...
DUDE, WHY ELSE WOULD CAPTAIN STACY TAKE THE RAP?
'CAUSE SPIDER-WOMAN IS HIS DAUGHTER! THAT'S WHY!
WE DID TOTALLY SEE HER TOSS THAT CREEPO COP THROUGH THE FREAKING DOLLAR DOG WINDOW.*
THAT WAS PRETTY METAL.
*FRANK CAS
SEE RADIOACT
SPIDER-GWEN #9, Y'ALL. --
WHAT?
WHAT WAS PRETTY METAL, BETTY?
HUH? UH...I...UM... NOTHIN'.
NOTHING?
SHE'S SAYIN' THERE'S NOTHI METAL ABOUT TR OR TREATIN' IN T SUBURBS OF NE JERSEY.
C'MON, Y'ALL, TIME A'WASTIN'

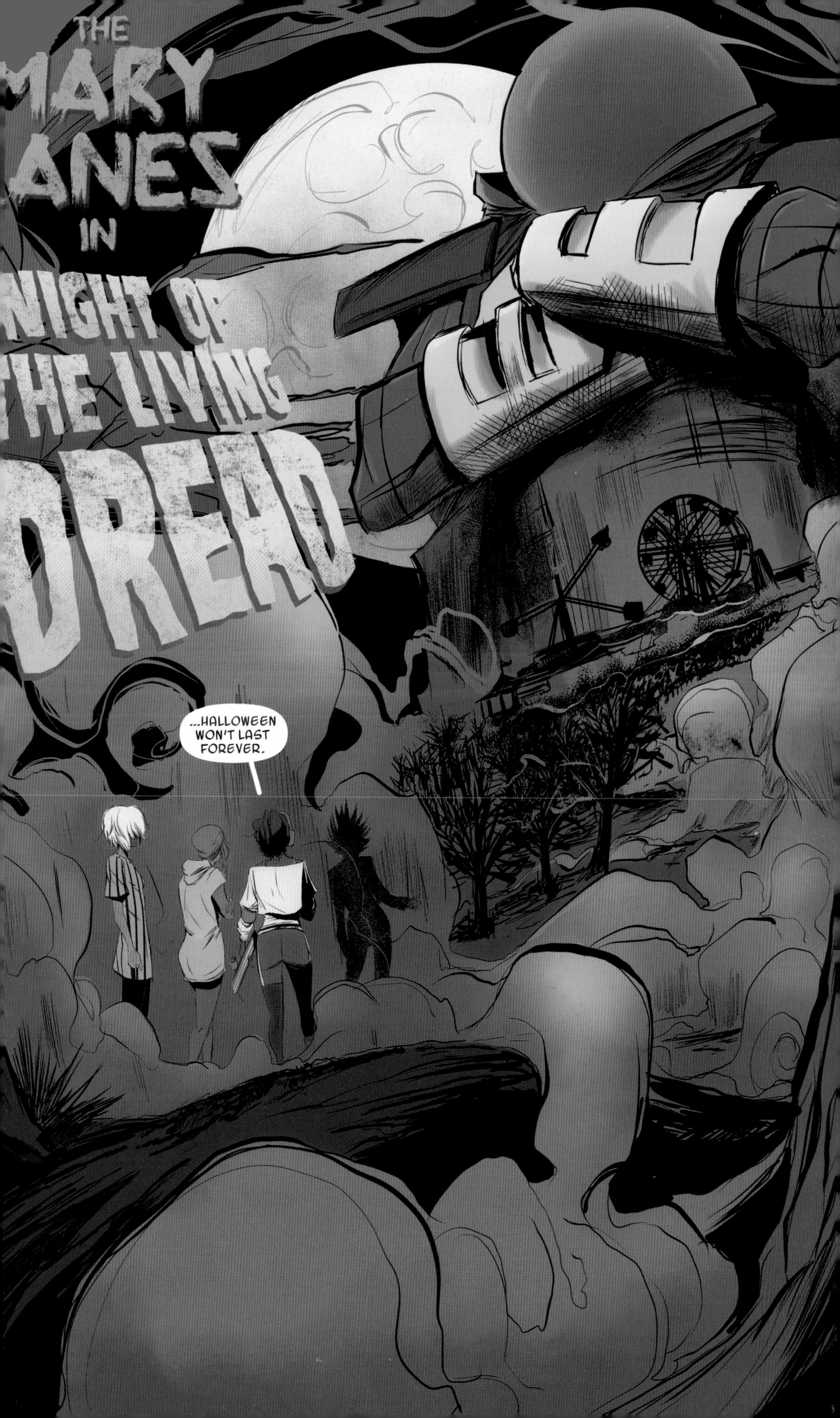
THE MARY JANES IN
NIGHT OF THE LIVING DREAD
...HALLOWEEN WON'T LAST FOREVER.

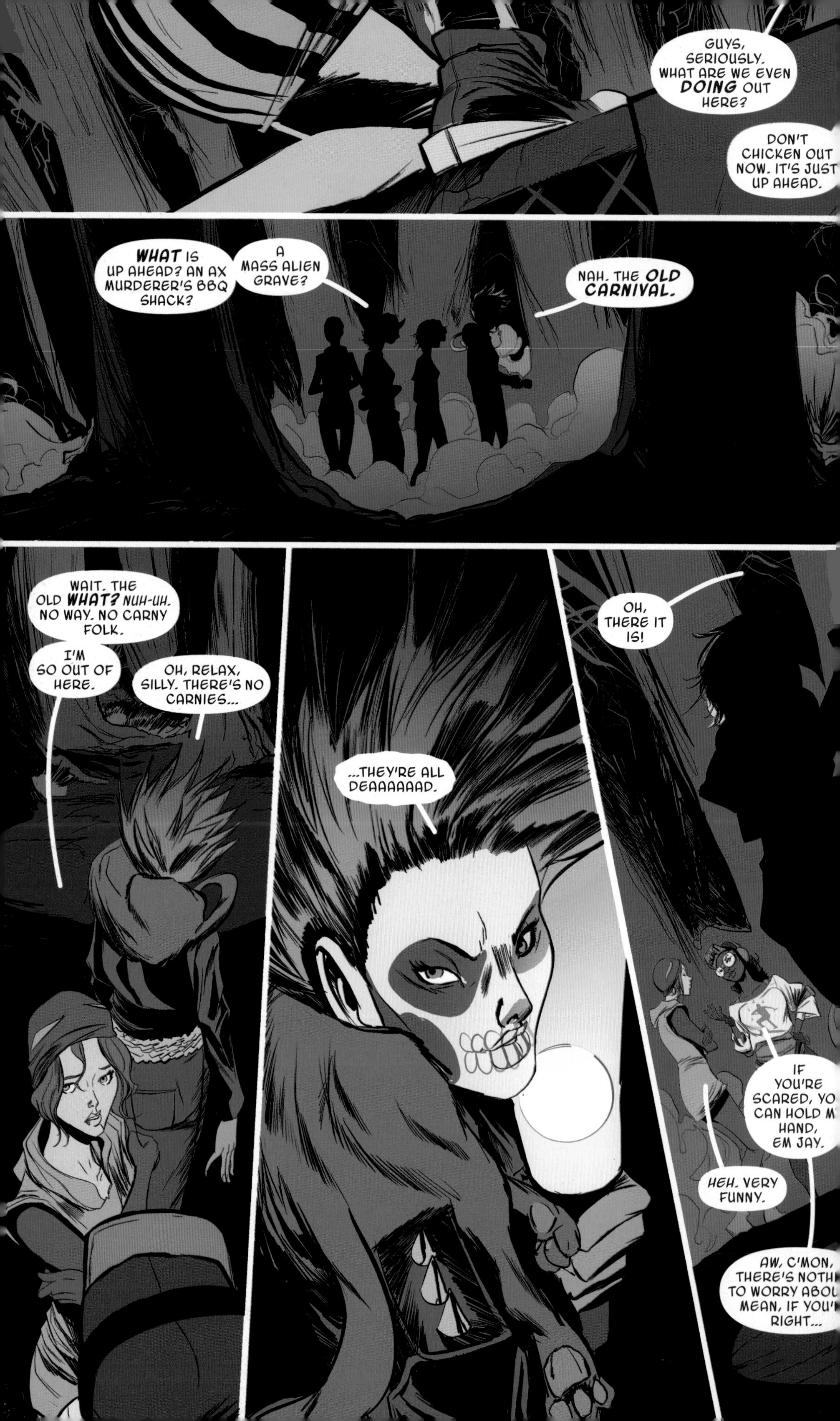
GUYS, SERIOUSLY. WHAT ARE WE EVEN DOING OUT HERE?
DON'T CHICKEN OUT NOW. IT'S JUST UP AHEAD.
WHAT IS UP AHEAD? AN AX MURDERER'S BBQ SHACK?
A MASS ALIEN GRAVE?
NAH. THE OLD CARNIVAL.
WAIT. THE OLD WHAT? NUH-UH. NO WAY. NO CARNY FOLK.
I'M SO OUT OF HERE.
OH, RELAX, SILLY. THERE'S NO CARNIES...
...THEY'RE ALL DEAAAAAAD.
OH, THERE IT IS!
HEH. VERY FUNNY.

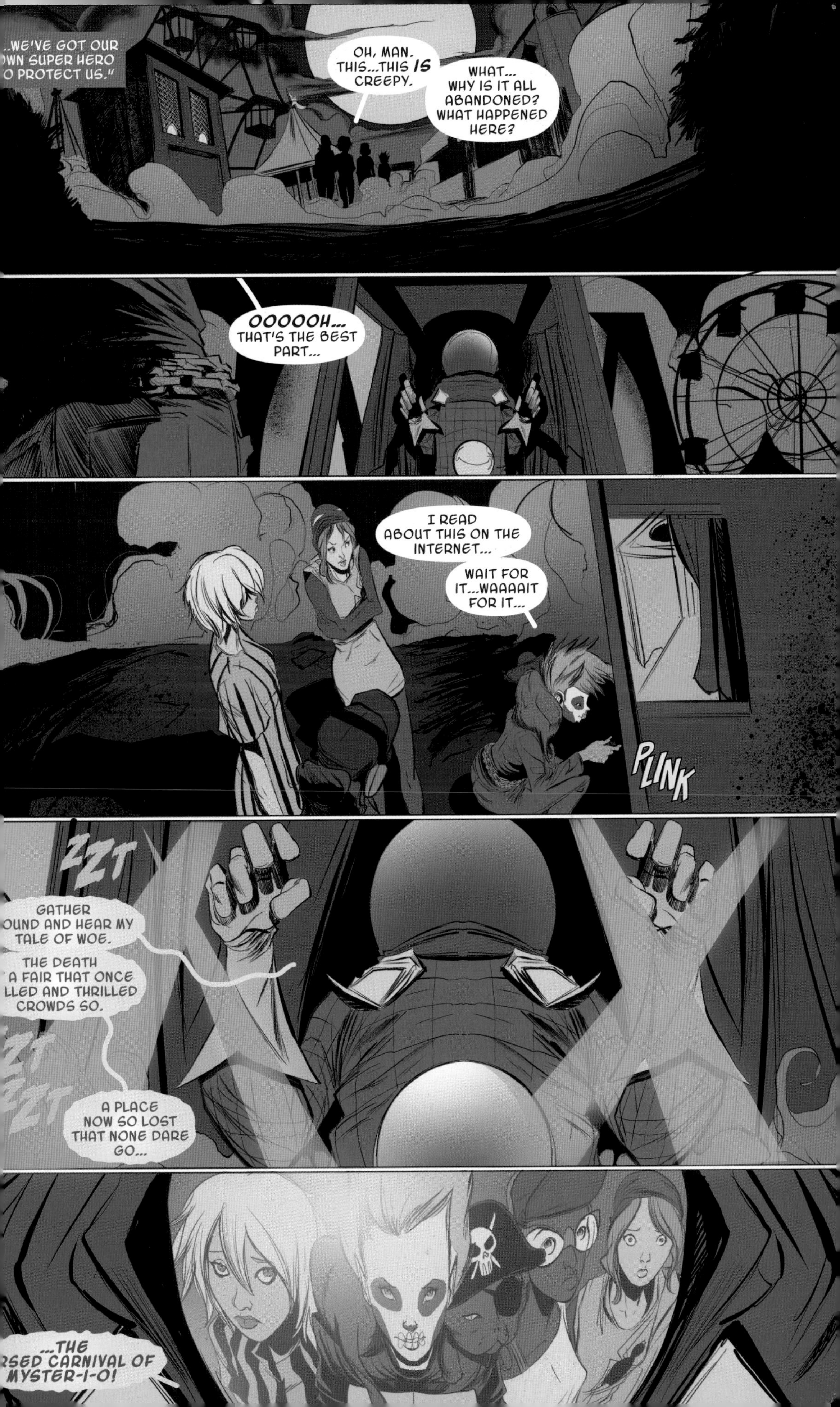

..WE'VE GOT OUR
OWN SUPER HERO
TO PROTECT US."
OH, MAN. THIS...THIS IS CREEPY.
WHAT... WHY IS IT ALL ABANDONED? WHAT HAPPENED HERE?
OOOOOH... THAT'S THE BEST PART...
I READ ABOUT THIS ON THE INTERNET...
WAIT FOR IT...WAAAAIT FOR IT...
PLINK
ZZT
GATHER
OUND AND HEAR MY TALE OF WOE.
THE DEATH
A FAIR THAT ONCE
LLED AND THRILLED CROWDS SO.
ZZT
ZZT
A PLACE NOW SO LOST THAT NONE DARE GO...
...THE
RSED CARNIVAL OF MYSTER-I-O!

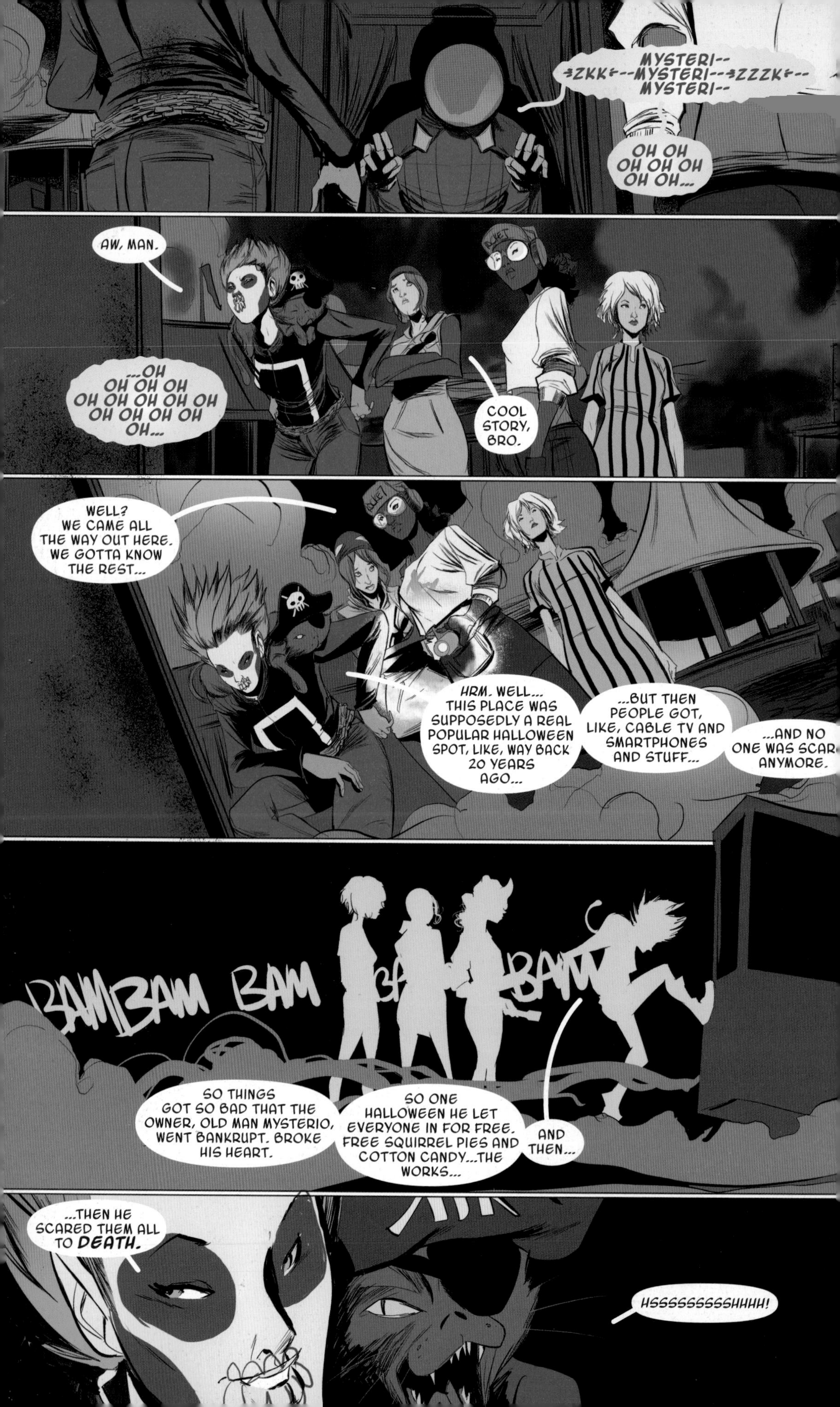

MYSTERI-- -ZKK- --MYSTERI-- -ZZZK- -- MYSTERI--
OH OH OH OH OH OH OH...
AW, MAN.
...OH OH OH OH OH OH OH OH OH OH OH OH OH OH...
COOL STORY, BRO.
WELL? WE CAME ALL THE WAY OUT HERE. WE GOTTA KNOW THE REST...
HRM. WELL... THIS PLACE WAS SUPPOSEDLY A REAL POPULAR HALLOWEEN SPOT, LIKE, WAY BACK 20 YEARS AGO...
...BUT THEN PEOPLE GOT, LIKE, CABLE TV AND SMARTPHONES AND STUFF...
...AND NO ONE WAS SCAR ANYMORE.
BAMBAM BAM BAM
SO THINGS GOT SO BAD THAT THE OWNER, OLD MAN MYSTERIO, WENT BANKRUPT. BROKE HIS HEART.
SO ONE HALLOWEEN HE LET EVERYONE IN FOR FREE. FREE SQUIRREL PIES AND COTTON CANDY... THE WORKS...
AND THEN...
...THEN HE SCARED THEM ALL TO DEATH.
HSSSSSSSSSHHHH!

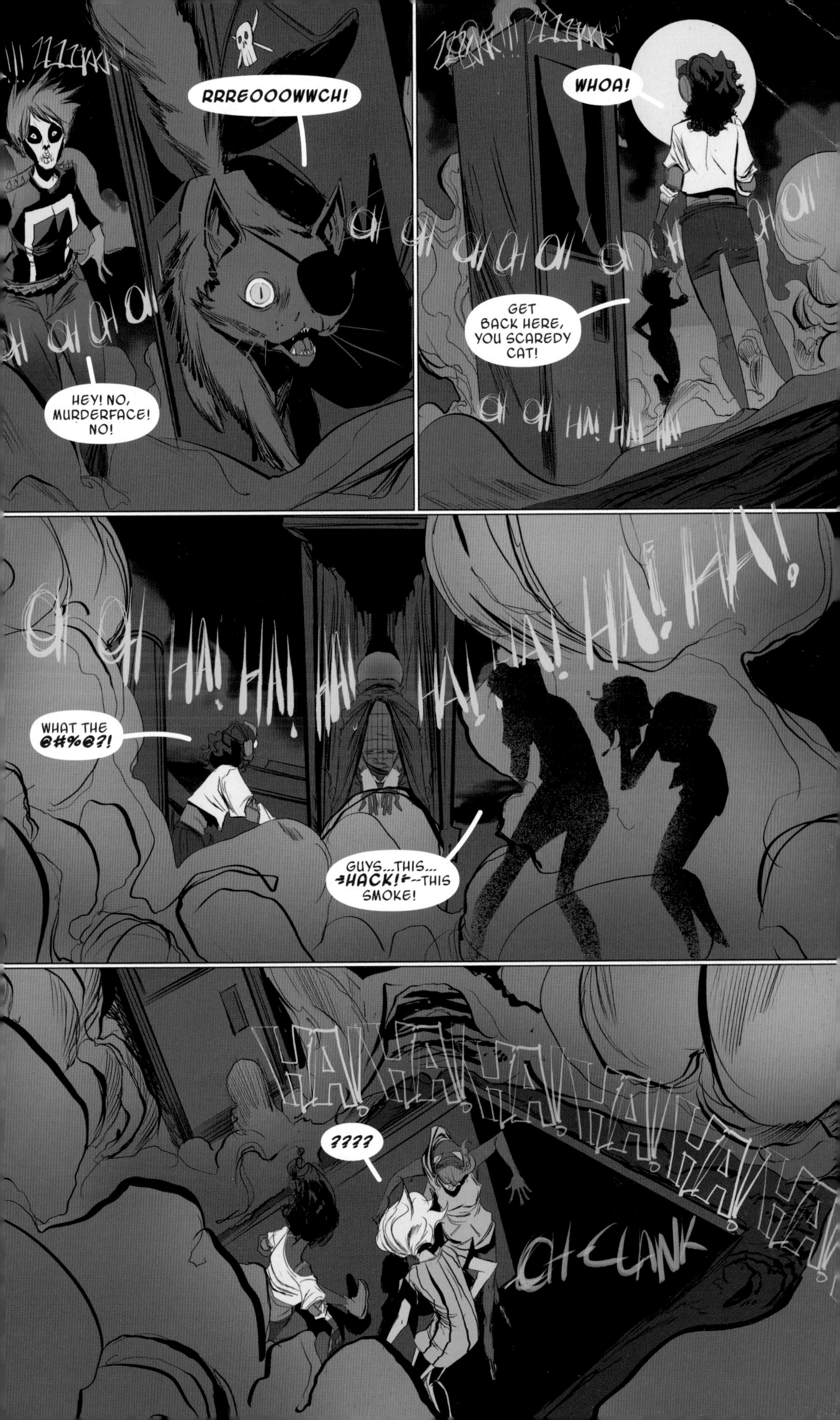
RRREOOOWWCH!
HEY! NO, MURDERFACE! NO!
WHOA!
GET BACK HERE, YOU SCAREDY CAT!
WHAT THE @#%@?!
GUYS...THIS... HACK!--THIS SMOKE!
????
CH CLANK

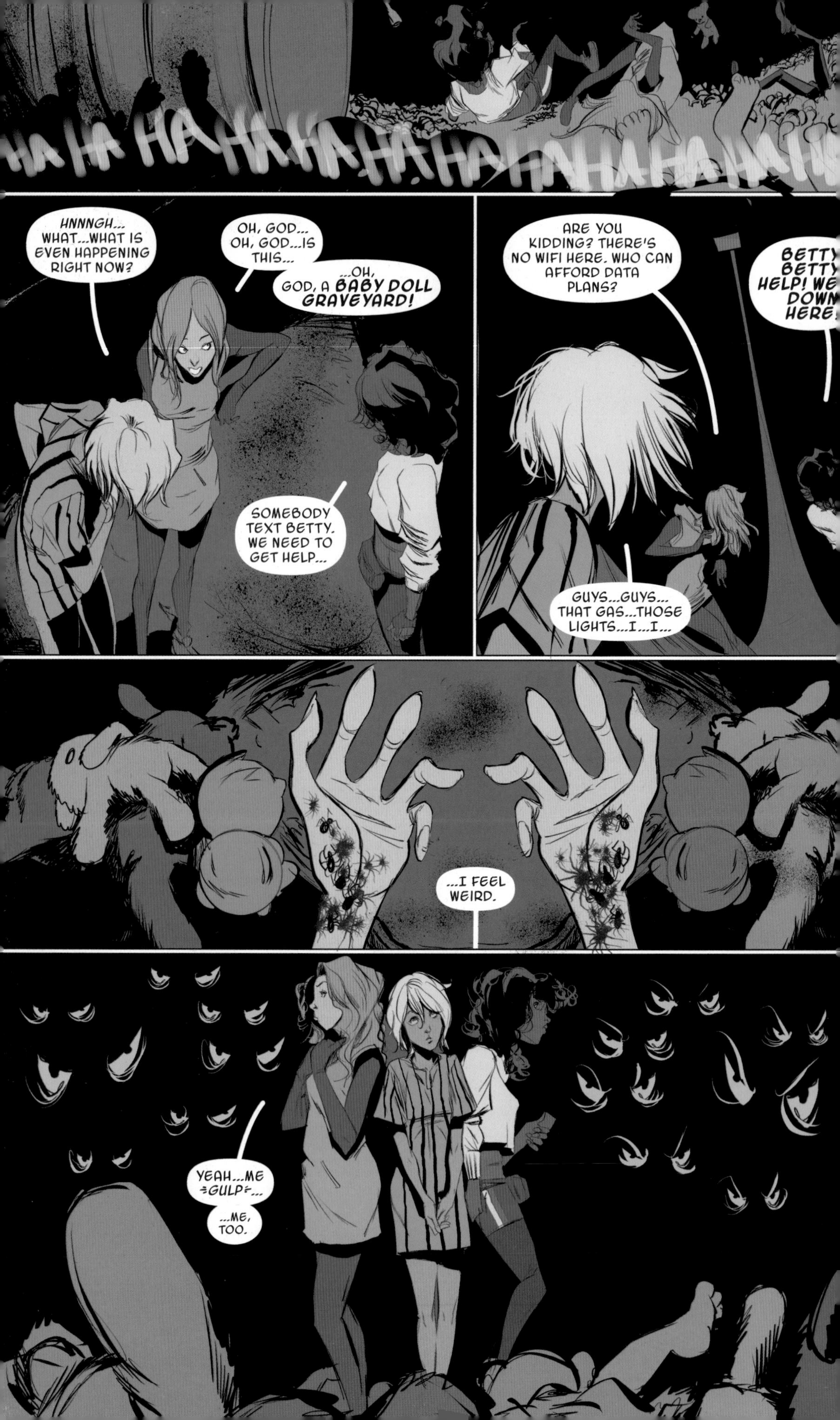
HA HA HA HA HA HA HA HA HA HA HA HA HA
HNNNGH... WHAT...WHAT IS EVEN HAPPENING RIGHT NOW?
OH, GOD... OH, GOD...IS THIS...
...OH, GOD, A BABY DOLL GRAVEYARD!
SOMEBODY TEXT BETTY. WE NEED TO GET HELP...
ARE YOU KIDDING? THERE'S NO WIFI HERE. WHO CAN AFFORD DATA PLANS?
BETTY BETTY HELP! WE DOWN HERE
GUYS...GUYS... THAT GAS...THOSE LIGHTS...I...I...
...I FEEL WEIRD.
YEAH...ME =GULP=...
...ME, TOO.

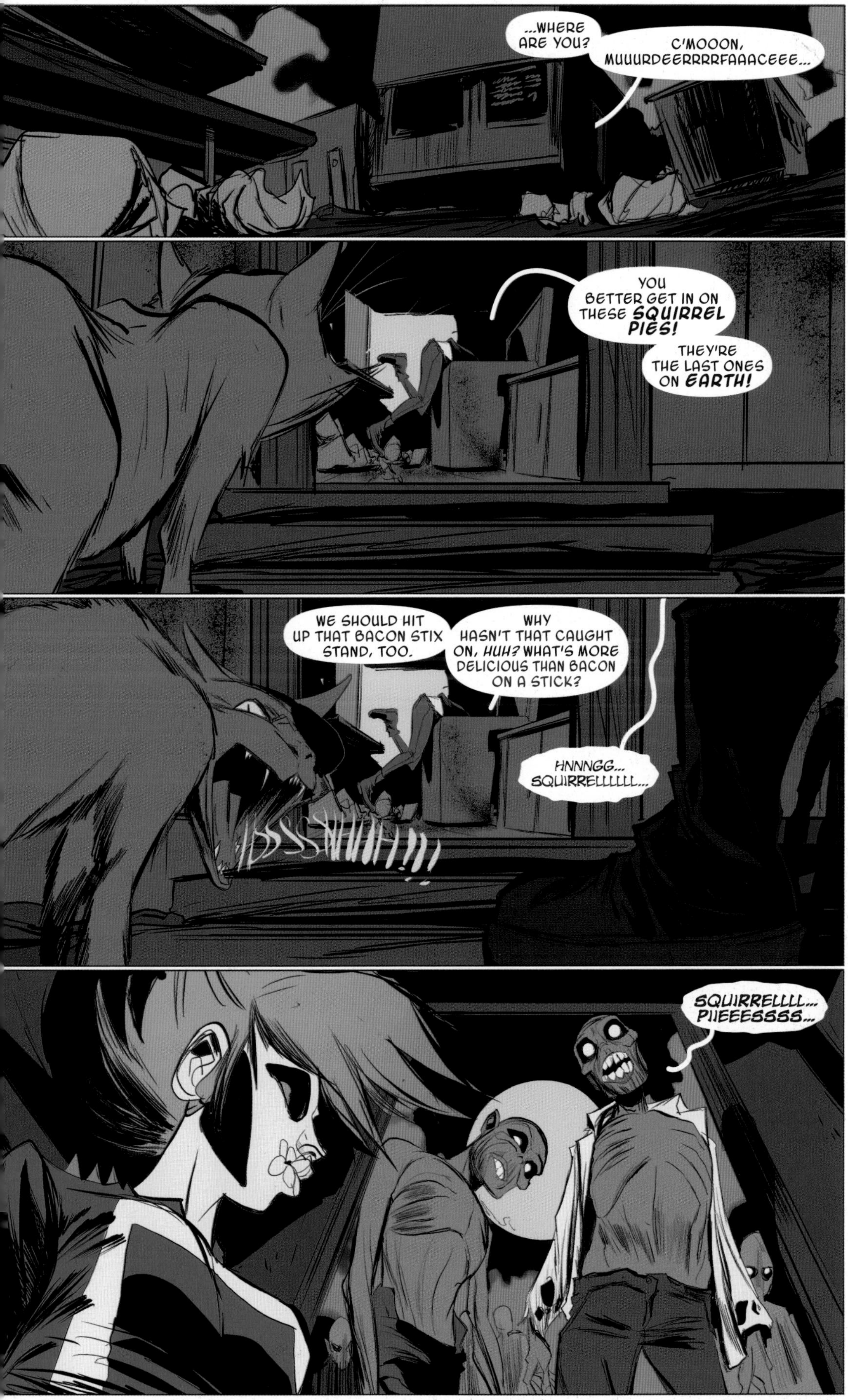
...WHERE ARE YOU?
C'MOOON, MUUURDEERRRRFAAACEEE...
YOU BETTER GET IN ON THESE SQUIRREL PIES!
THEY'RE THE LAST ONES ON EARTH!
WE SHOULD HIT UP THAT BACON STIX STAND, TOO.
WHY HASN'T THAT CAUGHT ON, HUH? WHAT'S MORE DELICIOUS THAN BACON ON A STICK?
HNNNGG... SQUIRRELLLLLL...
SQUIRRELLLL... PIIEEEESSSS...

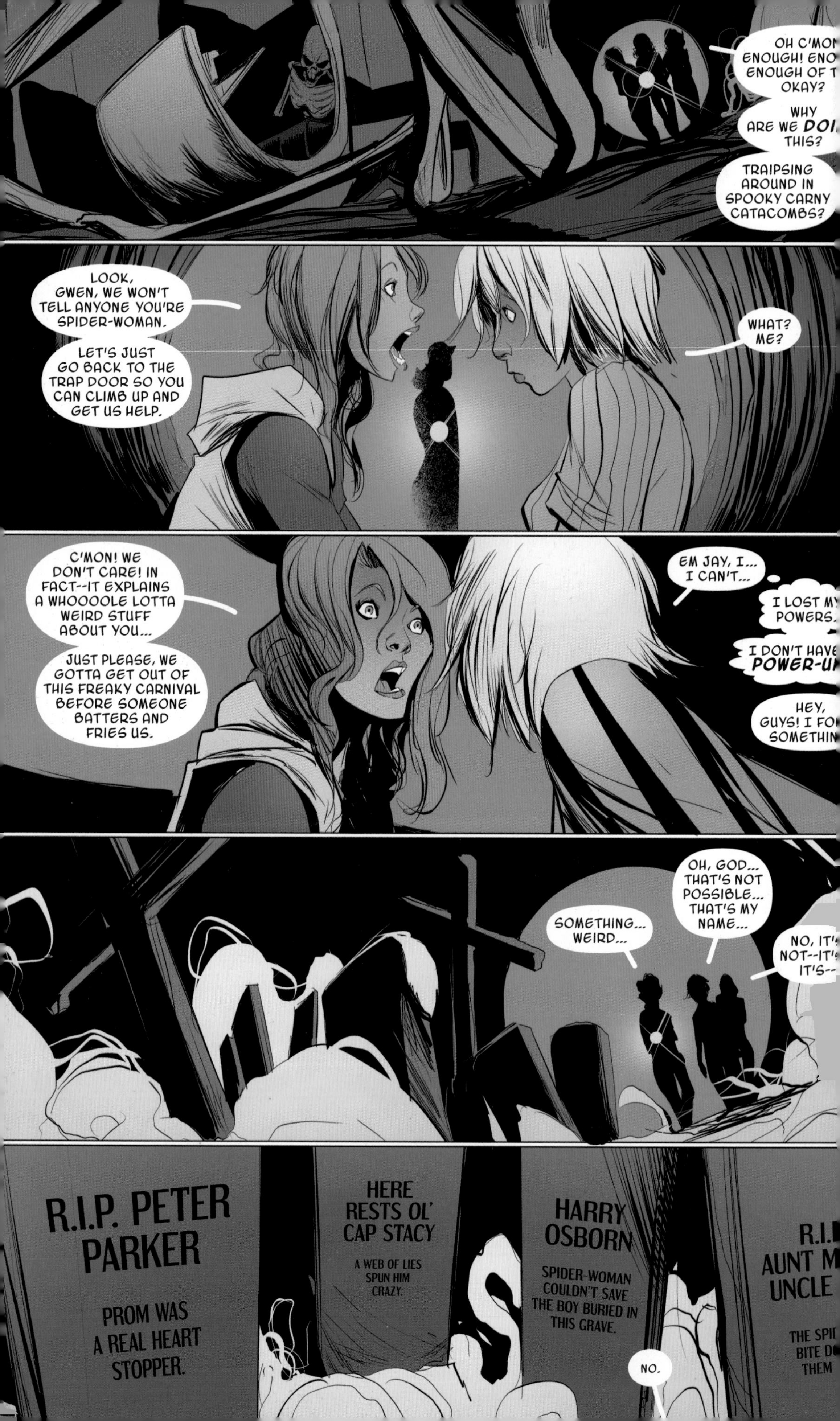
OH C'MON
OKAY?
WHY ARE WE
THIS?
TRAIPSING AROUND IN SPOOKY CARNY CATACOMBS?
LOOK, GWEN, WE WON'T TELL ANYONE YOU'RE SPIDER-WOMAN.
LET'S JUST GO BACK TO THE TRAP DOOR SO YOU CAN CLIMB UP AND GET US HELP.
WHAT? ME?
C'MON! WE DON'T CARE! IN FACT--IT EXPLAINS A WHOOOOLE LOTTA WEIRD STUFF ABOUT YOU...
JUST PLEASE, WE GOTTA GET OUT OF THIS FREAKY CARNIVAL BEFORE SOMEONE BATTERS AND FRIES US.
EM JAY, I... I CAN'T...
I LOST MY
I DON'T HAVE
HEY,
SOMETHING... WEIRD...
OH, GOD... THAT'S NOT POSSIBLE... THAT'S MY NAME...
R.I.P. PETER PARKER
PROM WAS A REAL HEART STOPPER.
HERE RESTS OL' CAP STACY
A WEB OF LIES SPUN HIM CRAZY.
HARRY OSBORN
SPIDER-WOMAN COULDN'T SAVE THE BOY BURIED IN THIS GRAVE.
NO.

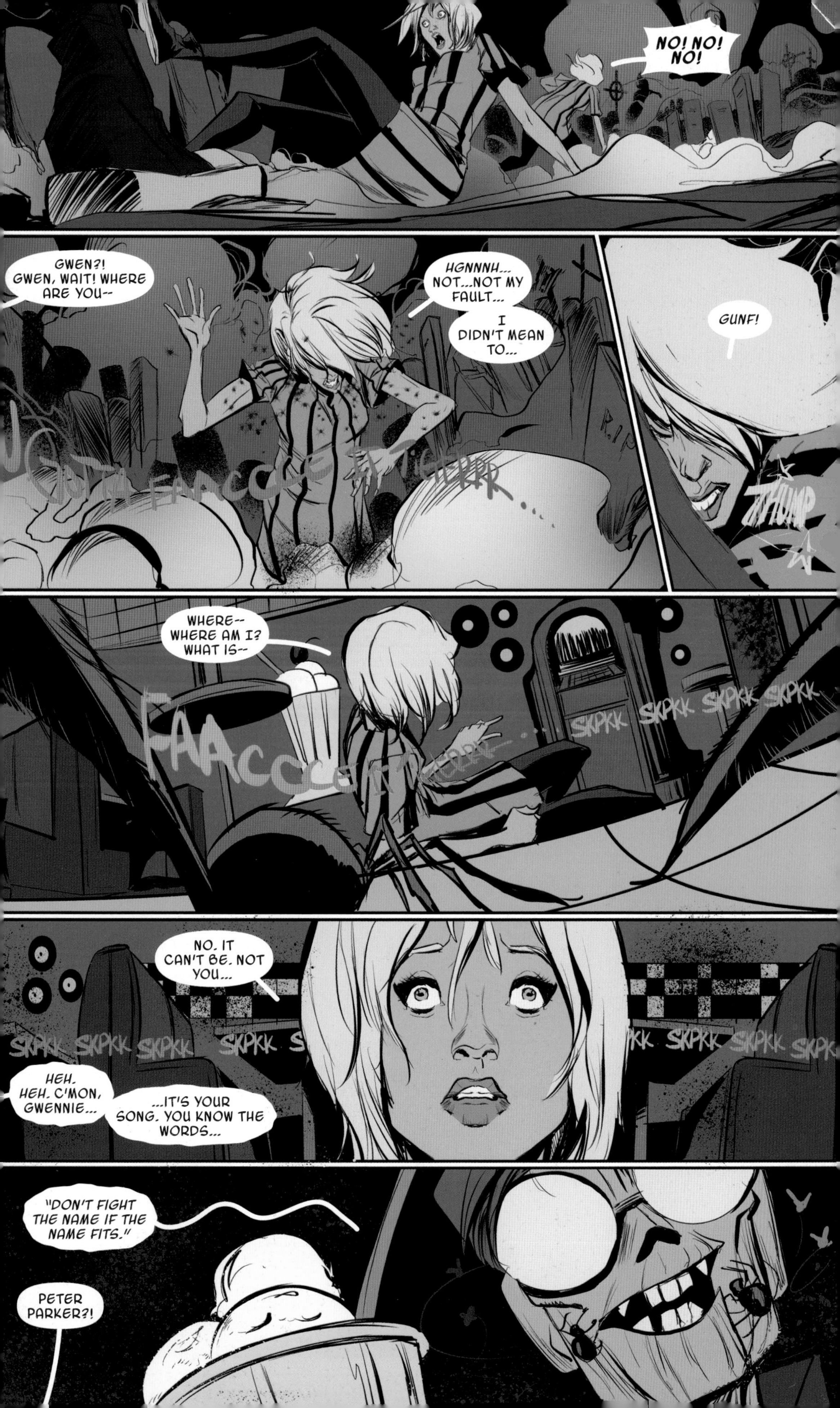
NO! NO! NO!
GWEN?! GWEN, WAIT! WHERE ARE YOU--
HGNNNH... NOT...NOT MY FAULT...
I DIDN'T MEAN TO...
GUNF!
THUMP
WHERE-- WHERE AM I? WHAT IS--
SKPKK SKPKK SKPKK SKPKK
NO. IT CAN'T BE. NOT YOU...
SKPKK SKPKK SKPKK SKPKK SKPKK SKPKK SKPKK
HEH. HEH. C'MON, GWENNIE...
...IT'S YOUR SONG. YOU KNOW THE WORDS...
"DON'T FIGHT THE NAME IF THE NAME FITS."
PETER PARKER?!

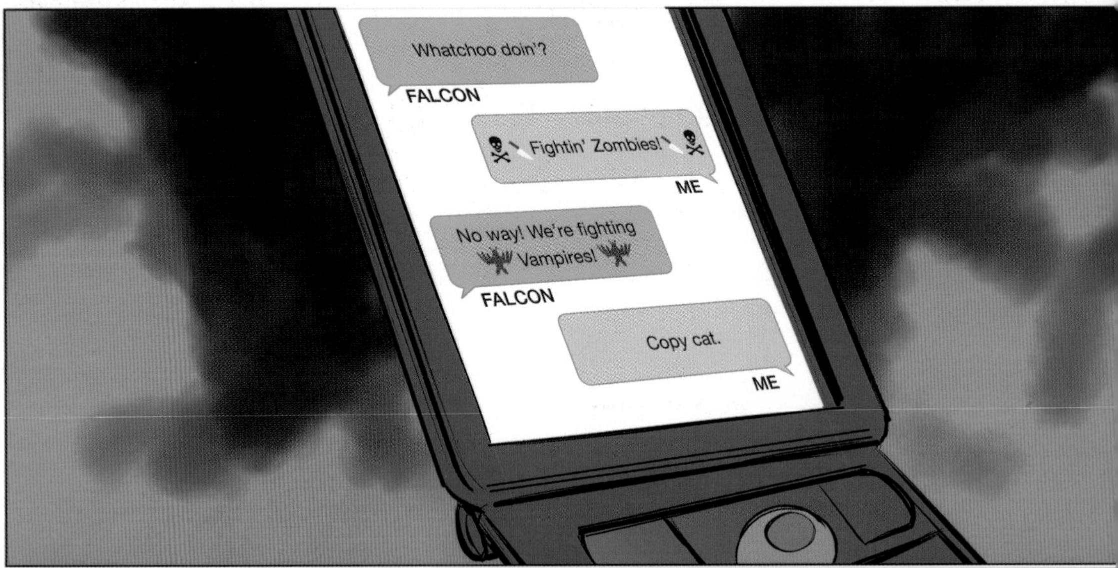
Whatchoo doin'?
FALCON
Fightin' Zombies!
ME
No way! We're fighting Vampires!
FALCON
Copy cat.
ME

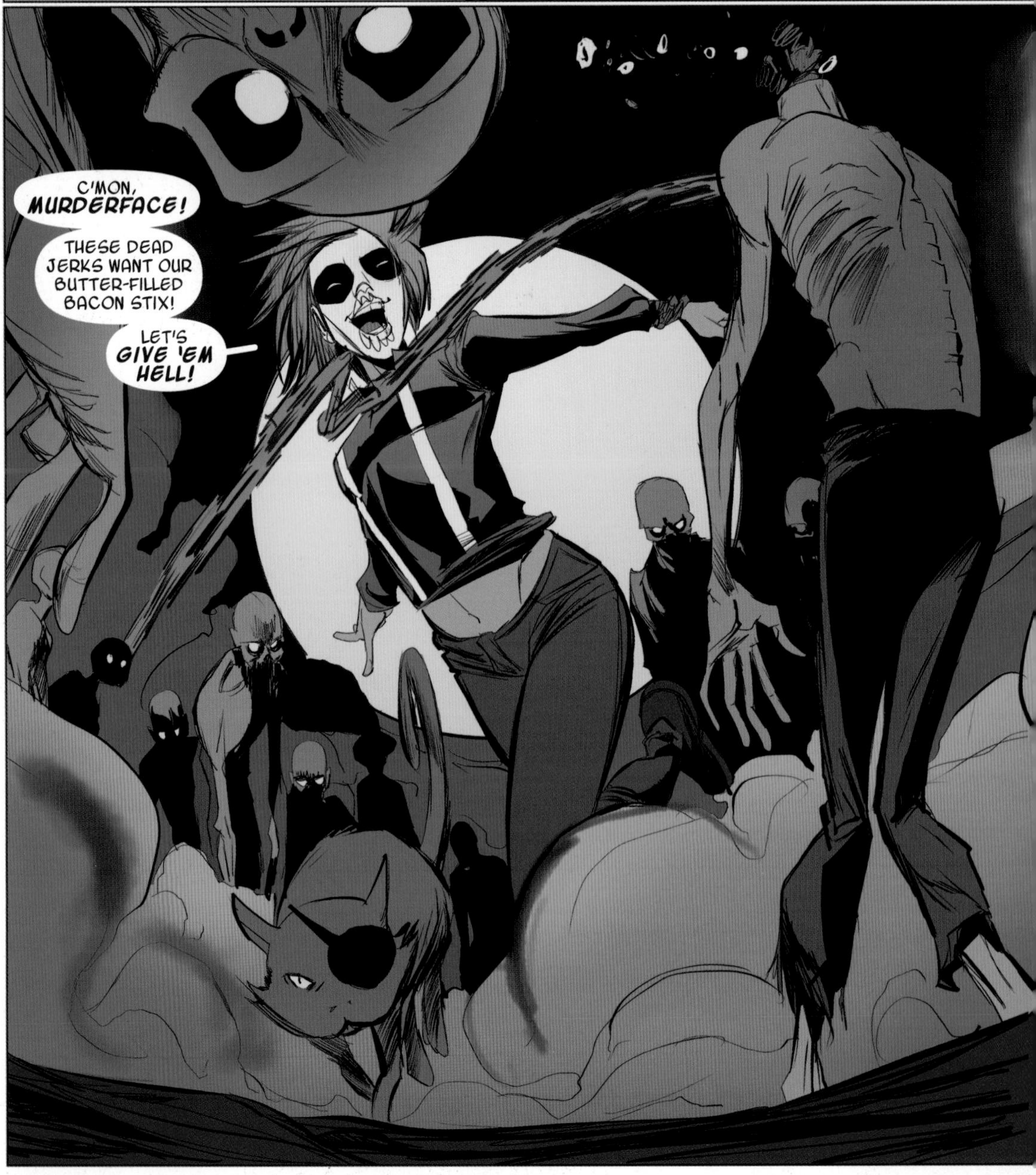
C'MON, MURDERFACE!
THESE DEAD JERKS WANT OUR BUTTER-FILLED BACON STIX!
LET'S GIVE 'EM HELL!

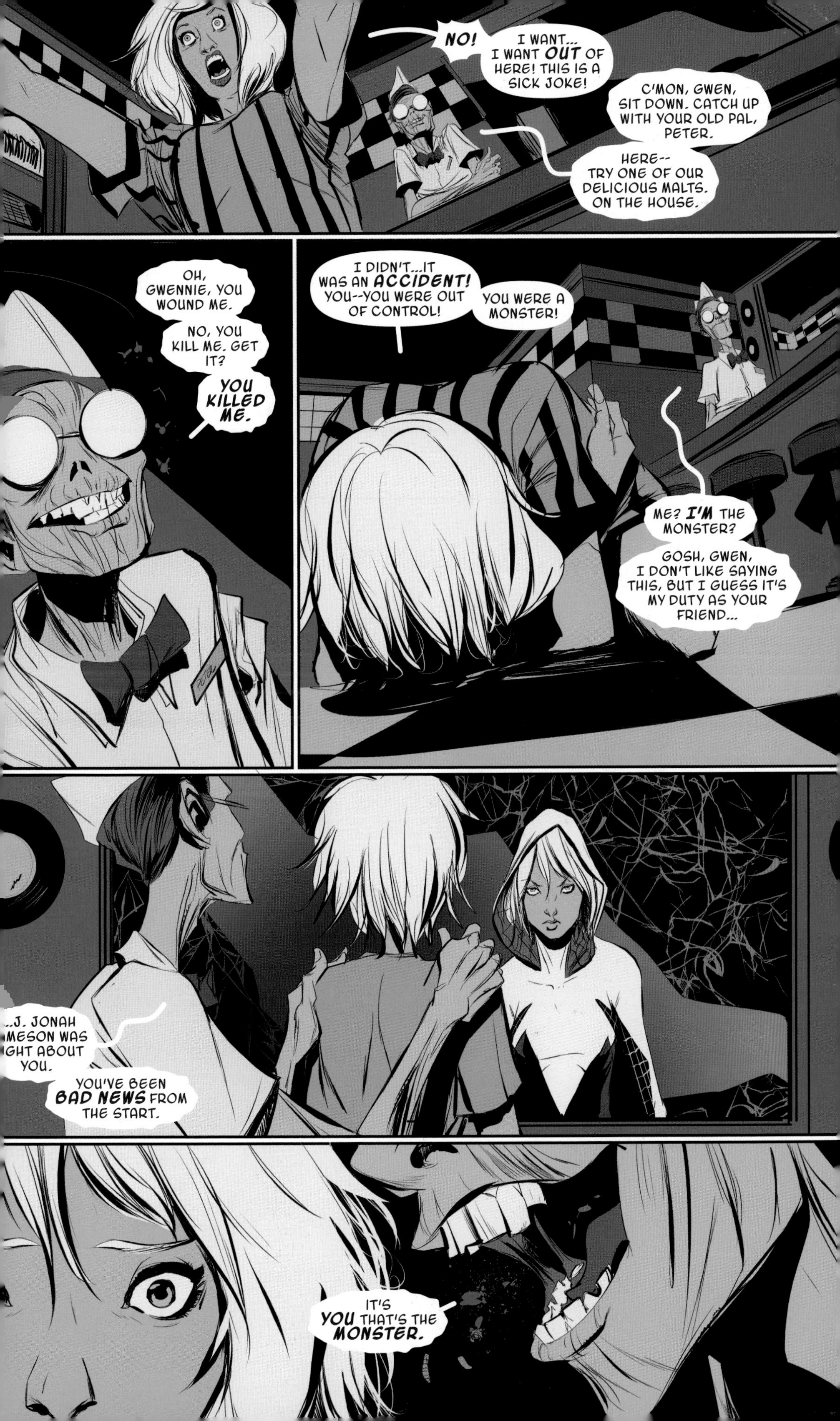
NO!
I WANT... I WANT OUT OF HERE! THIS IS A SICK JOKE!
C'MON, GWEN, SIT DOWN. CATCH UP WITH YOUR OLD PAL, PETER.
HERE-- TRY ONE OF OUR DELICIOUS MALTS. ON THE HOUSE.
OH, GWENNIE, YOU WOUND ME.
NO, YOU KILL ME. GET IT?
YOU KILLED ME.
I DIDN'T...IT WAS AN ACCIDENT! YOU--YOU WERE OUT OF CONTROL!
YOU WERE A MONSTER!
ME? I'M THE MONSTER?
GOSH, GWEN, I DON'T LIKE SAYING THIS, BUT I GUESS IT'S MY DUTY AS YOUR FRIEND...
YOU'VE BEEN BAD NEWS FROM THE START.
IT'S YOU THAT'S THE MONSTER.

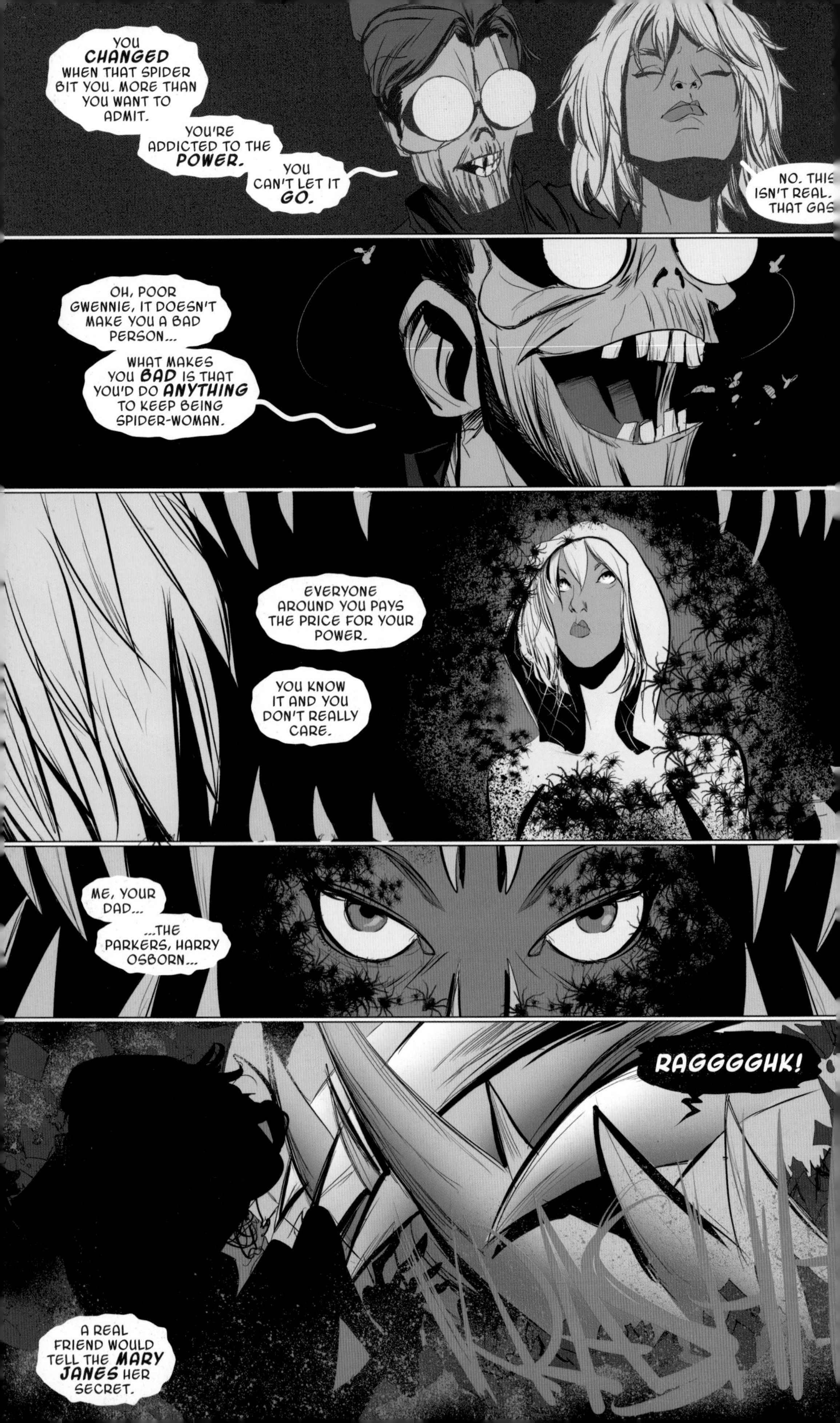
YOU CHANGED WHEN THAT SPIDER BIT YOU. MORE THAN YOU WANT TO ADMIT.
YOU'RE ADDICTED TO THE POWER.
YOU CAN'T LET IT GO.
NO. THIS ISN'T REAL. THAT GAS
OH, POOR GWENNIE, IT DOESN'T MAKE YOU A BAD PERSON...
WHAT MAKES YOU BAD IS THAT YOU'D DO ANYTHING TO KEEP BEING SPIDER-WOMAN.
EVERYONE AROUND YOU PAYS THE PRICE FOR YOUR POWER.
YOU KNOW IT AND YOU DON'T REALLY CARE.
ME, YOUR DAD...
...THE PARKERS, HARRY OSBORN...
RAGGGGHK!
A REAL FRIEND WOULD TELL THE MARY JANES HER SECRET.

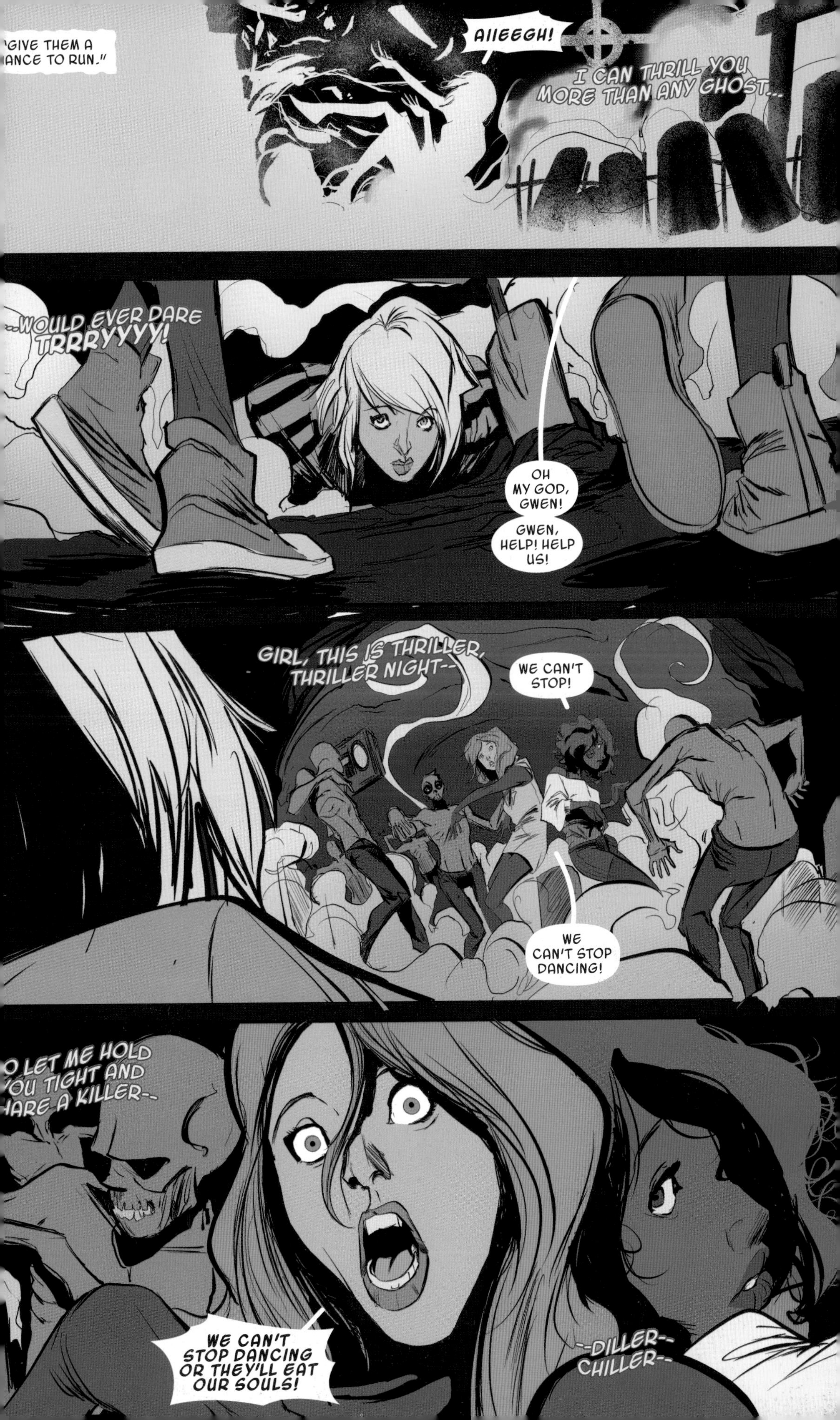
"GIVE THEM A
ANCE TO RUN."
AIIEEGH!
I CAN THRILL YOU MORE THAN ANY GHOST...
...WOULD EVER DARE TRRRYYYY!
OH MY GOD, GWEN!
GWEN, HELP! HELP US!
GIRL, THIS IS THRILLER, THRILLER NIGHT--
WE CAN'T STOP!
WE CAN'T STOP DANCING!
O LET ME HOLD YOU TIGHT AND HARE A KILLER--
WE CAN'T STOP DANCING OR THEY'LL EAT OUR SOULS!
--DILLER-- CHILLER--

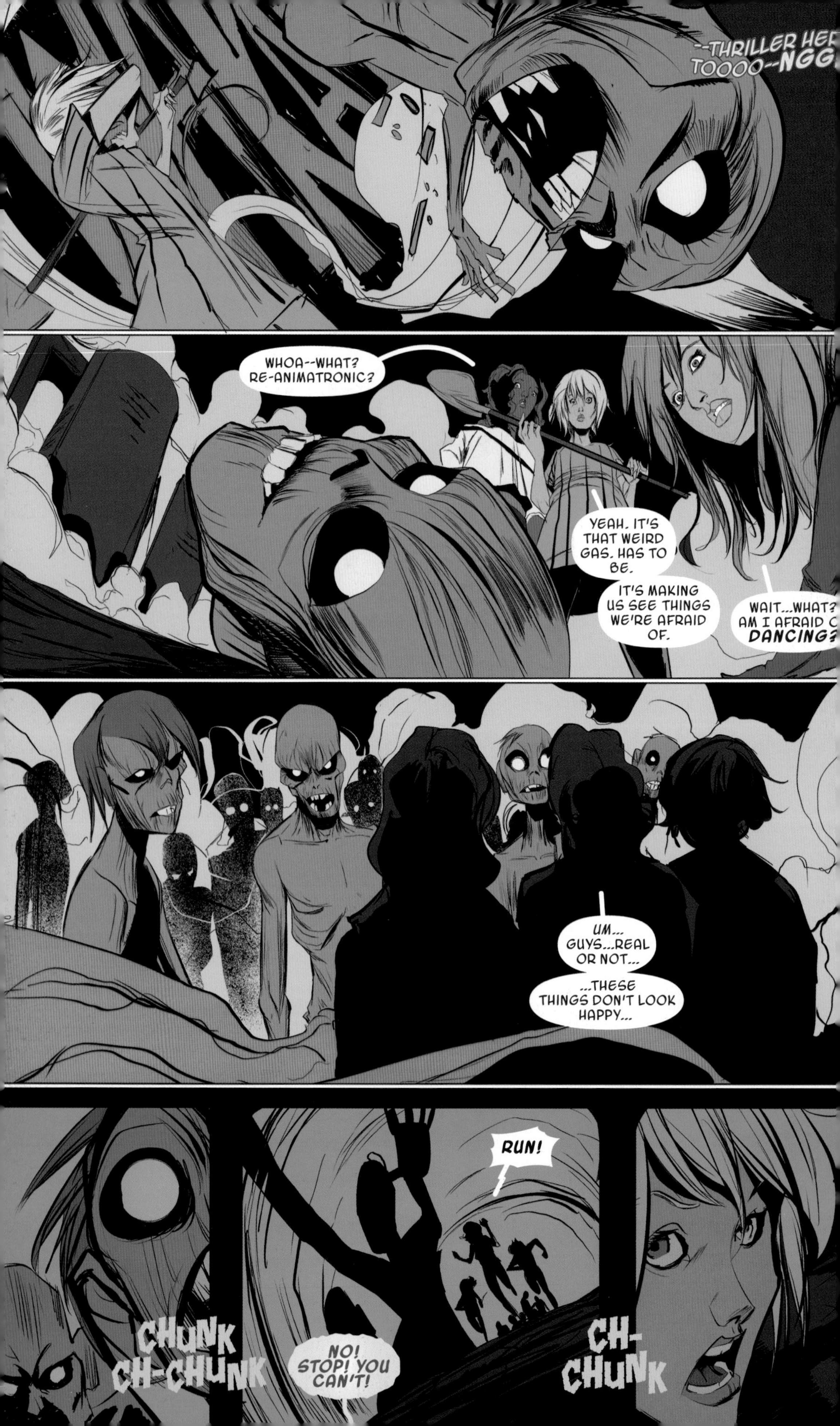
--THRILLER HER
TOOOO--NGG
WHOA--WHAT? RE-ANIMATRONIC?
YEAH. IT'S THAT WEIRD GAS. HAS TO BE.
IT'S MAKING US SEE THINGS WE'RE AFRAID OF.
WAIT...WHAT? AM I AFRAID O
DANCING?
UM... GUYS...REAL OR NOT...
...THESE THINGS DON'T LOOK HAPPY...
RUN!
CHUNK CH-CHUNK
NO! STOP! YOU CAN'T!
CH-CHUNK

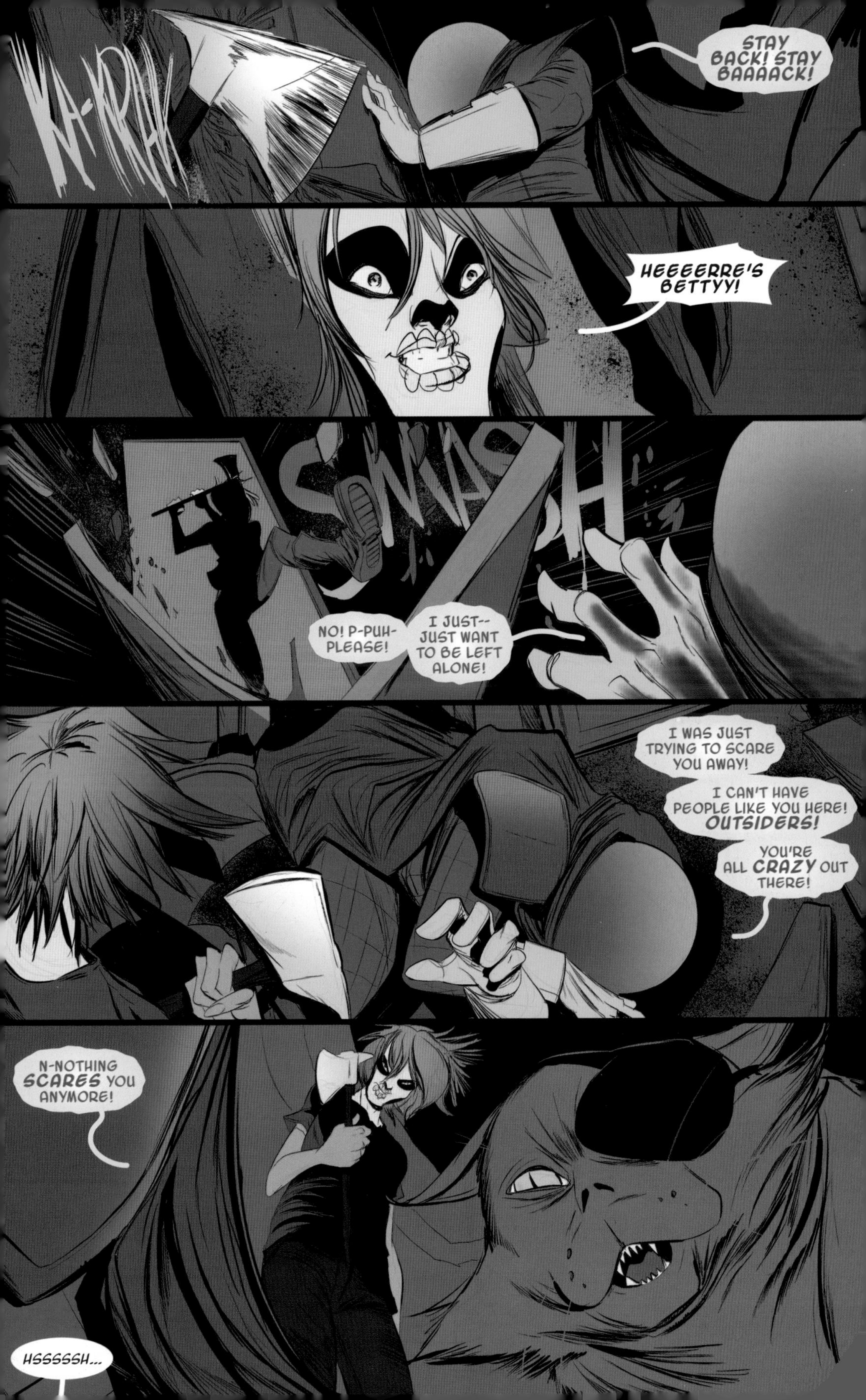
KA-KRAK
STAY BACK! STAY BAAAACK!
HEEEERRE'S BETTYY!
SMASH
NO! P-PUH-PLEASE!
I JUST--JUST WANT TO BE LEFT ALONE!
I WAS JUST TRYING TO SCARE YOU AWAY!
I CAN'T HAVE PEOPLE LIKE YOU HERE! OUTSIDERS!
YOU'RE ALL CRAZY OUT THERE!
N-NOTHING SCARES YOU ANYMORE!
HSSSSSH...

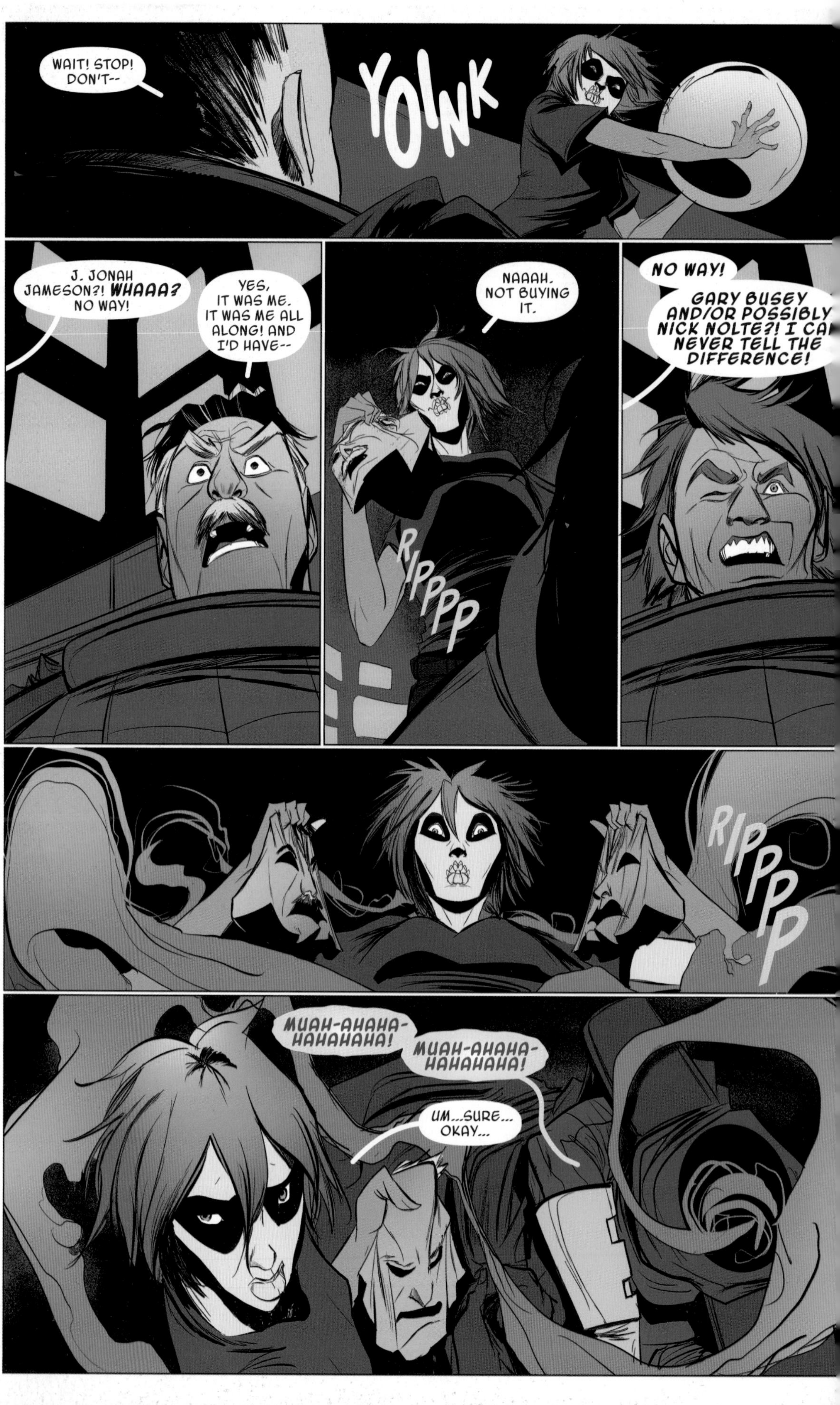
WAIT! STOP! DON'T--
YOINK
J. JONAH JAMESON?! WHAAA? NO WAY!
YES, IT WAS ME. IT WAS ME ALL ALONG! AND I'D HAVE--
NAAAH. NOT BUYING IT.
RIPPPP
NO WAY!
GARY BUSEY AND/OR POSSIBLY NICK NOLTE?! I CA
NEVER TELL THE DIFFERENCE!
RIPPPP
MUAH-AHAHA-HAHAHAHA!
MUAH-AHAHA-HAHAHAHA!
UM...SURE... OKAY...

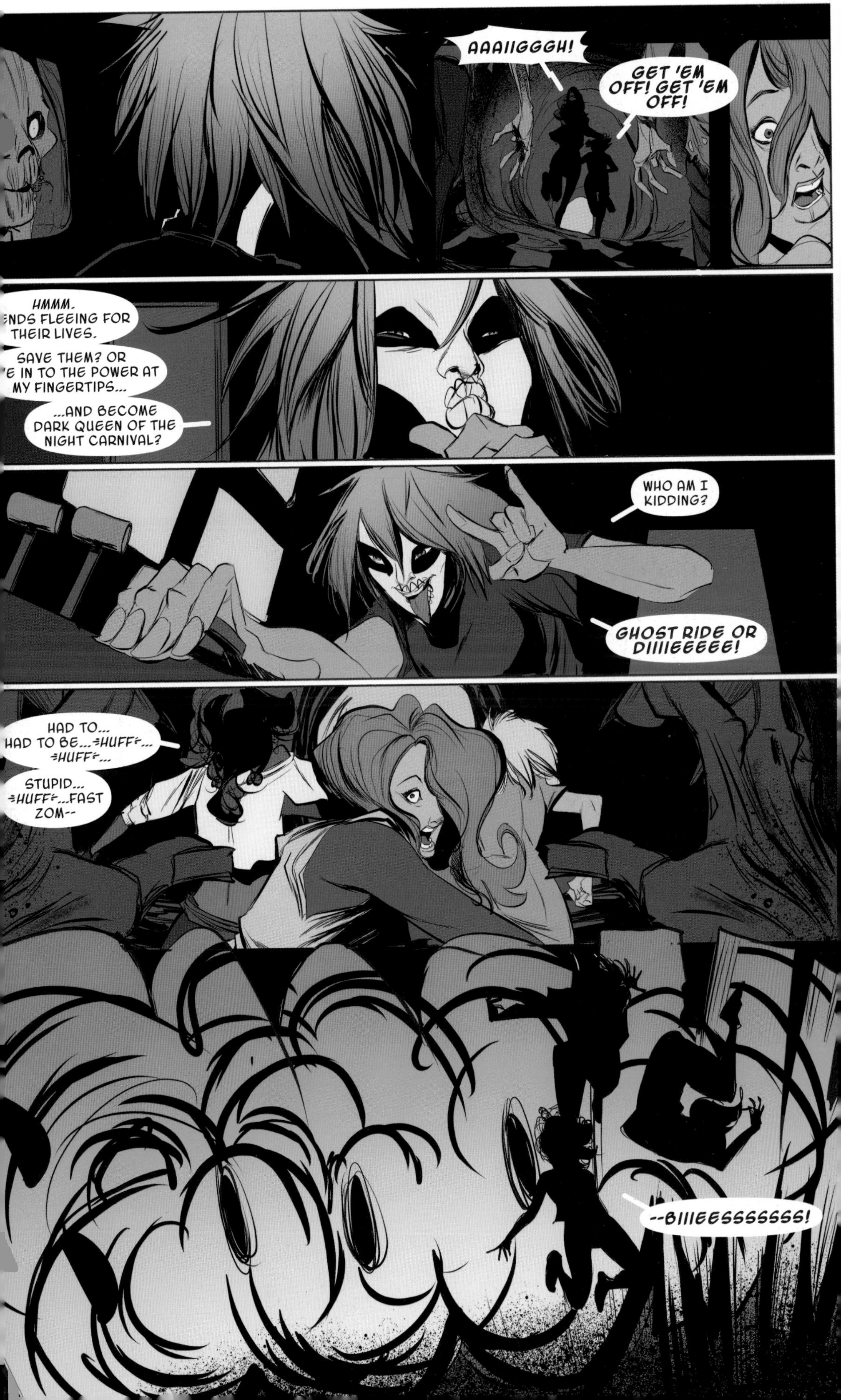
AAAIIGGGH!
GET 'EM OFF! GET 'EM OFF!
HMMM. NDS FLEEING FOR THEIR LIVES.
SAVE THEM? OR E IN TO THE POWER AT MY FINGERTIPS...
...AND BECOME DARK QUEEN OF THE NIGHT CARNIVAL?
WHO AM I KIDDING?
GHOST RIDE OR DIIIIEEEEEE!
HAD TO... HAD TO BE... =HUFF=... =HUFF=...
STUPID... =HUFF=...FAST ZOM--
--BIIIEESSSSSSS!

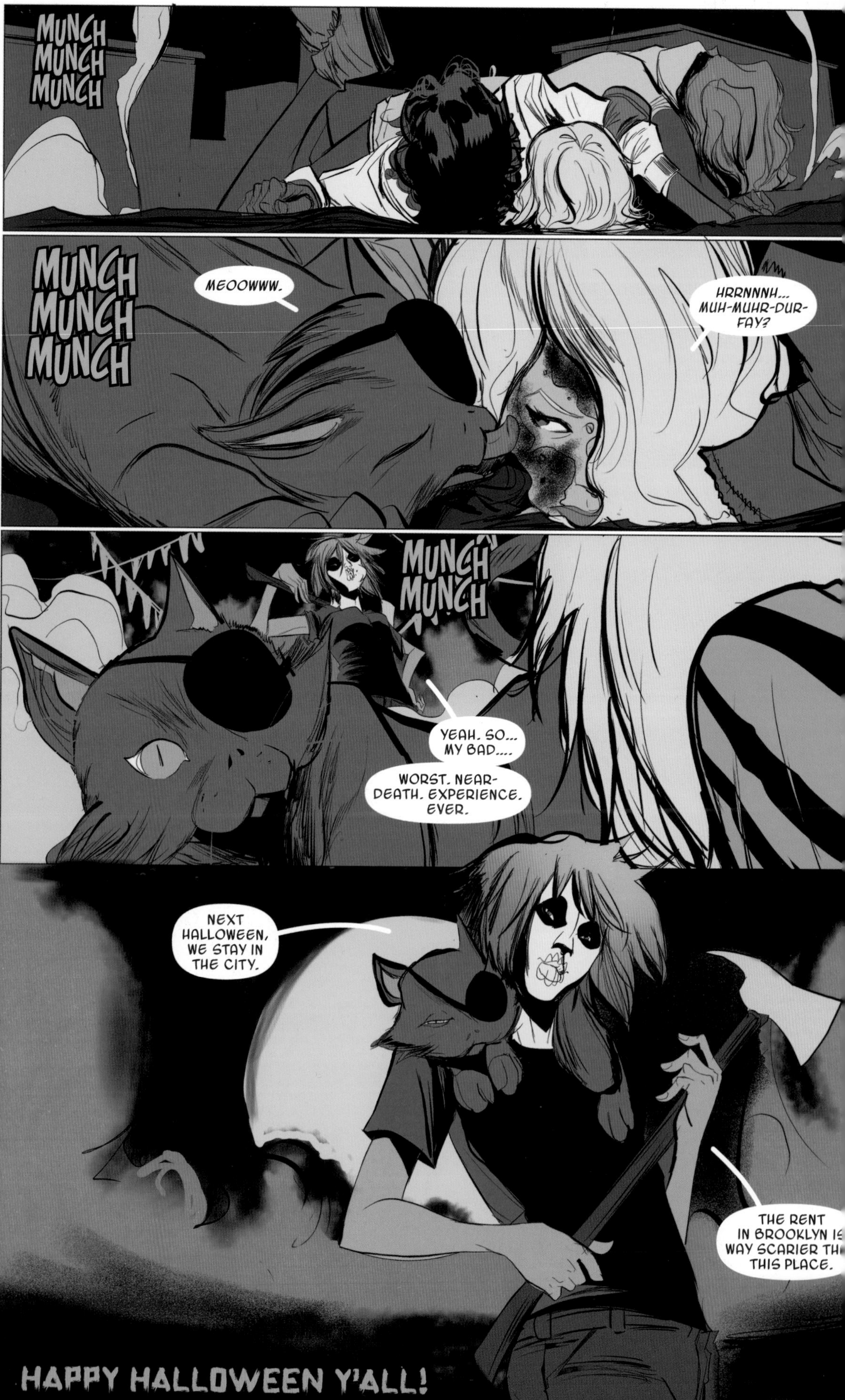
MUNCH MUNCH MUNCH
MUNCH MUNCH MUNCH
MEOOWWW.
HRRNNNH... MUH-MUHR-DUR-FAY?
MUNCH MUNCH
YEAH. SO... MY BAD....
WORST. NEAR-DEATH. EXPERIENCE. EVER.
NEXT HALLOWEEN, WE STAY IN THE CITY.
THE RENT IN BROOKLYN IS WAY SCARIER TH THIS PLACE.
HAPPY HALLOWEEN Y'ALL!

# THE GREEN GOBLIN

**REAL NAME:** Harold "Harry" Osborn
**OCCUPATION:** Former U.S. Special Forces operative, disavowed Agent of S.H.I.E.L.D.
**LEGAL STATUS:** American citizen, fugitive
**OTHER ALIASES:** None
**PLACE OF BIRTH:** Manhattan, NYC
**MARITAL STATUS:** Single
**KNOWN RELATIVES:** Norman Osborn (father), Emily Lyman (mother)
**GROUP AFFILIATION:** (formerly) S.H.I.E.L.D., U.S. Special Forces
**BASE OF OPERATIONS:** Global
**FIRST APPEARANCE:** Spider-Gwen (vol.2) #1

---

**HISTORY:** Harry Osborn is the only son of world-renowned billionaire scientist and industrial magnate Norman Osborn and tech innovator Emily Lyman. He is the sole heir to his estranged parents' company, the global conglomerate OSCORP.

After spending most of his formative years under the guardianship of his mother, Harry moved to Manhattan in his adolescence in order to take advantage of his father's power and influence over educational institutions in the area. Sharing his father's need to be viewed as "self-made", Harry began to show a distaste for the wealth and opulence of his social class at a very young age. By the time he reached high school, repeated run-ins with classmates and faculty at a string of prodigious private schools culminated in his expulsion. Seeking to give his son a dose of "real life", Norman Osborn enrolled Harry in his alma mater, Midtown High -- a public school. On his first day at Midtown, a pair of multisided dice fell from Harry's gym bag, prompting Flash Thompson to dub him the "Green Goblin" as a sarcastic play on Harry's interest in role-playing games and wealth. Unfortunately for Harry, both the nickname and bullying stuck.

However unlikely it may have been at his previous schools, Harry's role as an outcast led to a fast friendship with fellow students Peter Parker and Gwen Stacy. The three bonded over lunchroom role-playing sessions and a shared disdain for the school's social hierarchy. Despite this deepening friendship, it became clear that Harry deeply resented being socially ostracised. Frustrated by classmates who viewed him as coddled, spoiled, and weak, he began to channel his growing anger at his friends. Harry started to wrestle with his conflicted emotions towards Peter in particular, shifting between feelings of deep kinship and resentment at being grouped with such a "weakling". He also began to show a romantic interest in Gwen.

At the Midtown High prom Harry arrived stag, only to find Peter beaten at the hands of a group of bullies. Enraged, Peter morphed into a gigantic, mindless Lizard -- a result of his own scientific experiments and desire for revenge on his tormentors. Tossing Harry aside, the rampaging Lizard entered the prom where Gwen Stacy intervened in the guise of Spider-Woman. Seeking to protect her friends, Gwen masked her own agitation and fear with super-heroic bravado, pushing the Lizard to the limit in an attack that shattered him physically and emotionally. The humiliation caused the Lizard mutagen to overstimulate Peter's heart and accidentally killed him. Throughout all of this, Harry watched from afar. Frozen with fear and doubt, he was unable to inform Spider-Woman of the Lizard's true identity. Spider-Woman fled the scene, wanted for Parker's death.

Shaken by Peter's death, and driven to never again feel so powerless, Harry walked away from his civilian life and enlisted in the U.S. Army where he quickly rose to become a valued member of the U.S. Special Forces. This drew the attention of the world peacekeeping agency known as S.H.I.E.L.D., which recruited Harry into its ranks in order to exploit his connection to the vast resources of OSCORP. He enthusiastically accepted only to find himself relegated to a desk assignment with a personal assistant. Here, Osborn began to use the information that came across his desk to piece together a plan of his own -- a plot to avenge the death of Peter Parker.

*Art by Robbi Rodriguez*

# JESSICA DREW (SPIDER-WOMAN)

**REAL NAME:** Jessica Miriam Drew
**OCCUPATION:** Private investigator, adventurer, "retired" super spy
**LEGAL STATUS:** British/American citizen of Earth-616
**OTHER ALIASES:** You name it, she's been called it
**PLACE OF BIRTH:** United Kingdom
**MARITAL STATUS:** Single
**KNOWN RELATIVES:** Jonathan & Miriam Drew (parents, deceased)
**GROUP AFFILIATION:** The Avengers (616), S.W.O.R.D. (616), former agent of S.H.I.E.L.D. (616) and HYDRA (616)
**BASE OF OPERATIONS:** Manhattan, New York, USA (616)
**FIRST APPEARANCE:** Marvel Spotlight #32

---

**PARTIAL HISTORY:** The long and ridiculously convoluted history of Jessica Drew began on the Prime Earth (formerly designated Earth-616), when her parents moved from England to a small enclave on the outskirts of Wundagore Mountain in order to build and maintain a genetic research facility during her childhood. Poisoned by exposure to the natural deposits of uranium prevalent in the region, Jessica's life was saved by her parents' genetic experiments — chiefly an untested serum based on the regenerative and immunological properties of arachnids' blood. After a long coma-like stasis, Jessica awoke to find her parents missing. The experiment also granted her strange abilities akin to those of the spiders used in her parents' research.

Taking up residence in the area, Jessica's life took a tragic turn when her new-found bioelectric blasts accidentally killed a young man. Accused of witchcraft and murder, Jessica fled Wundagore, finding sanctuary with a wealthy benefactor named Otto Vermis, who — unbeknownst to Jessica — was also a high-ranking leader in the international terrorist organisation called HYDRA. Recognising her power, Vermis sought to mould Jessica into the perfect assassin and began training her in espionage and martial arts. But in her first and only field assignment for HYDRA, Jessica refused to assassinate S.H.I.E.L.D. Director Nick Fury. Rebelling against HYDRA, Jessica defeated Vermis in a battle to the death.

After time spent adventuring in Europe, Jessica moved to San Francisco where she put her talents and abilities to use as a private investigator and began her career as the costumed super hero "Spider-Woman". In a long career as Spider-Woman, Jessica found herself on countless adventures alongside the biggest and brightest super heroes of the Prime Earth. During this time, she served as a double agent of HYDRA/S.H.I.E.L.D., was captured, imprisoned, and impersonated by the queen of the alien race known as the Skrulls, and eventually became a key member of both the Avengers and S.W.O.R.D.

During the interdimensional war known as "Spider-Verse", Jessica was one of the spider-heroes recruited to face the vampiric clan of totemic hunters known as the "Inheritors". During this conflict Jessica played a key role in the Inheritors' defeat, using her skills as a spy to infiltrate their homeworld to gather vital information. Though historically averse to any sort of mentorship role, the Spider-Verse adventure required Jessica to serve as just that for Gwen Stacy, AKA the Spider-Woman of Earth-65 (see Spider-

Gwen) and Cindy Moon, AKA Silk of the Prime Earth. Despite her frustration over Moon and Stacy's inexperience, Jessica has become invested in both young women and continues to somewhat begrudgingly mentor them both to this day.

Returning from Spider-Verse, Drew found herself burnt out from grand, cosmic adventure. Seeking a quieter life, she quit the Avengers in order to focus on helping ordinary civilians. Resuming her role as a private investigator in Manhattan, Jessica decided to help people solve crimes.

However, as with all detectives and their retirement plans, Jessica's was ruined by yet another cosmic event. After rampant abuses and alterations of the space-time continuum, the fabric of reality began to fold in on itself. The result was the catastrophic collision of countless alternate realities. Called Incursions (known to you as SECRET WARS), these reality-destroying events resulted in a reshuffling of the entire Multiverse. During those eight months, Jessica mysteriously (just keep reading her comics, it'll be explained) became pregnant. Though pregnant, she continued her super-detective work by enlisting reporter Ben Urich and the reformed super villain Roger Gocking, AKA Porcupine, to help with her investigations while she was on the sidelines. As her baby approached term, Jessica was invited by her friend Captain Marvel to visit an intergalactic maternity ward run by Alpha Flight. But during her visit the hospital was invaded by an army of Skrulls. Despite this complication, Jessica's son was born healthy and unharmed as she led the other mothers of the maternity ward in turning back the Skrulls.

Jessica Drew remains active as a private investigator on the Prime Earth. She also serves as the mentor and de facto teammate of both Silk and Spider-Gwen. Due to the machinations of a mysterious Earth-65 spy organisation known as S.I.L.K., she is currently stranded on Earth-65, desperate to return home to her newborn son… ■

**HEIGHT:** 5'10"
**WEIGHT:** 130 lbs
**EYES:** Green
**HAIR:** Black

**SUPER-POWERS:** Spider-Woman possesses superhuman powers derived from the genetic experiment that granted her spider-like abilities. Her muscular density and strength have been extraordinarily enhanced and enable her to lift at least seven tons. As a result she also possesses speed, stamina, agility, and reflexes much greater than even the finest human athlete, and is greatly resistant to injury. Her rapid metabolism significantly increases her ability to heal as well as makes her far less susceptible to toxins, poisons, and drugs, and her body is totally immune to most forms of radiation.

Jessica's body possesses an inordinate amount of bioelectricity that she has learned to channel and discharge through her hands in controlled bursts of what she calls "Venom Blasts". She is capable of regulating their power from a simple stun blast to a lethal discharge. Via electrostatic attraction, Jessica is capable of adhering to most surfaces, granting her the spider-like ability to "wall crawl".

In the past, Jessica has possessed some control over the metabolic generation of certain types of pheromones that can create fear, elicit attraction and/or repulsion in others, depending on unknown factors. This ability currently seems to be dormant.

**SKILLS/TALENTS:** Due to her membership of several super-spy organisations, Jessica Drew is highly trained in the most cutting-edge espionage and intelligence techniques. She is also an expert martial artist and seasoned private detective, well-versed in the latest law enforcement protocols and methods.

**WEAPONS/EQUIPMENT:** As a result of Spider-Verse, Jessica possesses a wristwatch-sized device that grants her access to an alternate reality gateway, the most notable and frequently visited of which is Universe-65. Her preferred mode of transportation is a very fast, classic American motorcycle.

**FUN FACT:** Jessica Drew loves butter. A biscuit to put it on is nice, but not a deal breaker.

*Art by Robbi Rodriguez*

# SILK

**REAL NAME:** Cindy Moon
**OCCUPATION:** Adventurer, intern at FACT News
**LEGAL STATUS:** American citizen (Earth-616)
**OTHER ALIASES:** Cin, Bride, Analog
**PLACE OF BIRTH:** Washington Heights, New York
**MARITAL STATUS:** Single
**KNOWN RELATIVES:** Albert Moon Sr. (father, estranged), Nari Moon (mother, estranged), Albert Moon Jr. (brother)
**GROUP AFFILIATION:** Black Cat's Gang (undercover for S.H.I.E.L.D.), S.H.I.E.L.D. (freelance)
**BASE OF OPERATIONS:** New York City (Earth-616)
**FIRST APPEARANCE:** Amazing Spider-Man (Vol. 3) #1

**HISTORY:** Cindy Moon was born and raised in Manhattan, NY, of Earth-616, where she developed an early fondness for the sport of hockey equalled only by her aversion to schoolwork. Upon discovering that Cindy possessed an eidetic memory, Cindy's mother encouraged her to focus on her studies rather than a position on the school hockey team. This led to a heated argument in which Cindy was forced to attend a school field trip to the General Techtronic Laboratories Corporation.

While at General Techtronic Laboratories, a spider irradiated by a particle accelerator used in the demonstration bit both Peter Parker and Cindy Moon. Soon thereafter both manifested amazing spider powers. But while Parker went on to a lead a life of adventure as Spider-Man, Cindy Moon's fate took a very different turn. While Cindy's parents were aware of her new abilities and her mother was looking for a cure, a man named Ezekiel Sims found Cindy and explained that her powers made her the target of an extremely powerful totemic predator named Morlun. Fearing for the safety of her family, Cindy agreed to leave with Ezekiel. After training Cindy in the use of her powers, Ezekiel locked her in a bunker designed to block Morlun's ability to detect the spider totem within her.

Cindy was finally released by Spider-Man, who had learned of her history and location when the villain Orb revealed several of the Watcher's secrets. While travelling the city together, they discovered Cindy's family had moved, and their spider-senses alerted them to impending danger – suggesting that Morlun was not dead as Peter believed. Peter and Cindy also felt a powerful primal attraction to each other, which they continue to resist.

In "Spider-Verse", the interdimensional battle with Morlun and other spider-totem-hunting "Inheritors," Cindy was strategically important as the totemic "Bride", but her inexperience in battle and social situations brought her into conflict with other heroes, particularly the Spider-Woman of Earth-65, Gwendolyn Stacy. During this time, Cindy also forged a relationship with the Spider-Woman of her Earth, Jessica Drew, who has started mentoring Cindy.

Cindy returned to her home universe determined to find her family and to become a better hero and adult. As Cindy Moon, she's earned her G.E.D. and works at the FACT Channel with Jay Jonah Jameson, where Jameson took an immediate liking to both Cindy and her reporting on her alter ego, Silk. Jameson provided the first lead on Cindy's brother Albert, who had gotten involved in the Goblin Nation gang and landed in the hospital, recovering from an accident and drug addiction. Investigating and taking down the Goblin Nation became Cindy's top priority as Silk infiltrated the Black Cat's criminal organisation in order to pass information back to S.H.I.E.L.D. through her handler, Mockingbird.

In the Goblin Nation's underground hideout, Cindy learned that Albert had been on the street for two years before falling in with the gang, making her parents' trail even colder. She was also injected with the Goblin Serum, but was eventually cured by Black Cat. Although gaining a Black Cat's trust was part of Silk's mission, Mockingbird is concerned that Silk is getting too friendly with the criminal. Cindy has also been struggling to control her anger since the events in the Goblin Nation hideout.

On a trip to Earth-65, Cindy and Jessica Drew were stranded by S.I.L.K., the research organisation run by the Cindy Moon of that universe. While waiting for the Earth-65 Reed Richards to build a portal back to her home universe, Cindy visited the Albert, Nari, and Albert Moon Jr. of Earth-65 and located Cindy-65's secret laboratory. Back in her New York City, Cindy continues to work with Gwen Stacy and Jessica Drew to learn more about Cindy-65's history and plans in an attempt to make sense of her own past and destiny. ∎

**HEIGHT:** 5'7"
**WEIGHT:** None of your business
**EYES:** Brown
**HAIR:** Black

**SUPER-POWERS:** A bite from a "radioactive" spider granted Cindy Moon the ability to cling to walls, perfect balance and equilibrium, and superhuman speed and agility. Spider-Man (Peter Parker) has noted that she is faster than he is. Her musculature has been augmented so that she can lift (press) about eight tons.

Cindy also possesses the ability to organically produce her own silk webbing from glands within her forearms, possibly limited by her body's health and nutrition. These organic webs have a remarkable tensile strength and can also be woven into clothing. She releases her organic webbing through her fingertips. This same ability and webbing material allows her to form claw-like extrusions from her fingertips.

Having been bitten by the same spider as Earth-616's Peter Parker, Silk can find and sense Spider-Man anywhere in the Multiverse. Additionally, her "Silk-Sense" alerts her to danger.

**SKILLS/TALENTS:**
Intelligence
Eidetic Memory
Skating
Silk Weaving
On-the-Fly Clothing Design

**WEAPONS/EQUIPMENT:** Secondhand hockey gear and a sweet flip-phone.

**FUN FACT:** Cindy was recruited by several colleges to play ice hockey. Due to her time in the bunker, she was never able to fulfill that and many other dreams.

*Art by Robbi Rodriguez*

# CINDY-65 (SUPERIOR SILK)

**REAL NAME:** Cindy Moon
**OCCUPATION:** Scientist, social and industrial saboteur, spymaster
**LEGAL STATUS:** American citizen (Earth 65)
**OTHER ALIASES:** "Cindy-65", S.I.L.K. Superior
**PLACE OF BIRTH:** Washington Heights, New York
**MARITAL STATUS:** Single
**KNOWN RELATIVES:** Albert Moon Sr. (father, estranged), Nari Moon (mother, estranged), Albert Moon Jr. (brother, estranged)
**GROUP AFFILIATION:** Leader of S.I.L.K.
**BASE OF OPERATIONS:** New York City (Earth-65)
**FIRST APPEARANCE:** Spider-Women: Alpha #1

**HISTORY:** As a high school student attending a science exhibition at OSCORP Labs, Cindy Moon of Earth-65 (AKA Cindy-65) was nearly bitten by a radioactive spider irradiated by a particle accelerator used in the demonstration. With their daughter nearly bitten by a glowing spider, the Moons suspected an overt and harmful negligence on the part of the scientists at OSCORP. A lengthy lawsuit against OSCORP followed, during which Dr. Curt Connors, the acting chief of OSCORP's genetics division, testified under oath that effects of the irradiated spider's bite could have produced a wide range of symptoms in Cindy-65, ranging from superhuman abilities to death.

Increasingly filled with a lingering sense of loss since the near-miss of the spider's bite, Cindy-65 became dually fascinated and mortified with the possibilities of both the powers the spider could have granted and her own death. By comparison, the modest day-to-day life she lived seemed torturously insignificant. Now obsessed with maximizing her time in life, she sought answers to the questions that haunted her.

With her winnings from an out-of-court settlement with OSCORP, Cindy-65 invested heavily in her own obsessive study of genetics, seeking to recreate and improve upon the radioactive spider which nearly bit her. After years of work, Cindy-65's obsession had nearly depleted her funds and had forced her to cut ties with her own family, but she found herself close to a breakthrough.

That breakthrough came in the form of a S.H.I.E.L.D. agent and S.W.O.R.D. astronaut by the name of Jesse Drew. The lone survivor of a strange alien spider attack (which was totally not like the movie *Alien* at all…we swear), Drew's blood was infected with a seemingly lethal parasite. Brokering a deal with S.H.I.E.L.D., Cindy-65 began an experiment which ultimately saved Drew's life and also granted him enhanced spider-like powers. It seemed, however, that there was a cost to Drew's cure, as the parasite in his blood could only be kept at bay by a device which flooded his system with a rare isotope similar to the one OSCORP used to irradiate their radioactive spider.

When Cindy-65 refused to recreate or oversee the continuation of her experiments for S.H.I.E.L.D., she suddenly found herself at risk of losing all she'd built. Fortunately for her, the isotope and process used on Drew were known only to her. With this knowledge she blackmailed Agent Drew (AKA Agent 77) into stealing back her research.

The time after this confrontation with S.H.I.E.L.D. is buried in secrecy and redacted, unreliable intel. But what is certain is that a few short years thereafter, Cindy Moon re-emerged from the encounter determined to use her unique world view, experience, and intellect to form a countermeasure to S.H.I.E.L.D. and what she deemed "the secret masters of the world". Thus, with the help of Agent Drew, Moon formed the shadowy international espionage organisation known as S.I.L.K.

But as Cindy gained more and more influence in the world's affairs, she remained deeply and profoundly obsessed with what could have been. Tempted, yet fearful of the effects it might have if used on herself, Cindy claimed to have released her own irradiated, genetically modified spider into the world in an effort to study and refine the effects of its bite. This, of course, is probably a bunch of baloney, or at least not the full story. Either way, this spider in turn granted Gwen Stacy (see Spider-Woman, AKA Spider-Gwen) her powers with its bite.

Cindy-65 shadowed and studied Gwen as Spider-Woman, and S.I.L.K. began to gather data which it was presumably planning to use to develop a more powerful and effective version of the experiment that granted Gwen her abilities. During the course of their research, however, it was revealed that Stacy was in possession of an astounding interdimensional transportation device, which she used often to visit her fellow Spider-Women Spider-Woman (AKA Jessica Drew) and Silk (Cindy Moon-65's interdimensional counterpart) and share really awesome biscuits

After stealing the interdimensional teleporter from Gwen, Cindy-65 travelled to Earth-616 hoping to use Cindy Moon's identity to steal a vast array of the dimension's powerful and weaponized technologies. Confronted by Silk and Spider-Gwen, Cindy-65 revealed herself as Spider-Gwen's "benefactor", seemingly stripped Gwen of her powers for her defiance and bested the rookie Spider-Women in combat. With Spider-Gwen and Silk defeated, Cindy-65 returned home with her new-found arsenal.

However, Jessica Drew used intel of her gathered from S.I.L.K. to reveal to Agent 77 (Jesse Drew) that Cindy-65 had, in fact, cured him long ago and was using the false pretence of treating his afflictions to keep him loyal to S.I.L.K. In other words, Cindy-65 had been lying to Jesse Drew all along. As retribution, Jesse Drew gave Jessica the location of and access codes to Cindy's secret bunker. There Silk, Jessica Drew, and Spider-Gwen (A.K.A. "The Spider-Women") managed to defeat Cindy-65.

She is currently in the custody of Earth-65's S.H.I.E.L.D., confined to a bunker with only crappy old video game *Dangerous Street Garbage* to keep her company. ∎

**HEIGHT:** 5'7"
**WEIGHT:** 120 lbs
**EYES:** Brown
**HAIR:** Black

**SUPER-POWERS:** None.

**SKILLS/TALENTS:** In addition to world-class intelligence and eidetic memory, Cindy-65 is an expert in the field of genetics and provides gifted insight into advanced robotics, theoretical physics and several other fields of scientific study and application.

Combined with her intelligence, her experience with what lies behind the "secret veil" of the world, makes her a cunning and devious global strategist. As the head of the super-spy organisation S.I.L.K. she has on-the-job training in the most cutting-edge espionage and intelligence-gathering techniques.

She is also a competent martial artist due to her S.I.L.K. training.

**WEAPONS/EQUIPMENT:** Cindy is in possession of a wide array of advanced technological weapons, many of which were stolen or taken as spoils of war by S.I.L.K. Chief among them is a clawed power glove capable of recreating the schematics of any sufficiently studied weapon as a solid light 3D hologram. Among weapons it's recreated are older models of Iron Man's (Earth-616) and Doctor Doom's (Earth-616) armours, Doctor Octopus's (Earth-616) torso-mounted robotic tentacles, and the cybernetic tail of the Scorpion (Earth-616). It has also been shown to house an army of nanotech spider drones.

**FUN FACT:** Even before her encounter with the spider, Cindy-65 wanted to be so goth in high school that Winona Ryder from *Beetlejuice* was her hero.

*Art by Robbi Rodriguez*

# KRAVEN THE HUNTER

**REAL NAME:** Kravinoff, Sergei
**OCCUPATION:** Hunter, Soldier of Fortune
**LEGAL STATUS:** Unknown
**OTHER ALIASES:** None
**PLACE OF BIRTH:** Volgograd (Stalingrad), Russia
**MARITAL STATUS:** Presumed single
**KNOWN RELATIVES:** Vladimir Kravinoff (grandfather),
Louis ("brother")
**GROUP AFFILIATION:** Veteran of WAR MACHINE
**BASE OF OPERATIONS:** Global
**FIRST APPEARANCE:** Spider-Gwen (vol.1) #10

HISTORY: Sergei Kravinoff, AKA Kraven the Hunter, is the last remaining member of a long line of aristocracy that was decimated by the events of the Russian Revolution of 1917. After the presumed death of his parents, Kraven was taken in by his grandfather, Vladimir, a world-class spymaster, solider and big game hunter. Together they circled the world several times over, fleeing the many enemies which hunted the Kravinoff family as Vladimir trained Kraven to seek his family's revenge.

Decades later, with their family's enemies finally eliminated, Vladimir Kravinoff's hunt ended and the mantle of Kraven the Hunter was passed to Sergei. Resurfacing to the world at large, accompanied by his "brother" and servant, Louis, – Kraven found the landscape of the modern world to be a war-torn and adventurous place. Seeking to test his mettle, Kraven made his services available to the highest bidder as a soldier of fortune, serving in several arenas of conflict for various world armies and spy organizations until finally finding himself in the employ of Tony Stark's personal guard of mercenaries known as WAR MACHINE.

During his time in the employ of Stark, WAR MACHINE's involvement in skirmishes both domestic and abroad gained them a dubious, borderline notorious reputation as bloodthirsty hired guns. The veracity of such claims is up for debate, but many WAR MACHINE missions did in a fact put them at odds with the interests of the world peace-keeping agency known as S.H.I.E.L.D. During this time, Kraven became uneasy allies with a young soldier named Frank Castle. That allegiance that persists to this day, largely due to an secret blood debt between the two men.

Exiting from WAR MACHINE for as yet undisclosed reasons, Kraven retreated to one of his family's remaining American holdings, a vast estate somewhere outside of New York City. Here he retired from soldiering and attempted to restore his connection to his lost nobility through the hunting of exotic and dangerous game.

This retirement was, however, interrupted when Frank Castle called upon Kraven for help in capturing the Spider-Woman (see Spider-Gwen). Indebted to Castle, Kraven faced Spider-Woman in combat, ultimately failing to unmask her, but instead capturing a strange radioactive isotope which may in fact be the source of her powers.

During the course of their battle, Spider-Woman escaped Kraven's traps; he, however, is caught in the vice grip of infatuation and still totally crushing on how awesome she is. ∎

**HEIGHT:** 6' 0"
**WEIGHT:** 235 lbs
**EYES:** Brown
**HAIR:** Black

**SUPER-POWERS:** Kraven's strength, speed, agility, stamina, durability, senses, reflexes and life span have been increased and augmented to superhuman levels through a strange and arcane workout regimen and diet passed down by his ancestors.

**SKILLS/TALENTS:** Kraven is an Olympic-level athlete, a gifted tactician, and a world-class hunter and hand-to-hand combatant. He is an expert in field medicine and possesses an expert knowledge of nearly all known plant and animal life.

**WEAPONS/EQUIPMENT:** Kraven uses all forms of man-made weaponry, but favours knives, spears and bow weapons. He wears jungle cat pyjama work-out pants. Rawr.

**FUN FACT:** Kraven's brother is an orangutan named, Louis that he makes serve him food and wash his clothes and chauffeur him to opera houses or whatever rich weirdos do when they're not hunting men for sport.

*Art by Robbi Rodriguez*

## DeWOLFF, JEAN

**REAL NAME:** Jean DeWolff
**OCCUPATION:** Lieutenant, New York Police Department
**LEGAL STATUS:** American citizen (Earth-65)
**OTHER ALIASES:** None
**PLACE OF BIRTH:** Yancy Street, Lower East Side, NYC
**MARITAL STATUS:** Single
**KNOWN RELATIVES:** Philip DeWolff (father), Celia Weatherby-DeWolff (mother)
**GROUP AFFILIATION:** NYPD, former security chief of Oscorp
**BASE OF OPERATIONS:** New York City (Earth-65)
**FIRST APPEARANCE:** Spider-Gwen (vol. 0) #1

---

**HISTORY:** Born and raised on the Lower East Side of Manhattan, Jean DeWolff followed in the footsteps of many of the youth of her neighbourhood and joined the Yancy Street Gang (AKA YSG) as a means of positive change and public service. Seeking a way to expand her role in the community in a greater sense, DeWolff found inspiration in several of the revered but ostracized former members of the YSG who'd gone on to join the NYPD. So upon graduating from her general studies at Empire State University, DeWolff swallowed her pride, took the hit to her street rep and joined the police academy.

Proving herself a quick and natural police officer, she was soon assigned to the Special Crimes Unit as partner to rising NYPD star, Lieutenant George Stacy (see Captain Stacy). Though a decade removed, the two shared a bond as former members of the YSG and formed a brief but intimate partnership. Together they gained renown throughout the NYPD after their efforts dismantled the criminal empire of Wilson Fisk, AKA the Kingpin of Crime.

After Stacy's promotion to captain, DeWolff continued to serve the NYPD with honour and distinction, but police corruption and the narrow prospect of promotion eventually took such a toll that DeWolff accepted an offer to move into the private sector as a security chief for OSCORP.

However, during her short absence from the NYPD, news mogul J. Jonah Jameson led a charged media campaign blaming the adventurer known as Spider-Woman (see Spider-Gwen) for the death of Midtown High student Peter Parker. A groundswell of public support led to the appointment of a police task force designed to bring Spider-Woman to justice. Racked with guilt over his inability to help the Parker family, Captain Stacy soon took charge of the investigation. But upon discovering that Spider-Woman was in fact his daughter, Gwen Stacy, Captain Stacy found himself in moral crisis and began to do what little he could to end the hunt for Spider-Woman. Stacy's ability to conduct the case was soon in question, and he was relieved of command of the task force.

Promoted to the head of the case in advance of Stacy's pending departure, Captain Frank Castle handpicked DeWolff as his partner, luring her back to the NYPD by giving her the opportunity to police the way she'd always hoped to. This, however, was at least in part due to DeWolff's knowledge of Captain Stacy, whom Castle suspected was somehow in league with Spider-Woman.

Despite his radical methods, DeWolff gained a swift appreciation for Castle's direct and unrelenting sense of justice. But as Castle's investigation began to target Captain Stacy as a Spider-Woman conspirator, DeWolff became sceptical, believing that whatever Stacy's involvement, he was certainly well-intentioned. This belief is only increased when Stacy asked for her assistance in solving the mysterious disappearance of the Midtown High Lizard, Spider-Woman's strange combatant on the day of Peter Parker's death.

The off-book investigation led DeWolff beneath NYC, where she aided both Spider-Woman and Samantha Wilson, AKA Captain America, in a battle with several mutated lizards. On a tip from Captain America, DeWolff investigated Peter Parker himself. She became concerned by the obvious holes, missteps and media influence on the Spider-Woman case and was further worried when Captain America informed her of Frank Castle's chequered past as a soldier for billionaire Tony Stark's personal private army, "War Machine".

But as Castle's case began to draw tighter around George Stacy and Spider-Woman, it was derailed by a change of public opinion when Spider-Woman was shown as a public ally of Captain America. Presented with the evidence, District Attorney Foggy Nelson suspended Castle's investigation, fearing the negative blowback from implications of an NYPD police captain secretly aiding its most-wanted suspect.

Insistent that Gwen Stacy is secretly Spider-Woman and in criminal conspiracyw
Lt. Jean DeWolff is currently on stakeout, torn between her loyalty to her job, the Stacy family, and her partner, Frank Castle. The only thing that troubles her nearly as much as her conscience is sharing a car with the dietary choices of Ben Grimm. ■

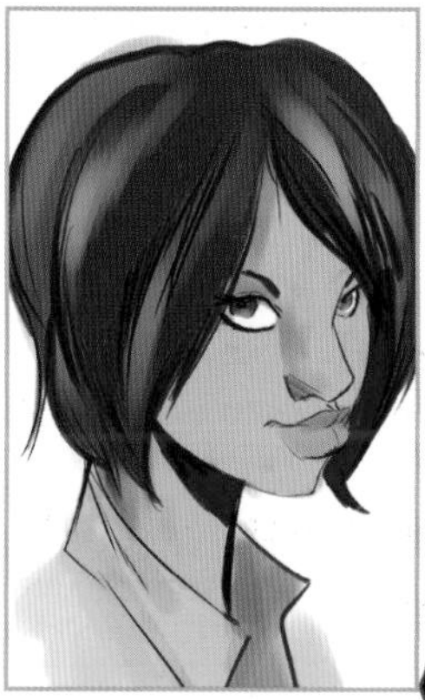

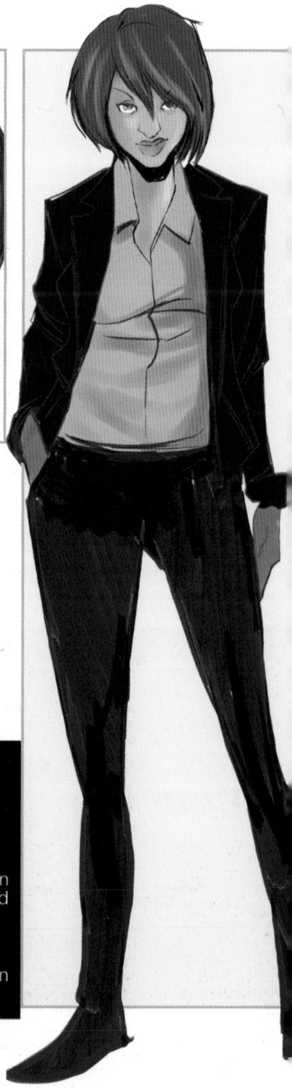

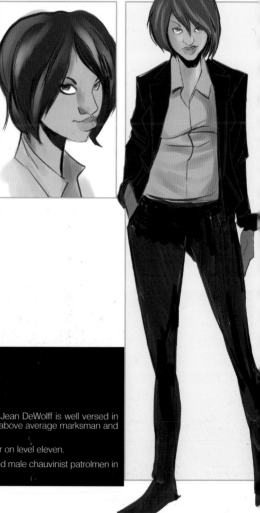

**HEIGHT:** 5'8"
**WEIGHT:** 135 lbs
**EYES:** Brown
**HAIR:** Auburn

**SUPER-POWERS:** None.

**SKILLS/TALENTS:** As a lieutenant in the New York Police Department, Jean DeWolff is well versed in the latest police protocol and methods. She is a skilled detective, an above average marksman and has been trained in several different self-defence techniques.

**WEAPONS/EQUIPMENT:** Standard police issue 9mm handgun. Swagger on level eleven.

**FUN FACT:** Jean DeWolff has wedgied the underwear of more jerk-faced male chauvinist patrolmen in the New York Police Department than any officer in its history.

***Art by Robbi Rodriguez***

## RICHARDS, REED

**REAL NAME:** Reed Richards
**OCCUPATION:** Student, amateur scientist
**LEGAL STATUS:** American citizen (Earth-65)
**OTHER ALIASES:** None
**PLACE OF BIRTH:** Brooklyn, New York
**MARITAL STATUS:** Single
**KNOWN RELATIVES:** Nate Richards (father), Dr. Evelyn Richards-Foley (mother)
**GROUP AFFILIATION:** None
**BASE OF OPERATIONS:** New York City (Earth-65)
**FIRST APPEARANCE:** Spider-Gwen (vol. 1) #7

---

**NOTABLE HISTORY:**

-Six months old: Learns to read. Writes his first sentence: "This ends in flames."

-Age 3: Visited by an older Reed Richards from an alternate timeline/parallel dimension, Reed becomes aware of the existence of the Multiverse and the legacy and responsibility of being a Reed Richards.

-Age 4: Learns to tie his shoes with quantum superstring.

-Age 6: Begins high school at Van Dyne-Pym Academy of the Sciences. Expelled when school's main wing goes up in a conflagration of cosmic flame after Reed burns a textbook on robotics written by Tony Stark.

-Age 7: Takes the Scholastic Aptitude Test in order to attend college early and get out of high school gym class, scores a perfect 1600.

-Age 8: Enrols for a semester at the Von Doom Academy. Expelled when the semester ends in more cosmic flame.

-Age 10: Granted enrollment in the prestigious FUTURE FOUNDATION. Expelled for ice this time. So. Much. Ice.

-Age 11: Begins a summer internship under the Reed Richards of Earth-56. Notable for a surprising lack of cosmic ice and flame.

-Age 12: Avenges death of his mentor, Earth-56's Reed Richards by defeating his killer, Rogue Richards of Earth-161 in a duel with, you guessed it, cosmic flame.

-Age 13: Reed is approached for aid by Jessica Drew, a super hero stranded on Earth-65 after an encounter with the spy organization S.I.L.K. Reed helps Jessica and the other Spider-Women (see also: Silk and Spider-Gwen) by building and opening his first interdimensional gateway out of toy construction bricks and parts of an old stereo. He later assists the Spider-Women by altering their weaponry for their final battle against his Earth's Cindy Moon (see Superior Silk, AKA Cindy-65).

-Shortly thereafter the radioactive isotope device that currently gives Gwen Stacy her spider-powers is damaged in a battle with the mercenary Kraven the Hunter. Reed aids Stacy by repairing and upgrading the device.

-Reed Richards is currently between schools. What's a diploma but a piece of paper anyway? ■

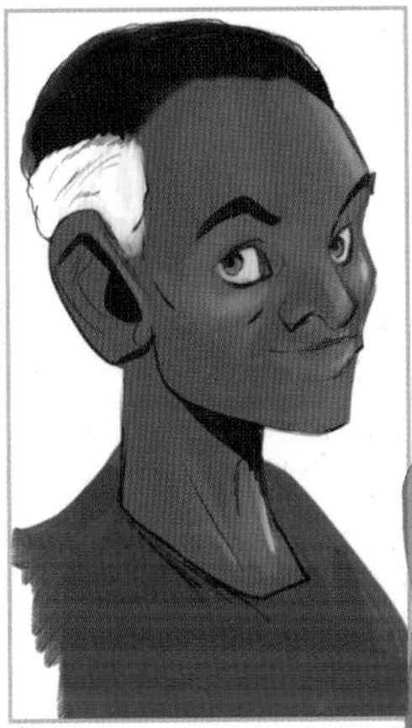

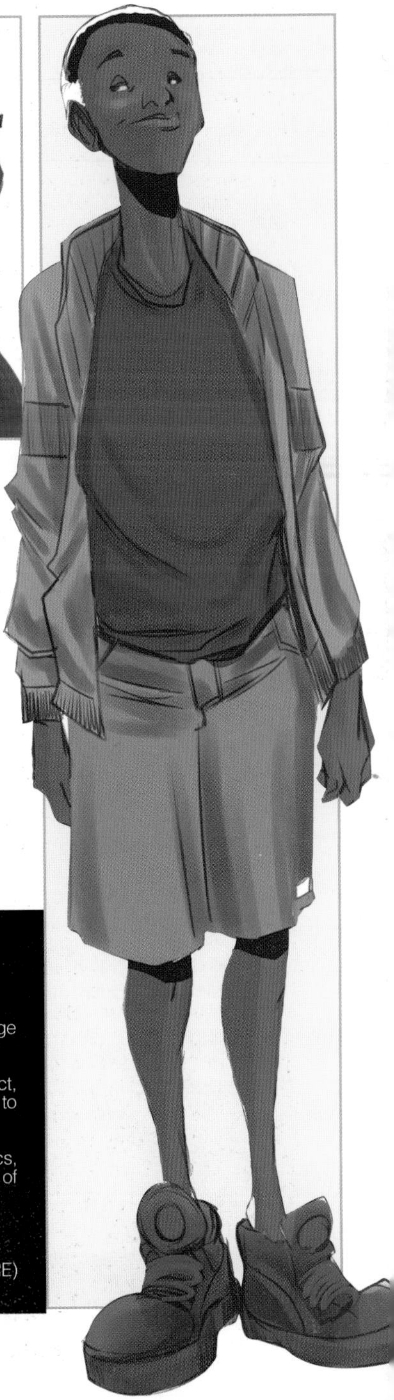

**HEIGHT:** 5'7"
**WEIGHT:** 140 lbs
**EYES:** Brown
**HAIR:** Black, premature white

**SUPER-POWERS:** If you call possibly being one of the smartest people to ever walk Earth-65 at age 13 a super-power, then that is what Reed Richards's super-power is.

**SKILLS/TALENTS:** Reed Richards possesses a Multiversal-class intelligence. As an ultra-autodidact, he is largely self-taught over a wide array of subjects, largely focussing on but not exclusive to scientific research and study.

Despite his youth, he is already a near expert in several fields of theoretical and applied physics, with a gifted insight into advanced robotics, genetics and many other wide-ranging fields of scientific study and application.

**WEAPONS/EQUIPMENT:** Seems to have a predilection for harnessing cosmic flame.

**FUN FACT:** The Multiverse is REAL. There's probably even another (INSERT YOUR NAME HERE) out there somewhere reading a handbook entry about YOU!

***Art by Robbi Rodriguez***

## THE MARY JANES

**OCCUPATION:** Musicians.
**BASE OF OPERATIONS:** New York City (Earth-65).
**FIRST APPEARANCE:** Edge of Spider-Verse #2 (AKA Spider-Gwen #0).

---

**BRIEF HISTORY:** During their senior year at Midtown High, a lunchroom altercation between Mary Jane Watson and Glory Grant led to a week of after-school detention. Bound by trash pick-up duty the two then-mortal enemies found common ground passing the time by singing and writing nonsensical pop songs. A band was shortly formed to play the Midtown High senior prom, with Mary Jane as lead vocalist and guitar, Glory as chief songwriter and keyboardist, and Glory's best friend Gwen Stacy as drummer. Betty Brant entered the fold after highjacking the school's morning public address with her recreations of Swedish Death Metal songs. Brant created the band's first gig poster announcing band under the name MURDER FACE.

However, this first gig was brought to a screeching halt by the battle between the monstrous Lizard and the Spider-Woman, a fight which ended in the tragic death of their mutual friend and classmate, Peter Parker. In mourning, the band temporarily disbanded, reforming only after Mary Jane Watson booked the band, now THE MARY JANES, a gig without the consent of the other members. Despite their misgivings, the other members joined Watson on stage and channelled their grief and frustration into the best set of their lives, a performance they've struggled to recreate since.

It was during this performance the group drew the attention of the *Daily Bugle*'s young music reporter, Randy Robertson. Sensing the band's potential, Robertson joined the band as manager and quickly brokered the introduction of a second vocalist, a young Parisian street performer with a checkered past named Felicia Hardy. The introduction of Hardy led to a creatively fruitful but tumultuous period in the band's history, during which Mary Jane was nearly strangled to death by a mic cord. Hardy would soon leave the band and find international success as a pop star (see *Felicia Hardy & The Black Cats*). After two years of struggle, the band was presented with a major headlining opportunity at a local rock venue. With their drummer Gwen Stacy missing due to secretly being Spider-Woman, the Mary Janes were taken to the stage only to once again be dramatically interrupted, this time by a confrontation between Spider-Woman and Aleksei Sytsevich (AKA the Rhino).

This, however, proved to be a major windfall for the band, as the media coverage of the destruction that followed also drew attention to the Mary Janes. Within days their single "Face It Tiger" became an overnight viral internet sensation, garnering hundreds of thousands of online plays and nearly one hundred whole dollars in revenue.

This success, however, was fleeting. Stacy was temporarily booted from the band for her absence, a move which caused a rift between the commercial and creative aspirations of the members. chiefly those of Watson and Grant. After struggling to replace Stacy, she was invited back when the band was presented with a major opportunity to open for Felicia Hardy's international tour. Once again the gig was interrupted. This time by ninjas.

To date, the band continues to gig around NYC but has struggled to recreate the success of "Face It Tiger", to manage the personalities within the band, and to make any money doing what they love. They recently survived a haunted carnival, though, so at least life isn't boring. ■

---

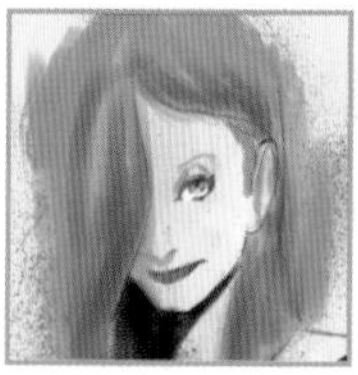

**WATSON, MARY JANE**
Lead vocals, guitarist

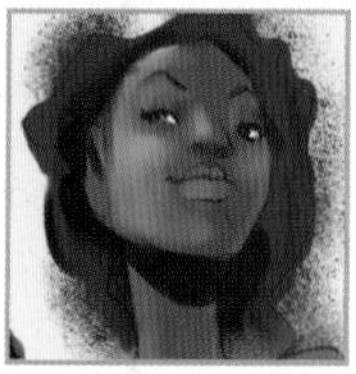

**GRANT, GLORY**
Songwriter, Keyboards

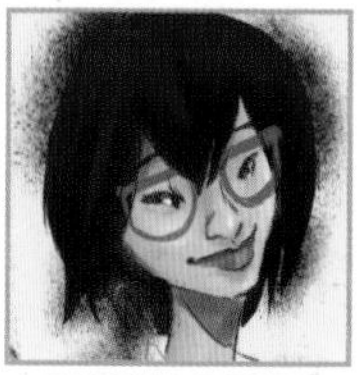

**BRANT, BETTY**
Bass Guitar

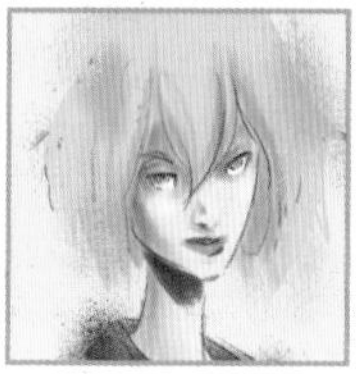

**STACY, GWEN**
Drummer,
Spider-Woman

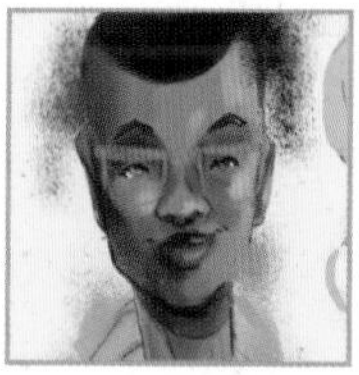

**ROBERTSON, RANDY**
Band Manager,
Music Reporter

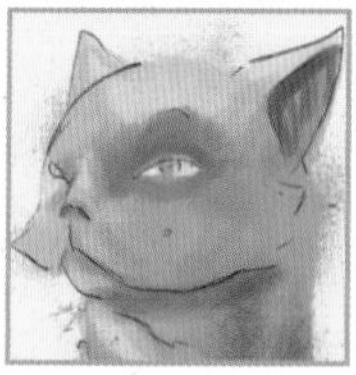

**MURDERFACE**
Mascot

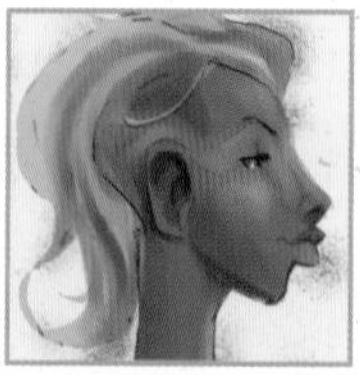

**HARDY, FELICIA**
Former vocalist,
pop star, thief

**FUN FACT(S):** The band's pet cat, MURDERFACE, may, in fact, be a demon that Betty summoned from the fiery depths of hell.

***Art by Robbi Rodriguez***

# SPIDER-GWEN VARIANT COVER GALLERY

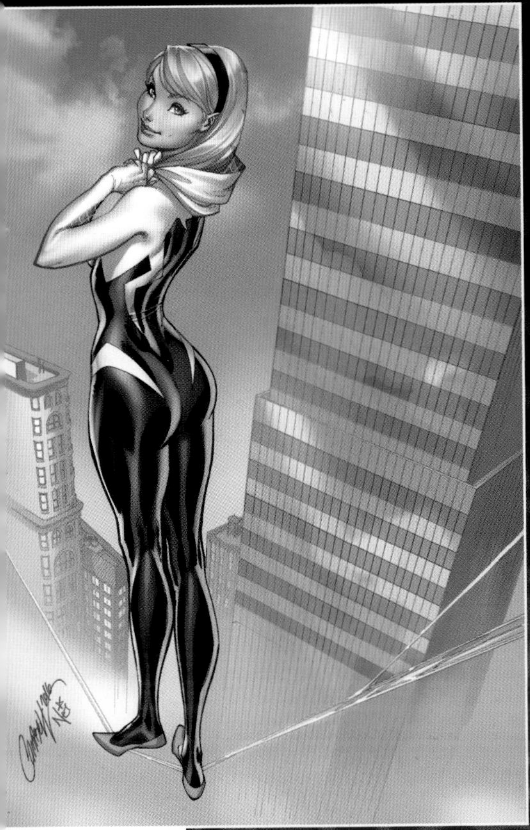

pider-Gwen #9
J. Scott Campbell

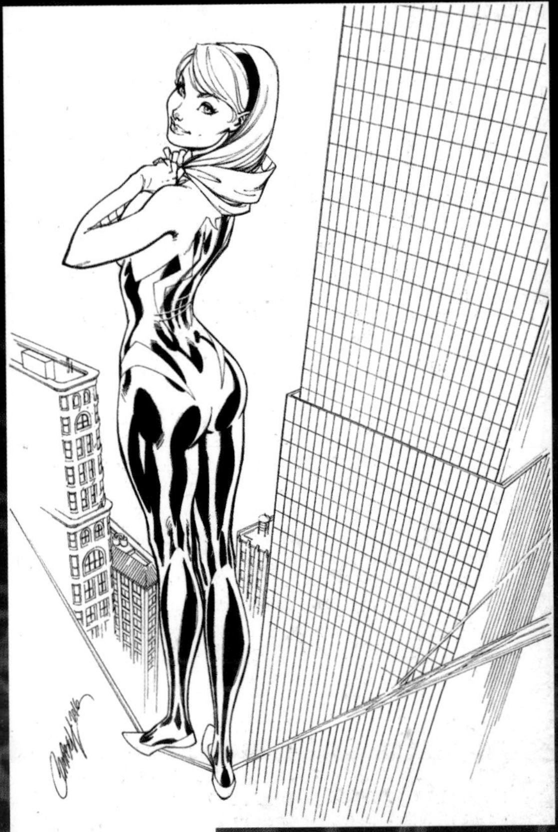

Spider-Gwen #9
by J. Scott Campbell

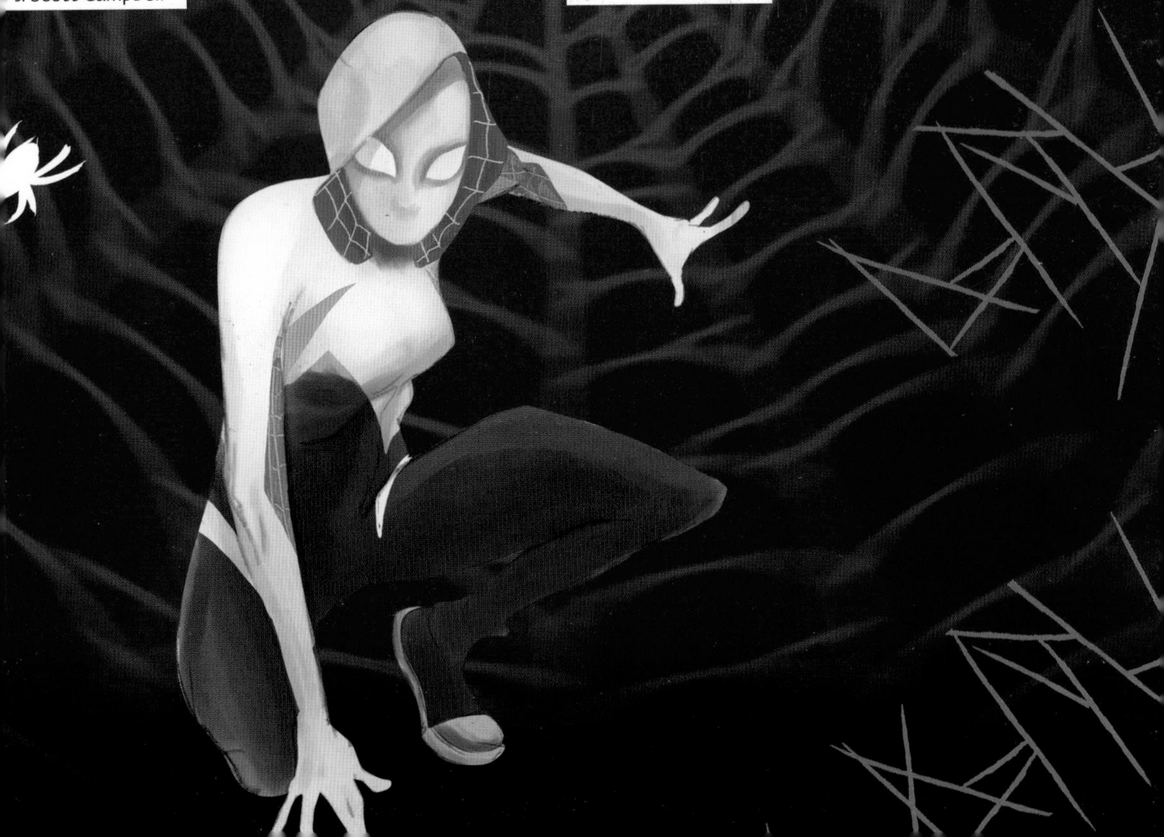

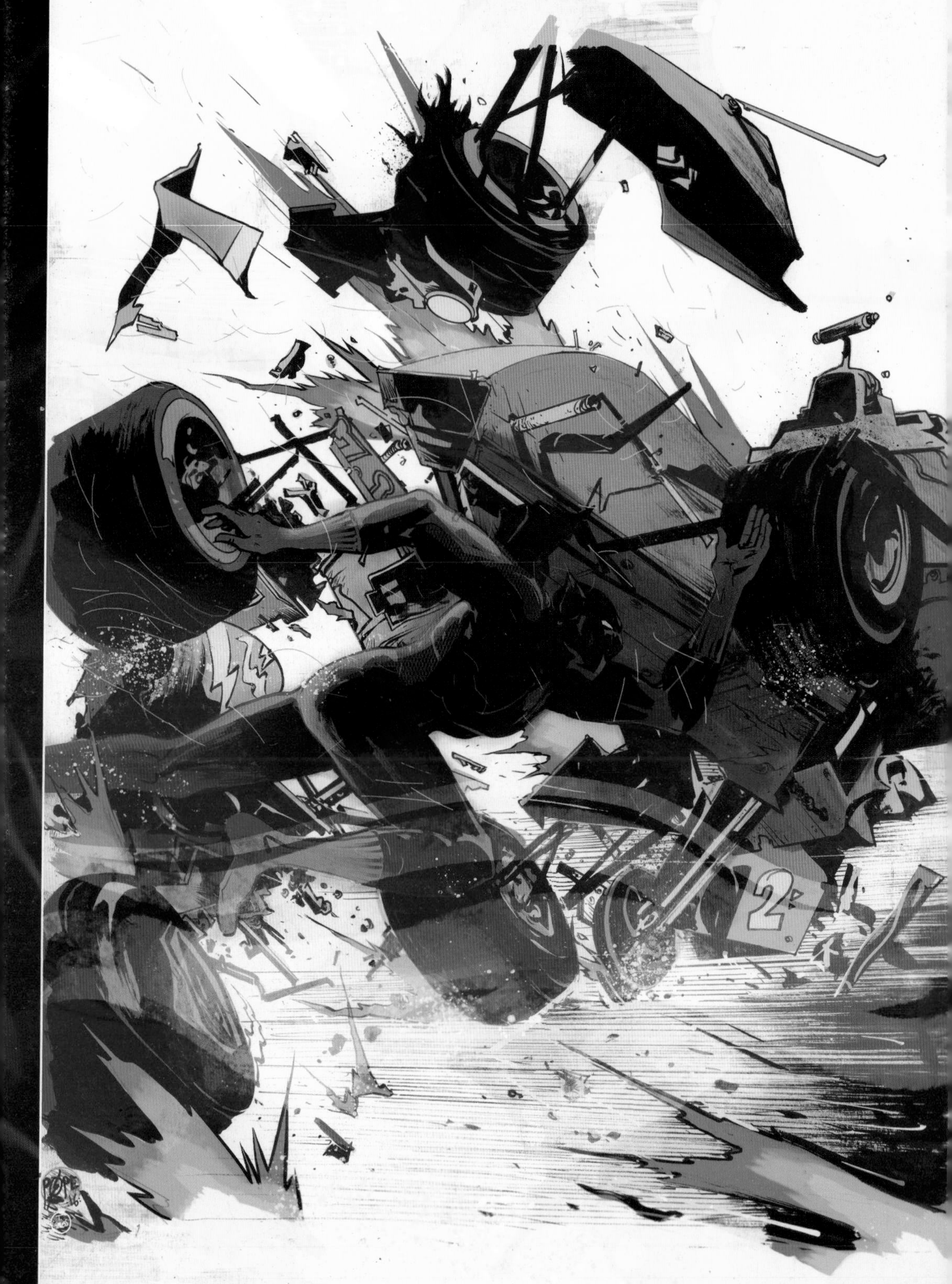